DUCKWORTH OVERLOOK

This edition first published in the UK
in 2018 by Duckworth Overlook

LONDON
30 Calvin Street, London E1 6NW
T: 020 7490 7300
E: info@duckworth-publishers.co.uk
www.ducknet.co.uk
For bulk and special sales, please contact
sales@duckworth-publishers.co.uk
or write to us at the address above

NEW YORK
141 Wooster Street, New York, NY 10012
www.overlookpress.com

A catalogue record for this book is available
from the British Library

ISBN 978-0-7156-5252-7

1 3 5 7 9 10 8 6 4 2

Printed in the UK by TJ International Ltd, Padstow, Cornwall

THE FRIENDSHIP CURE

KATE LEAVER

120 YEARS

DUCKWORTH
OVERLOOK

Contents

CHAPTER ONE

What is friendship?

IT'S THE FIRST WEEK of university. Cambridge, 1998. That tender, exhilarating week, when you feel like you have to choose your friends for life, right there, on the spot. Gillian is 19 years old; Liz is 18. They meet and they like one another, but they toy with the idea of befriending other people.

Days into university life, Gillian and Liz discover they're both reading English. They're sat next to one another in a class about playwrights and on this particular day they're studying Harold Pinter. The teacher calls for two women to read one of Pinter's scenes out loud. It's called 'The Black and White,' from *A Night Out*. It's from a collection of tableaus by Pinter; a series of little life stories. This one is about two old ladies dunking bread in soup and watching the world go by. It's one of those flawless sketches — mundane in perfect measure, like it's been written straight from life.

Gillian and Liz are nominated to read the scene. They giggle, as teenagers do, even that close to 20. The teacher (Peter? Ed? They only remember that they were already on a first name basis) reads the stage directions aloud.

THE FIRST OLD WOMAN is sitting at a milk bar table. Small.

A SECOND OLD WOMAN approaches. Tall. She is carrying two bowls of soup, which are covered by two plates, on each of which is a slice of bread. She puts the bowls down on the table carefully.

Gillian is THE FIRST OLD WOMAN, Liz is A SECOND OLD WOMAN. Or was it the other way around? Whatever; they take an old woman each and they read the scene, which is a quaint little meditation on hot soup, social interaction, bus timetables and the dangers of talking to strangers as an older woman. They taunt each other about flirting with strange men, imply they used to be troublemakers and peer out the window to check when the bus is coming. It is a rather perfect little glimpse into friendship between old ladies.

During that scene, with the ease of youth, Gillian and Liz become best friends.

That was nearly two decades ago, that class. Gillian and Liz are now in their late thirties and they're still best friends. In fact, in homage to the Pinter play that cemented their friendship, they have a standing date for the year 2040. It's a Facebook event with only two guests: Gillian and Liz. In roughly two decades, they'll go back to Cambridge, find a diner within walking distance of a bus stop, and order tomato soup with complimentary bread. They'll natter on at one another about public transport, the audacity of the young, men in uniform and the passage of time. Maybe they'll recite the

Pinter scene, maybe by then they'll have their own grievances with hospitality and strangers. Either way, they'll be there, a lifetime into a friendship that started one day in 1998. They'll have a language only they understand and that curmudgeonly way of speaking that you have to earn with old age. Their kids will have had kids, their husbands might still be around, their families will keep them alive. But after all those years, they'll be the ultimate ambassadors for lifelong friendship: THE FIRST OLD WOMAN and A SECOND OLD WOMAN. And oh, what a glorious achievement that will be.

When I try to predict my own future, there's one thing I know to be true: my friends will be there for it. When I daydream about my life to come, the elements of existence dance uncertainly. Marriage? Sure. A long and fascinating career? Yes, please. Kids? Probably. But friendship is my non-negotiable, my definite, my always. I can see it now: five or six of us playing lawn bowls in the sunshine, drinking wine, squabbling about decades of shared history. There'll be a few new hips and knees between us, several dentures, a couple of hearing aids. We'll have some kind of mutual vice that our doctors and children wish we didn't have — alcohol with our blood pressure medication, a regular stash of hash cookies, an old-timer gambling ring, some late-in-life mischief we can cackle over. We'll have our own shared language; maybe it's bus timetables, maybe it's the creeping heat of summer, maybe it's the proper rules of Balderdash. In my ultimate fantasy of old age, we live together — or at least, on the same street.

We're within shuffling distance from one another, possibly with walkie-talkies for ease of communication. Whatever happens between now and then, we choose to close our adulthood the way we started it: next to one another.

To me, that's the ultimate in friendship. It's the promise of soup and cantankerous behaviour decades from now. It's a tacit pact to stay in each other's lives by choice, not because biology compels it. That's what friends literally are, after all, they're the family we choose. Or, perhaps it's better to say that staying friends until the end is the gold standard in friendship. It's the dream. There are so many complex, lovely, toxic, frantic, fleeting manifestations of friendship for all of us. It's what defines us at every turn: the people we choose to keep and the people we leave behind. Every time we interact with someone new, we work out whether we want them in our lives and if so, in what capacity. Each new acquaintance has the potential to be elucidating, destructive, fabulous, painful and sublime. How we manage our relationships with other human beings is what makes us who we are.

There are the legacy friends we've had since preschool or primary school, the ones we can't quite let go of because the longer we are friends, the more accumulative history we have in common. There are the family friends we just kind of adopted from our parents, like pseudo cousins who grew up around us. The high-school friends we originally chose out of necessity because adolescence is a game of survival and you grab whoever's closest to you on the first day. The university friends we actually consciously select using our almost fully developed frontal lobe. The work friends we spend more time with than just about anyone else in our lives. The accidental friends we collect along the way and keep until it's too late to discard them. The casual friends we get on with at parties but don't bother to pursue beyond that. The Facebook friends we make partly out of social obligation, partly because on some days, somewhere in our souls, we still count the number of social media connections as a measure of who we are. The Twitter friends we banter with when we should be doing work. The Instagram friends with whom we only ever really exchange 'likes'. And every accidentally on purpose acquaintance in between: our ex-boyfriend's particularly fabulous mother, our sister's friend, our friend's sister, our old drama teacher, our swimming coach, our gender studies tutor, our trainer, our psychologist, our grandmother's doctor, our favourite barista.

There are infinite incarnations of friendship — and there's a spectrum of quality on which they fall. We all need friends who genuinely lift us up, who hold on to us through the drudgery, who keep us afloat and who make our lives better. If we're lucky, we have one of those friends in our lives. If we're extremely, wonderfully, impressively lucky, we have several. Just think of that sublime feeling you get when you know you're about to become friends with a new person: the nerves, the awkwardness, the warmth, the anticipation. It's a little like falling in love, in that peculiar way your heart tethers itself to a new person, willing them to cross over from acquaintance into something more. And just like romantic love, there's that feeling of not quite knowing where you stand, or how enthusiastically to offer your affections. Just like romantic love, there's hope and fear and it's all so desperately wound up with who we think we are and what sort of love we feel we deserve. Just like romantic love, you want to spend all your time with this person all of a sudden, like you can't get enough of them. Making friends can be extremely daunting, but I'll eat my favourite navy-blue beanie if there's a better feeling than finding a soul buddy and inviting them into your life. You feel lighter, somehow; buoyant, even. When you successfully recruit a new person into your friendship circle, you're essentially confirming that you are a likable human being, worthy of someone's time and emotional investment. It can make you feel funnier, smarter, better about who you are — and more sure about your place in the human race. Real friendships are just the most glorious, life-affirming things. They're some of our greatest achievements as human beings.

Friendship is so enchanting, so complex, I almost feel dissatisfied with the nuance we get from the English language when we talk about it. There's the word 'platonic', of course, to describe the unromantic love between two people, but we usually use that as a disclaimer to prevent people from thinking we're in love with our mates ('it's purely platonic', 'we're just platonic'). There isn't an English word that does real justice to the loveliness of camaraderie. Other languages have had a go at getting in that nuance, though. The Ancient Greeks famously had six words for love, one of which is 'philia', which describes profound friendship. It's not a casual kind of friendship; it's the sort of thing you only really achieve by going into battle together (perhaps the Ancient Greeks meant literal battle, but I like to extend it to mean figurative battle; going through adversity together). Philia is all about fierce loyalty, emotional transparency, confidence and even sacrifice in the name of friendship; it's the real deal, the ultimate in friendly commitment. That's perfectly congruent with what Aristotle said about friendship, too; that it's not for the faint-hearted or the ill-willed. It's a serious commitment and not available or possible for everyone. Greeks take friendship seriously and I love them for it. They also have the word 'philotimo', which translates to the 'love of honour' and refers to the importance of honouring your buddies. So it is more than liking them or even admiring them, it is respecting and honouring them like members of the family. They're right, too; there should be honour in friendship.

The Japanese have the word 'nakama' to identify a best friend, a close buddy, or someone for whom you feel true non-romantic love. It's stronger than 'friend'; it's someone who is embedded in your emotional life. The Spanish have 'camarada' to describe a dear friend or possibly housemate and they use 'compadre' as a respectful term for a male friend. There's an Aboriginal Pintupi word, 'kanyininpa', which refers to the relationship between people holding each other. It's meant to imply an intimacy between friends that's more like the relationship between a parent and their child; a familial bond that transcends genetics. The Korean word 'sarang' refers to someone you want in your life until you die. Slightly more casually, the Hungarians talk about the process of 'pertu' as a form of bonding between mates, usually over some kind of alcoholic drink, and of course there is the now-famous Swedish word 'hygge' to evoke the sense of cosiness and comfort you get from doing something like sitting by the fire with a glass of wine and your best friends. Perhaps my favourite way to explain how you might sometimes feel about your beloved friends is the Indonesian word 'gemas' and the Tagalog word 'gigil', which describe the urge to squeeze, pinch or cuddle someone because you cherish them so. I get that all the time with people (and dogs) I love.

There are other lovely linguistic odes to friendship, too. With your friends, you might share a 'binnenpretje', the Dutch word for an in-joke or private joke between friends. You might feel inclined to 'cwtch' with your friends, the Welsh word for cuddling, or finding a safe space with someone. They might make you experience 'geborgenheit', the German word for feeling protected and safe from harm, or you might engage in 'gezellig' together, which the Dutch use to evoke the warmth and happiness of a shared experience.

We are immeasurably lucky if we get to experience any of these incarnations of friendship (and you may, with my blessing, use as many of these beautiful foreign words as possible to impress your friends). Sharing confidences, swapping secrets, exposing vulnerabilities, talking through our perspectives on the world, learning who we are, training ourselves to trust that someone will be there for us when we need them, promising to be there for them in return — these are all the most vital skills and profound pleasures of being human. Good friends are, as they say on the Internet, 'everything'.

And then there are those friends who aren't really friends at all. For some reason, we all have them. They don't belong in our lives, not really, not truly, not if we're honest with ourselves. But we keep them there out of fear and complacency. At best, they slightly upset the equilibrium of our life every time we make contact with them — at worst, they steal from our sense of self-worth until we have nothing left. We cling to these inappropriate friends — people who are incapable of good friendship, people who have drifted from our lives or people we've outgrown — because we believe we have no choice, because we are too frightened of the confrontation required to erase them from our lives, or because we suspect we might deserve them. Everyone, at some stage in her life, has kept an unworthy friend around for the sake of convenience, cowardice or that private, but necessary sense of belonging. Any friend is better than no friends, we think. The more, the better. Any company is better than solitude.

But is that true? Evolution can make fools of us all, sometimes. We can be so scared of being alone and so biologically programmed to seek out mates that we'd rather surround ourselves with toxic or false friends than be on our own. We are so busy building our identities from our careers, hobbies, romance and offspring, we forget how important proper friendship is for survival — and how much work it takes to maintain it. As a society, we are simultaneously terrified of being alone and already desperately lonely.

We may technically be in possession of many friendships — online, at work and in real life. And yet we are smack-bang in the middle of the greatest loneliness epidemic in the history of our species. We are literally dying of loneliness; our hearts weakened and our immune systems ravaged by it. Scientists can detect loneliness in our blood streams. It's a public health crisis the world over and can cause early death, dementia, heart attack, stroke, diabetes, high cholesterol, homelessness, broken marriages, mental health problems and physical pain. It is one of the greatest threats to humanity and one of our most primal fears. Increasingly, we don't just die alone; we die because we are alone.

Of course, there's a difference between being alone and being lonely. You can be happy and self-sufficient in your own company — that kind of solitude is vitally important to our durability as humans. Conversely, you can be utterly lonely in a room full of people — that kind of solitude is dangerous and scary. I think we're caught in a great modern paradox: scared of being alone but lonely in company. We've lost something of our ability to truly connect with each other. We've built a culture of individuality without knowing how to be alone successfully or how to truly combat loneliness. It's tempting to blame the Internet or Tinder or Pokémon Go. It's tempting to blame the next generation of young people, like every generation has before us. But really this is our own doing, and it's far more complex than that. It's not about youth or technology; it's about evolution, science, health, grit, empathy, romantic comedies, honesty and priorities.

We need to relearn the art of friendship because we need each other more than ever. The only way we can end this era of acute loneliness is to start a new era of proper, loving, restorative camaraderie between human beings. That means prioritising friends in our lives. It means deliberately, brazenly choosing who deserves to be in our lives in the first place. It means investing time and energy into people outside our own families and marriages. It means compassion for people who've lost their way. It means kindness and action for asylum seekers and the disenfranchised on a political level. It means a wilful revival of empathy above things like professional success, ambition and profit.

That's what this book is about: the revival of friendship. It's about the science, psychology and curative nature of having mates in your life. It's a manifesto on the loveliness of good friendship and the dangers of bad.

I said before that some of us are extremely, wonderfully, impressively lucky to have several true friends in our lives. I'm one of those people: extremely, wonderfully, impressively lucky. Friendship hasn't always come easily to me. I've lived long stretches of my life lonely, holding onto life and my family through bouts of mental and physical illness. In a vulnerable teenage moment, I once told my mama that friendship wasn't for me because one-on-one conversation is really hard and talking in a group made me feel invisible. I've had bad friends, false friends and friends who shouldn't have been called friends at all.

But one way or another, here I stand after three decades on this planet, with the most astonishing group of friends.

They've got integrity, warmth, kindness and wit. They're smart, compassionate, inspiring and capable. They've been there for me and I for them, throughout some hellish circumstances. We've been heartbroken and headstrong, we've been in love and in danger, we've been right next to one another and flung to opposite sides of the globe. We've survived things nobody should ever have to go through. We've seen the very worst of humanity and through it, found the very best of it. We gravitated towards one another originally because we have a common respect for good grammar and bad puns, but also because we've all seen genuine darkness in life. I, for one, frankly don't know what I'd do without my core group of friends. They're the people I go to for advice on everything in my life, they're the people I workshop every major decision with, they're the people who make me laugh and cry and know for sure who I am. They've helped me claw back sanity on many occasions, understand the world I live in, and nestle into the adult person I've become.

If you're looking for an expert on friendship, I'm your girl. Not because I'm a flawless friend or because I've spent formal academic time or resources studying it. I'm your girl because I've spent my lifetime so far trying to understand what makes friendship work. I've always been fascinated by the choices we make when it comes to forming, keeping or discarding friendships.

For this book, I've interviewed strangers from the Internet, friends of friends, academics, scientists, psychotherapists and my closest mates. I've asked why some friendships last a lifetime and others crumble at the first disagreement. Why some people make our hearts light and others don't. What we get from friendship that we don't get from romantic relationships, family or work. How much time we need to invest in a friendship to keep it alive. Why you can leave some friendships for years and return to them as though no time has passed, while others disintegrate if you neglect them for a few weeks. How the Internet has changed the way we stay in touch and whether digital closeness is a blessing or an illusion. What curative qualities friendship can have for people with mental illness. How we could use friendship to cure loneliness and why we haven't already done so. Whether it's possible for a man and a woman to be best friends. How to make friends as an adult. How we can deploy friendship to live longer, better lives.

I've asked best male friends what makes a lasting bromance. I've asked great women how they'd get through life without their girlfriends. I've met men and women who are best friends. I've spoken to people who met at primary school, high school, college, work, through their families, on public transport, on Twitter, by accident and in online fan forums for 1990s teen stars. I've listened to stories about cancer, depression, grief, anxiety, heartbreak and emotional abuse. I've made new friends in a new city and asked them what it was like to be recruited into my life. I've heard enough to know that friendship is at the centre of humanity and that to understand it is to understand ourselves.

CHAPTER TWO

We are social animals

FIVE TEENAGE GIRLS are sitting on the tube in London, late afternoon, freshly changed out of school uniforms. Three of them are whispering and hooting, their arms and legs splayed over seats and each other's laps, as physically close to one another as possible. The remaining two sit across the aisle, one pulling the other's hair into a long plait down her back. This amateur hair stylist picks up a thick bunch of her friend's hair, parts it and inspects her scalp — they could be chimps in that moment, one picking the nits out of the other's hair while David Attenborough narrates from the sidelines in head-to-toe khaki. I observe this behaviour with a quiet little grin and go back to my book (eye contact on public transport is strictly forbidden in all unwritten codes of appropriate social behaviour — besides which, teenage girls only usually speak to me in public if I'm wearing my 2013 One Direction World Tour T-shirt). But the tableau stays with me — partly because I remember being one of those young girls, physically attached to my friends as though they might simply float away if they weren't secured. But partly, also, because I've been reading about evolutionary psychology and social grooming. Science says that we, like primates and hyenas and prairie voles, develop close relationships through physical contact. So when I see these lovely girls playing with each other's hair, draped over one another as though they truly couldn't bear to have the distance of an armrest between them, it occurs to me that they're right in the middle of some social grooming. They're bonding in the most primal way we know how: by touching one another. Teenage girls, as it happens, are the perfect example of how we've evolved as a species to foster and maintain friendships. They're very fond of physical contact, they partake in a great volume of gossip and they like to choreograph synchronised dance routines at sleepover parties (more on that in a moment). They're also perhaps at peak vulnerability when it comes to friendship formation.

Teenage girls evolved from primates, just like the rest of us, only they seem to need the validation of linking arms as they walk between classes more than anyone. Their incarnation of friendship is demonstrative — and heavy on the social grooming. Social grooming is a very popular way for animals of all kinds to make friends, actually. Primates spend inordinate amounts of time licking, nit picking and stroking one another — far more time than required simply for hygiene. Researchers have observed again and again that monkeys and chimps groom one another, both their family members and what we would call friends. There's plenty of evidence in the animal kingdom that physical touch is an important foundation for kinship, and that certainly translates to human behaviour. Physical touch on our skin releases endorphins, those lovely feel-good rushes we also (allegedly) get from exercise. Touch also triggers the release of the chemical oxytocin, which is colloquially known as 'the cuddle chemical', 'the love hormone' or 'the hug hormone' for its intimacy inducing properties. Oxytocin tends to make us feel relaxed and comfortable, so much so that its production can even make us sleepy. It's involved in our development of generosity, empathy and as you probably know, orgasm (that last one is less related to friendship, though please see my chapter on whether men and women can ever truly be friends). Oxytocin is a pleasure hormone and its release is linked to our neural reward and social memory systems, which explains why we tend to repeat whatever behaviour produced it. Researchers at the Max Planck Institute in Germany found that chimps who bonded with other chimps using social grooming had higher oxytocin levels than those who did not. It is reasonable to assume there's a similar reaction in human bodies, and it points to our evolution as a species that enjoys physical touch. Some scientists even call the skin a 'social organ' because of how deeply and instantaneously affected we are by touch. Just think about the last time someone you love hugged you when you needed it (if you're 'not a hug person', I can't help you), or a colleague rested their hand on your shoulder in a gesture of support. It was lovely, no? It communicated things to you wordlessly, things that maybe couldn't be articulated? Then think about the opposite sort of feeling you get when someone touches you without your consent or desire; how quick you are to feel repulsion and how powerfully it can move you to anger or fear. Our skin is a receptor for emotional communication in many ways, and humans absolutely use physical touch as a way to gauge someone else's intentions — be they friendship or enmity.

Now, for chimps, social grooming has all sorts of important purposes. It sets the social hierarchy and establishes a power balance between peers because, for instance, chimps are more likely to share food with chimps who've groomed them before. Social grooming can be a really effective way to dispel tension after a fight or conflict between chimps, so it can actually affect their chances of survival. We have a lot in common with chimps (DNA, sense of humour, fondness for bananas), but we are also, in many ways, not chimp-like. Perhaps the most obvious way humans digress from chimp behaviour is spoken language. Humans have evolved to speak to one another, and that should go some way to reducing our reliance on physical touch to communicate all our feelings or intentions. We communicate with body language and spoken language, and we use both those things to establish camaraderie. In his book *Grooming, Gossip and the Evolution of Language*, eminent British anthropologist and evolutionary psychologist Robin Dunbar argues that because language is so important to us , gossip has in some ways replaced grooming as a bonding agent between humans.

We gossip strategically, too, to get close to people who are viable or desirable companions for us. We're a sophisticated species, what can I say? And that is perhaps why you won't see as many people at work or school licking their fingers and straightening out someone else's eyebrow hair. It is also why mothers tend to do exactly that kind of thing to their kids: because grooming is our most primitive gesture of love.

And so, let's go back to those teenage girls as an example here. The whole ecosystem of adolescence is, for better or worse, built on gossip. Young people trade secrets, spread rumours, tarnish reputations and establish a social hierarchy in whispered or texted exchanges. Do you remember high school? It's all about trading gossip for social status. Gossip is a vital, and fascinating, form of human currency, used to build people up, tear people down, bring people together and push them apart. There is no faster way to bond with someone new than to share a hatred for a third party or, even better, have something salacious to divulge about them. I have no idea what those girls on the tube were whispering about that day, it could have been anything. But I have been a teenage girl and I remember only too vividly how much your survival at school depended on your gossip capital.

The power of gossip extends into adulthood too, of course; secrets and rumours are equally destructive and unifying in college, university and the office. There's nothing better than office gossip! Oh, boy. I've known entire workplace friendships that exist on nothing else. Adults are just as culpable when it comes to gossiping. But it's not always sinister. Sometimes, yeah, telling a secret that is not yours to tell can damage another person and certainly spreading lies is dangerous. But simply exchanging social information with someone can be incredibly bonding. Think how great it is to be the one with the goss, how much fun it is to be the one hearing it and how close you feel after the exchange. Gossip doesn't have to be cruel; it can also just be the exchange of information to do with what someone is doing or wearing, who someone is dating, marrying or shagging, where someone has been seen, employed or propositioned. We build alliances with gossip in a delicate, sometimes ominous way that probably does mirror the way primates use grooming.

It's not all about gossip, though. I'd go as far as to say any verbal exchange could emulate the evolutionary significance of touch. Kind words, commiserations, whispers of support and whoops of delight are all ways we communicate our intentions of friendship. They affect us in much the same way stroking and petting might calm or endear an animal. And, of course, you can put vast, aching distance between you and another human being in the space of a coolly uttered phrase.

Language is, obviously, an enormous part of our communication as humans. But it ain't everything. We know now that social grooming is an effective way of forming friendship ties between people, but you know what else is? Dancing. Singing. Anything done in sync with other human beings. If there's alcohol involved, all the better. There's something magical about moving and making noise with other people — and it doesn't matter whether you have the correct pitch or any sense of rhythm at all. It couldn't matter less, really, whether you're singing the right lyrics to the Venga Boys or dancing the Macarena technically correctly. The point is that moving in relative unison with other human beings, in close proximity and usually with joy, triggers our endorphin system in the same way as physically touching one another does. If you imagine that each person is wrapped in a string of figurative fairy lights, activities like dancing and singing light them right up. That's why we dance at weddings, birthday parties and celebrations: not just because it's tradition and not just because it's good fun. It's because these are occasions when we ask for spontaneous friendship between newly introduced strangers and we reinforce the closeness of our existing connections. To return to the teenage girls for a moment, this is precisely why One Direction or Ariana Grande fans are so united as a fan base and so desperate to go to concerts; these are the venues of their social bonding. Shouting lewd or loving things in the general direction of Harry Styles, along with 30,000 other people who agree, creates the most joyous sense of belonging. Strangers become friends, friends become closer. Concerts are friendship festivals with a good soundtrack — teenagers know that better than anyone.

When I was growing up, the single most popular activity at sleepover parties and school camps was spontaneous, earnest choreography. I played Lou Bega in a deeply inappropriate public dance performance of Mambo No. 5 when I was in my first year of high school, and I can still picture the consternation with which we choreographed that dance. There was one girl who was a trained dancer, so she took the lead with choreography and we all threw in a move or two. Presumably my casting as the male singer had something to do with my strong masculine presence at the time (despite my girlish curls, I was always getting cast as men). The act of learning, rehearsing and then performing that ridiculous dance was powerfully bonding for that group of girls. It brought us close to each other, in a way that other getting-to-know-you activities organised by teachers simply didn't. It set us apart from the other girls in our year, secured our positions in a group of people we were tentatively beginning to call friends. It was not the first time, nor the last, that I used synchronised dance (clumsy, melodramatic, oddly sexual) as a way of bonding with other teenage girls. We did it all the time, and it didn't even matter whether we ultimately had an audience. This wasn't about wanting to be seen by outsiders, it was about wanting to be seen by each other. Twelve was probably the age at which this sort of boogie ritual was most popular, and there obviously wasn't any alcohol involved. Give it a few years and that heady, dreamy state of intoxication only exacerbated a) the need to dance, even if it involved a minimalist approach like gentle swaying or raising your arms in the air and b) the feeling of closeness with your drinking/ grooving companions. The disgusting beer I sampled from my stepbrother's mini fridge circa 14 years old inspired me to sing loudly, dance emphatically and bond with my fellow under-agers in a way we simply wouldn't have done without the 4.9 per cent alcohol content. That was, of course, just the beginning. As I got older and hit my twenties, drinking, dancing and yelling lyrics at each other in public places became a deeply important social ritual. Of course, for all time, alcohol has facilitated romantic and sexual dalliances. But to me, the more interesting thing is how it initiates and strengthens friendship (or, let's be honest, has the capacity to destroy it — many a fight goes down on the d-floor).

Perhaps this is why we form so many significant friendships in our teenage years and early adulthood: because it's probably the most concentrated period of drinking, dancing and singing along to Elton John/The Killers/Destiny's Child in our lives. It's also the time, I think, that we naturally have the greatest number of friends. If I could draw the general patterns of my friendships over my life so far on a graph, it'd start off tentatively with my childhood friends, dip when I became inseparable from my first best friend, increase moderately through primary school, jump slightly at high school, spike at university then, happily, settle down a little as I found my true friends in my late-twenties, with little peaks for new work friends along the way. We tend to collect a lot of friends when we're entering adulthood because we're still working out who we are and what we want from our companions in life. Having spoken to so many people my age about friendship, I notice a definite trend of shedding friends as we head into our thirties. By this age, our barometers for friendship quality have improved and we're really starting to fill our lives with things like career goals, romance, marriage, family and financial responsibility, so we tend to close ranks a little as the available slots for friends in our lives become more precious. It is tempting, at different times in our lives and as we establish our own identities, to pick up as many friends as possible. But as we become adults, that ambition for popularity wanes a little and we're able to make smarter friendship decisions. Then we start arranging friends into a hierarchy, determined by how close we are and how much we value them.

Pleasingly, we can use maths and evolutionary science to work out both the maximum number of friends we should have in our social circles, and how many might be in each league.

Researching friendship in any sort of academic sense will inevitably lead you to the office of evolutionary psychologist Dr Robin Dunbar at Oxford University in the United Kingdom, whose book on gossip as evolutionary strategy we've already mentioned. Dunbar is what you'd call the authority on friendship studies. He began his academic career studying evolution but ended up brain-deep in the theory of friendship when he started applying what he'd learnt about primates to human beings. He invented something he rather modestly called 'Dunbar's Number', which is the maximum number of friends and acquaintances one person can realistically keep within their social network. He arrived at the number in the '80s, when the Machiavellian Intelligence Hypothesis — now known as the Social Brain Hypothesis — had just become popular in anthropological circles. The hypothesis suggested that primates have large brains because they live in socially complex societies, meaning you could theoretically tell the size of a primate's social group by the size of their brain. Building on this idea, Dunbar did some fancy maths (using the ratio of neocortical volume to total brain volume in the human brain) and arrived at a number. A number that should, according to Dunbar's hypothesis, be the size of a human's social group. That number was 150. We have what Dunbar calls 'cognitive constraints' that prevent us from maintaining meaningful relationships with any more people than that. That is to say, there are limits to the amount of information our brains can process and retain, which means we are restricted when it comes to the number of people we can assimilate into our social network. It's directly correlated to the size of our neocortex, which is the most recently evolved part of the cerebral cortex that concerns hearing and sight in mammals. Our brains are simply not capable of having infinite friendships — we have to stop somewhere and evolutionary psychology says that's at the 150 mark.

Within that 150, there are several groups of friends with whom we have varying levels of intimacy: we typically have five very close friends, 10 close friends, 35 friends and 100 acquaintances. There's a secret inner layer of 1.5, which is usually your romantic partner (they take so much time and love, they're worth 1.5 humans — which you're welcome to tell them, but do credit me for the romance of it). It's as though we're given a quota of intimacy that our brains can handle, and we've learnt to distribute that intimacy among the people in our lives according to how much we care about them. The way we allocate that intimacy has a lot to do with the sort of people we are. Introverts are more likely to have a smaller group of intense friendships, where extroverts might have a larger group of shallower connections. We might spend a lot of intense time with a few people, a lot of quality time with a couple of people, occasional time with a lot of people, or any variation of the time-to-intimacy ratio. This is what Dunbar would call our 'social fingerprint'; our own unique pattern of friendship distribution. We may all have this evolutionarily determined group of 150 friends, but the way we treat them is entirely over to us.

Now if, like me, you can't quite conceive of such an exact friendship system without seeing it applied to your own life, grab a pencil. Map out your own social network by drawing a small circle with your favourite five people in it, surrounded by concentric circles containing your 10, your 35 and finally, your 100. You may include family members, if you wish. Start with the people you're most likely to call in an emergency or emotional crisis, then fan out until you reach the people whose existence you mainly acknowledge via Facebook on their birthday. You should end up with a scribbly diagram of roughly 150 names in layered circles. We say 150, but it could range from 100 to 200, depending on how open to socialising you are.

When I met with Dunbar, having travelled by train from London to Oxford with a copy of his book *How Many Friends Does One Person Need?* in my backpack, I told him I couldn't resist making my own friendship map using Dunbar's Number.

'I sat down with a pencil and tried to map out my friends in circles,' I say, rather proudly.

'What, both of them?' Dunbar says in reply, attempting what I can only assume is just one of the friendship-themed jokes he keeps up his sleeve for occasions such as this. We chuckle.

'Am I mad or can you actually feel the cognitive constraint when you're doing it?' I say. And I stand by that — arranging the people in your life into categories of closeness is quite difficult. The most important friendships, the ones you can count on one hand, are easy. I jotted mine down fairly quickly. But it gets harder the further you get from that first layer of intimacy. By the time I got to the final 100 people in my social network, I was struggling to list names and I could have sworn I could feel that strain in my brain. I have an active imagination; I was envisaging those cognitive constraints. I did actually cave and have a cheeky look at my Facebook friends list to remind myself who I might count as an acquaintance. At the end of all that, I did, rather pleasingly, arrive at around 150. Beyond that, I couldn't think of anyone else I'd comfortably call a friend or acquaintance.

Dunbar tells me the outer limit of our memory is 1,500. That's the maximum number of names we should be able to put to faces. If you were shown photographs of people you've encountered in your life, you should be able to identify 1,500 of them. But facial recognition is hardly a basis for friendship and 1,500 is much bigger than our natural social networks, regardless of how many followers we have on Instagram. What keeps us down at that 150 mark for real connection is partly the cognitive constraint of memory, partly our willingness to invest time in a particular relationship. In what world could you possibly maintain more friendships and acquaintances than that? The quality of a friendship is directly related to how often you see or speak to someone. Friendships are not like relationships with family members, whom you can ignore from time to time because you know you have a biological contract to love one another. They require temporal and emotional commitment, or they simply disintegrate. If you're not diligent with friends, they drift out of those inner layers of intimacy and end up in that rather cold group of people you once knew.

Sitting in a plump burgundy armchair across from Dunbar, I sigh as I picture the people I used to know spilling out of the acquaintance circle like lemmings over a cliff. It's a funny thing, the way some friends come into your life and then later vanish from it. There are so many reasons people come and go or move between those layers of intimacy, I almost want to do a second drawing of all the people who no longer belong in my 150 (seems a little bleak, though). As you'll find out if you try and make your own social network map, it's a strangely exposing thing to do. The make up of our social circles is a deeply personal thing; you're literally counting out the people who matter to you. And who are we, really, but a reflection of all the people who sit in those circles?

Dunbar explains to me that the line-up of 5 — 10 — 35 — 100 friends and acquaintances seems to be human nature — whether we're talking about my personal friends list, or the composition of Indigenous tribes around the world. The humbling reality is that we may live in a hyper-modern world with infinite technological possibilities for connection, but we're still beholden to our neocortex for the size of our social network. The closer we have to work or live with other human beings, the more likely it is we will reach that number; that's why nomadic tribes or subsistence villages almost inevitably reach a population of between 100 and 250. Dunbar says it's 'almost spooky' how often the number 150, or thereabouts, pops up. For your reference, 150 is the size of a clan within the world's remaining hunter-gatherer societies. It's the size of a Neolithic farming village, a Roman army and a self-governing commune of the Anabaptist sect, the Hutterites. It's the number of academics typically found in a specialisation at a university. It's the smallest self-sufficient military unit in any Western armed force. It's the total number of people Brits send Christmas cards to each year, according to a study Dunbar did in the '90s. And it's become the standard number of employees some firms around the world will house in one office, before they build another one (the firm W.L. Gore & Associates was the first business to explicitly use Dunbar's Number to determine the size of their individual branches). Dunbar's Number — 150 — is a magic formula for meaningful interaction, whether we're talking about personal companionship, military strategy or an office population. It seems to be the limit of people we can meaningfully interact with, in any context.

If we're talking about the number 150 in a friendship context, each of those layers within that number — the 1.5, the 5, the 10, the 35, the 100 — require different levels of intimacy. Obviously, we start with the 'significant other' and circle outwards until we reach people we don't see that often. The people in each of these layers serve different purposes, too: the closest 5 (or 6.5, if you count your romantic partner) are the people you rely on for primary support. They're the ones you'd ask if you needed to borrow cash or cry on someone's shoulder; your first line of emotional defence. Once you ripple out to include the next 10, bringing us to a total of 15, that's more what your social network looks like. It's called the 'Sympathy Group' in your social circle. These are the people you actively seek to hang out with, the people you'd want to see on your birthday. They're people whose deaths would devastate you. Imagine the sort of mourning you might do if someone died, and you get a pretty clear idea of how much they mean to you now. The Sympathy Group might include friends and family. They're your people, your important people. The next layer out (made up of 35, which brings us to 50) is ... well, Dunbar's not entirely sure, to be honest. The field of evolutionary psychology hasn't exactly decided what purpose that layer serves — maybe the exchange of slightly more distant intimacies, maybe meeting at the school gate picking up the kids or looking after each other's children. Maybe they'd get an invitation if you had a particularly big wedding; maybe you'd pay your respects at their funeral. They're a pleasant lot wedged in between your closest buddies and your acquaintances, on the outer limits of what you might definitively call friends before you get to acquaintance territory.

That final layer (made up of 100, bringing us up to the total of 150) is made up of what we call weak ties. This is usually 75 per cent acquaintances, 25 per cent extended family. The people here are largely useful for information; they form your idea of what's going on in the world. They're sources of gossip, the people you like to casually check in on via social media, subjects of salacious interest more than an actual emotional connection. It's satisfying to know what these people are up to — Did they just get engaged? Where did they get married? Are their kids cute? Who got divorced? Who nailed their dream job? — but there's not a lot going on between you otherwise. You might actually see them in person once a year, if that, and that's not really enough to sustain a proper friendship (unless, as we'll cover later, you're communicating and swapping secrets online regularly). If you bumped into anyone from the outer limits of your social circle, or happened to be in a foreign city at the same time, you'd probably get a drink and catch up. But there's probably minimal concerted effort to see each other otherwise.

In his research, Dunbar has analysed a lot of Facebook and Twitter data, looking for evidence of this 150 breakdown. He says it's all there: if you look at the number of people we communicate with very frequently and span out to the ones we barely interact with, you get roughly the same groupings we've been working with so far. We can afford to take our number of acquaintances out to 500 on social media, to include all sorts of transactional friendships like the people we work with, the barista who makes us coffee, the guy we always see on the commute to work, the friend we inexplicably made at that music festival in Berlin one time and never spoke to again. This is casual beer in extenuating circumstances territory, even more so than the people who make it into your 150. If anything, their primary purpose is to prop up our egos, assuring us that we have successfully collected hundreds of people in our lifetimes with whom we have affinity. It's nice to have a lot of friends — that's why we prize popularity so highly in our list of desired attributes. The emotional quality of these friendships may be low, but gazing at the number of your Facebook 'friends' gives you a pleasant little jolt to the ego. We shouldn't go as far as to define ourselves or our social value by the number of friends we have; we're more sophisticated and friendship is more complex than that. But, evolutionarily speaking, that may actually have been why people made friends in the first place.

Scientists and psychologists are, shall we say, perplexed by the very notion of friendship. It doesn't, at first glance, have an obvious evolutionary purpose. We know a lot about finding kin in the early days of humanity, and how we were motivated to reproduce. We know comparatively little about why we might have sought out connections with non-kin. The prevailing theory is that popularity might protect you in crises or danger. Strategically, the more you can rely on the loyalty and protection of people when you need them, the safer you'll be. In the early days of human existence, this might have been the people we could count on to defend us in a fight between or within tribes, or even in a showdown with a predator like a tiger. There would have been a contract of loyalty between pairs and groups of people that ensured you would have their back if it was needed and vice versa. For men, that would most likely have been a guarantee of physical back-up. For women, especially when they found themselves trying to make alliances in their partner's family, it was more of an emotional or social back-up system. This sort of set-up is outlined in a theory called 'reciprocal altruism', whereby it's understood between friends that they will exchange favours. You help me and I'll help you, that kind of mentality. Evolutionary psychologists thought that was the evolutionary motive for friendship: purely an exchange system between human beings trying to assure their own survival. But that theory is limited and a bit grim, really, and it only accounts for certain types of friendships — the ones where we truly count favours and expect to get out what we put in. Researchers have realised that modern friendship is more complex (and lovelier) than that. Reciprocal altruism can only go so far; after a certain point in a friendship, it becomes irrelevant how many favours one person does for the other. In fact, in a genuine, loving friendship, it's nice to deliberately lose track of who owes whom what. It's less materialistic or pedantic than that (in fact, if you have a mate who insists on counting pennies or gestures of friendship between you, I'd suggest re-evaluating the friendship).

That brings us to something called The Alliance Hypothesis, as outlined by Peter DeScioli and Robert Kurzban. According to them, friendship is, in part, caused by 'cognitive mechanisms designed to assemble support groups for potential conflicts'. That's the physical, moral, social or emotional back-up we can expect to get in fights. Conflicts between people tend to be resolved by counting who or what principle has the most supporters. So it's logical that having more friends on whom you can rely for a vote of confidence in those situations makes you more powerful. The more friends you can rally to a particular cause, the more valuable you are. In this way, friendship works less like an exchange of altruism and more like alliance politics. Perhaps that's where friendship began: in the desire to have the most support in times of conflict. Strategically and, in our most primal states, for survival, it makes sense. Now that we are more self-sufficient for survival (or more dependent on things like currency, economics, access and proximity to food, water and shelter, defence, emergency services and medical aid for survival), we have the luxury of defining our friendships by other things: kindness, familiarity, sense of humour, that often inexplicable feeling of just being fond of someone. Sometimes, these days, we choose friends quite against our survival instinct; people who nudge us to smoke or drink or binge eat or escape our responsibilities. We can build our networks of allies however we wish. It's a modern indulgence, to compile our social circles based on loyalty as much as a sense of fun. That explains why you've got your old reliable friends who would do anything for you, as well as those low-key useless ones who make you laugh. But, to me, whatever the friendship is based on, it's got to have an unspoken level of alliance; the sense that you are in something together.

In an experiment published by William Austin in the *Personality and Social Psychology Bulletin* in 1980, pairs of people were given a joint task to complete in return for a reward. Some of the pairs were strangers, others were friends. The participants were told their reward for completing the task together would be divided by contribution. That is, the person in each pair who contributed more would get a greater share of the reward. If you were in it for the reward, it would make sense for you to tally up your contribution as you went along so it would be clear what you'd done and what your partner had done. The pairs made up of strangers tended to use different coloured pens so they could clearly see who came up with what. The pairs made up of friends made no such effort to monitor contributions; they were happy to let that go and share whatever prize they were given. I think this is lovely. It's the unspoken alliance I am talking about; the sense that you're in this friendship together and happy to share whatever goodness comes your way, regardless of what you get out of it in return. This little scenario happens again and again between good friends: when the bill comes at the end of dinner, when it comes to giving birthday presents, how much time you spend talking about one person's life, how much emotional support each person needs and receives. There's this lovely sense of longevity implied in the decision not to count favours, like you know that you'll always be in each other's lives and it will ultimately balance out.

The teenage girls I saw on the tube that day are right at the beginning of all that. They are, in some ways, wiser than we tend to give teenagers credit for being. They've been through that excruciating, tender stage of childhood where you learn what it is to have friends and, in the playground, what it is not to. They've sampled loneliness, they've known self-doubt, they've compared themselves to people who seem more popular and wondered why they don't look or sound like them. They're smack-bang in the middle of that delicate phase where they're trying to work out how much space to take up in the world, how much they're allowed, how much they've earned. And most importantly, they're choosing their allies for the long lives that stretch before them. Some of those friendships will last the distance, others will falter and fall apart. It's all about learning who they are and who they want by their side through all the angst that's yet to come. Of course, ideally, we make new friends throughout the later decades of our lives, too. I hope I'll always be open to the idea of a new friend. But at their age, they're in a more precarious position. Physically, their frontal lobes have not fully developed yet so they don't have an adult mental or emotional capacity to necessarily make the best decisions for themselves. And yet, at what time in our lives other than adolescence do we spend as much energy ferociously trying to get to know ourselves? Making friends at that stage is like compiling elements of your soul; you are who you choose to hang out with and you're going to make both wonderful and terrible selections. I wish every teenager the wisdom to start working out what they stand for, the strength to stick to it, and the humility to evolve. When it comes to friendship, we're using all our faculties: our hearts, our brains, our egos and our bodies. We're using language, both verbal and physical. We're using social lubricants, like alcohol and music. We are social animals and our very instinct to survive compels us to make friends. There is scarcely anything more important in those girls' lives than the friendships they have and will have, and I hope that in time, like me, they'll realise that.

CHAPTER THREE

Squad goals and girlfriends

REBECCA WAS 17 YEARS OLD when she joined the Royal Air Force (RAF). She was spritely and plucky, looking for mischief as much as work. And she found it — when she found her partner in crime. She met Nina on a Thursday; Nina's first Thursday on camp. Like the other new girls, Nina looked lost at first — she was, after all, just a teenager signing up for military service. Rebecca, being slightly older and more accustomed to life on the base, took Nina and the others out for their first boozy night on the town, to a cheesy place nearby called The Box, where the bartenders plied you with alco-pops no matter how young you looked.

From that night on, Rebecca and Nina were inseparable (except during the torturous months they were sent on different assignments and were separated by oceans). They were in the same squadron and lived on the same block, so they would work hard together during the day and drink hard together every night. It was a strange, heady time, with all the discipline of a military career by day and all the sweet abandon of underage rebellion by night. They had that inextricable type of best friendship, like they were invisibly conjoined or bound at the feet in a lifelong three-legged race. They were rarely seen apart — they became a set, a pair, a two-for-one.

One time, Rebecca and Nina turned up to a military party dressed head to toe as Tweedle Dee and Tweedle Dum. Nobody else was in costume, not one person. They could scarcely have found a better metaphor for their relationship: two beautiful idiots dressed in identical outfits, wading through a crowd of people in plain clothes. They lived by their own rules and they may as well have had their own language. Women in other squadrons used to ask management if Rebecca and Nina could join theirs; their friendship was so enviable and infectious, people just wanted to be around it.

When Rebecca and Nina were together, they moved as one. When they were sent on different assignments, to different corners of the world, they wrote to one another. Between them, they've got enough letters to fill a book. Rebecca's favourite telegram from Nina is in a frame. It says, 'Hi Muppet, we are nowhere. Miss you loads, Nina.' Nowhere is spelt 'k-n-o-where' and the message would have had to go through security to reach Rebecca because it was official military correspondence. In fact, Rebecca kept every telegram, every letter, every memo between them.

The girls might have had fun, but they held onto one another through some rough times, too. Nina's mother was an alcoholic, so there were explosive fights followed by stretches of silence between them. Rebecca wasn't on speaking terms with her parents. Both women suffered from bulimia and depression.

They each tried to take their own lives, at different times. They drank too much, they slept too little and they crashed into one another for support. They fought and made up. They kept each other alive in a hyper-masculine environment that didn't put much effort into keeping its women safe.

It was a strange place for two women to find themselves, the RAF. It was exactly the kind of tense, lonely experience that would foster a friendship like Rebecca and Nina's. It's fitting that both girls would enlist at around the same time and also make the decision to leave together to pursue their true dreams. Four years into their service, around the year 2000, the girls were in a nightclub. They were on the dance floor, having a life-changing conversation at full volume, over the music. They both just said, 'This is mad! Let's leave!' Rebecca said, 'I don't want to do this any more, I want to be an actress and a writer!' Nina said, 'I want to be a nurse!' And so, in sync as always, they went straight to the administration centre the next day and registered to leave the RAF. Six months and one last assignment later, they were free to get on with the rest of their lives — together, obviously. They moved to London, where Rebecca went to drama school and Nina trained as a nurse. They both got married. Nina has kids and Rebecca is their honorary aunt.

'We have plans to be friends forever, 100 per cent. As we get older … Well, Nina had a problem with her thyroid … I don't know …' Rebecca says, getting staccato with emotion. 'I've sort of dealt with how one day your parents will die and I know that, but like, your friend? I don't know, I can't deal with it, it's bigger. It's bigger. The light in my life would go out. I'm going to cry, oh God.'

The idea of existing without Nina is so offensive to Rebecca, she gently sort of dry retches. Her best friend's mortality is too much for her to think about, so we move on to a more general philosophy. What is it about female friendships that's so special? What kind of chemistry is going on between two women who adore one another platonically? How has Nina become the single most important person in Rebecca's life?

'It's just on a different level, female friendship,' Rebecca says. 'I think sisterhood is rooted in us, tribally, from generations past.'

Rebecca hit on exactly the thing I've been thinking about female friendship. What she has with Nina is exactly what I picture when I think of intense, lifelong female friendship. In fact, so much so, that when she said what I've just relayed to you here, I made a funny sort of squawking noise in response. I do that in interviews sometimes, when someone says exactly what I hoped they'd say. Rebecca, whom I liked immediately (and not just because she's written a cabaret show about being in the RAF with her best mate Nina, though it certainly has something to do with it), just happened to back up my own theory on female friendship: that woman-to-woman friendship is entirely different from male-to-male friendship. It doesn't matter if it's between a pair of people, like Rebecca and Nina, or a bigger group, like, say, Taylor Swift and her 'squad'. The very experience of being women unites us in a way men simply can't know. We might not all be literally in the RAF, surviving it with our best buddy, but we are all, to varying extents, fighting to live in a world that still belongs to men. Friendship is the alliance we have to have, just to get through.

If you were to look at the DNA of a friendship, you'd inevitably find gender in there as a defining factor. Female friendship is a support system predicated on our experience as women. Now, I don't imagine every set of best friends or group of girlfriends necessarily sits around discussing the suffragette movement or quoting the latest statistics on the gender pay gap to one another (I lied, I do imagine exactly that). What I'm talking about is a less formal exchange of solidarity; a more casual sort of feminist support that we offer each other.

My girlfriends and I do it all the time. We live in different corners of the world, so we have a WhatsApp conversation going between four of us: Jemma, Ayla, Sammie and me. The conversation is called 'Bridesmaids' because we recently wore matching dresses and cried all over each other at Sammie's wedding. There are thousands of messages between us (WhatsApp, for the uninitiated, is an app that allows you to text multiple people at once in a private conversation that's run through Wi-Fi rather than your phone's network data.)

We write to each other in that group every day, one way or another. Some days it's absolute nonsense: private jokes, bad puns, emojis and photos of dogs we saw on the street. But most days it's a little treasure trove of advice — about everything. We talk about holidays, breakfast, clothes, depression, anxiety, Beyoncé tickets, insomnia, Taylor Swift's relationships, cancer, men, wine, heartbreak, unrequited love, what we're eating for dinner, some cute kids we saw at the park, TV shows we binged on, books, notable cookies we've eaten, Britney Spears's comeback, candles, movies and careers. It's a higgledy-piggledy little stash of every conversation topic we could ever need to cover. But it's also full of conversations I'd quietly categorise as feminist: how to get through a presentation for a roomful of male executives, how to get people at work to stop calling you by a diminutive nickname, how to ask for a promotion, how to get a pay rise, how to start a professional networking group for women, how to have kids and have a career. And then there are the conversations I'd put under 'shit women have to deal with': guys starting conversations on public transport, dudes who touch you without an invitation, men who deliberately undermine you at work, anyone who wilfully underestimates your capacity to do something based on your biological traits. Our WhatsApp thread is full of personal silliness, but it's also our way of constantly negotiating how to be women. It's a private focus group of the comrades we trust the most.

That WhatsApp group is proof, to me, that we use female friendship for confirmation of our own existence. We work out how to behave and react and be in the world, as women, by talking to other women. Obviously, our differences define us too and we need people to challenge who we are and what we do as much as confirm it. I'm not saying we should seek out clones to prop ourselves up in life; I'm saying we tend to gravitate towards people with similar life experiences.

This is not all conjecture from me, by the way. You know who else is on my side, when it comes to the unique nature of female friendship? Evolutionary science. A landmark study conducted in the year 2000 argues, basically, that women have evolved to seek out female friendship in a way that men simply haven't.

The findings came when a group of American scientists were working on a study to investigate the way women respond to fear. They wrote about it in a paper called 'Biobehavioral Responses to Stress in Females: Tend-and-befriend, not fight-or-flight'. The paper was published by the American Psychological Association in a journal called the *Psychological Review*, so we know it's legit. Dr Laura Cousino Klein, Dr Shelley E. Taylor and their team's findings suggest that women don't necessarily respond to danger or fear in the way men do. You've heard of the phrase 'fight or flight' before; we use it colloquially now to talk about the way we respond to stress. That is to say that when we're confronted with some sort of threat, our instinct is usually to either fight or to flee. This 'fight or flight' model of behaviour has been around since the 1920s, but as Klein and Taylor point out, the majority of studies in this area have been conducted on men. So what we really know is that *men* have a fight-or-flight instinct, but there hasn't been enough female-specific research to know if the same thing applies to women. That's mainly because women have periods and the hormone fluctuations they entail confuse everyone, including scientists. So, basically, for ages most tests that might include hormones as a factor were done on the males of our species. Back in 2000, Klein and team counted 200 studies that included 14,548 people and found that 66 per cent of those subjects were male, with just 34 per cent female. What if women react entirely differently to stress but we don't actually know because all this damn time we've been testing so many men?

That's precisely what Klein and co. propose. They concluded that women respond to stressful conditions with a 'tend-and-befriend' instinct more than a fight-or-flight one. They say women are biologically motivated to protect themselves and their babies, and that this maternal instinct actually stops women from fighting or fleeing because both those options could be dangerous for the tiny human in their care. Instead, Klein and Taylor believe women respond to stress by calming and comforting their baby, and making friends for protection from danger.

So when life throws a stress curveball in the direction of a woman, her response is to check her baby's alright (if she has one handy) and then reach out to other women for companionship and safety in numbers. The single greatest source of danger to a woman is now, and possibly always has been, the male of the human species. Women are killed by their partners in alarming numbers the world over, so even though #notallmen is a hashtag on Twitter, women have a biological imperative to protect themselves from man-folk. This might be one of the reasons why they seek out female friends — for solidarity and protection. Men have little biological reason to fear women and they've always been dominant, so they haven't developed any such mechanism.

When humans are in stress, their bodies have a hormonal response to threat, which includes the rapid release of oxytocin.

It is generally accepted that oxytocin is enhanced by the oestrogen in the female body. Oxytocin can have a calming effect — and if that's true, it explains why women are better able to make buddies in times of stress than men, who tend to react with aggression.

Klein et al. say the female instinct to make friends (or 'strong tendency to affiliate' as science would put it) is 'one of the most robust gender differences in adult human behaviour'. Women crave the social connection of other women as a product of their evolutionary needs — and they will seek it out more than men at all life stages. Teenage girls, female college students and adult women are all more likely than their male peers to get same-sex support when they need it. As fully-grown humans, women rely less on their spouse for socialisation than men and appear to be generally more buoyed by a small group of same-sex friends. At every age, women are just drawing strength from other women like it ain't no thang. They seek support, of course, but they're also more generous in giving it. In fact, research reveals that women are 30 per cent more likely than men to have given support in response to life stressors like money and work problems, personal issues, death and health concerns.

Rhesus and squirrel monkeys demonstrate similar behaviour in the way they maintain matrilineal social systems. Mothers, daughters and sisters in primate groups treat one another in much the same way they treat unrelated females — mainly by licking them and protecting them (I know that's how I make friends). They spend between 10 and 20 per cent of their time grooming one another, which is an expression of friendship and status. I don't want to go on too much of a monkey tangent — I'll only start making simian puns and nobody wants that — but suffice to say a lot of monkey research appears to confirm my whole 'female friendships are special' theory. And I don't know about you, but when I put forward any kind of cultural hypothesis, I like to have monkey back-up before I publish anything.

I also wanted to talk to one of the authors of the 'Tend-and-befriend' paper. Partly because it was published in 2000 and surely they've thought of something new to add in the past 16 years. But mainly because I wanted to ask one of the female scientists whether her personal life experiences matched her research. So, on a Friday evening UK time, I skyped Dr Laura Cousino Klein, who was sitting outside a Starbucks in Colorado.

Unsurprisingly, Klein has lived out some of her own theory. When she started this research, she was a female scientist in male-dominated territory, trying to challenge something we took to be true about evolution. Since the study, and as she continues her work in the area of gender difference and resilience, Klein has become a mother and felt that biological pull of loyalty towards her family that she once wrote about in theory. At times of stress (walking into Penn State University as one of just three women in her department, multiple miscarriages, a husband who left her with three children under 12) Klein has reacted precisely the way she predicted: by tending to her children and finding solace in her friendships.

'Since the research has been published, I have become an advocate for valuing our social relationships and finding ways to help people prioritise them,' says Klein. 'We're so caught up in our computers and our work, are we really taking the time to cultivate relationships that are biologically satisfying?'

Now I want to tell you an extraordinary story that is, more than anything, all about biologically satisfying friendship. Natasha Bakht is a family law professor living in Ottawa, Canada. She wanted to have a child, so she became pregnant via sperm donor and planned to raise her son as a single mother. When Natasha was pregnant and working at the University of Ottawa, one of her colleagues — an environmental lawyer called Lynda Collins — suggested she could be Natasha's birth coach. At the time, Lynda just thought it might be cool to see a human being come into the world. She wasn't a mother yet herself and she was naturally inquisitive about the process — and besides, she wanted to be helpful. Natasha gave birth to a little boy, whom she called Elaan. Elaan is a beautiful child, but his arrival on Earth was not simple. Complications during labour left the little boy with severe disabilities. Six months into his life doctors discovered part of his brain was dead. He now lives with spastic quadriplegia, epilepsy, asthma and visual problems. He cannot speak. For his mothers, watching Elaan grow — he's now seven — is both heart-achingly wonderful and devastating.

Right from the very first day of Elaan's life, Lynda was by his side. She lived about 15 minutes away from Natasha and Elaan, and visited frequently. What started out as hour-long visits became three-, six-, nine-hour visits, where she'd just spend all day playing and hanging out. Elaan was only truly comfortable in the company of two human beings: Natasha and Lynda. Any other carer who turned up would inevitably make him despair. In every respect except biology, Lynda was as much Elaan's mother as Natasha. So by the time Lynda started thinking about whether to have her own child, she realised she already had one. She'd become besotted and Elaan took over her life in a spectacular, unexpected way. The three of them became this totally unconventional, completely lovely family unit. Lynda looked into adopting Elaan, but because she and Natasha are not in a conjugal relationship, she couldn't legally do that without Natasha giving him up. Still, they wanted something to officially acknowledge Lynda's relationship with Elaan, because it truly was the connection between a parent and a child. Elaan knows Lynda as 'Aunty Lyndy' and nobody can make him laugh quite like she can. Conveniently, remember, Natasha is a professor in family law. She'd heard of something called a declaration of parentage, which could legally make Lynda Elaan's mother. If they were successful in their legal bid, they'd have Elaan's birth certificate changed to include Lynda's name as well as Natasha's. They were the first pair of close friends to try and become co-parents of a child in Canada and the legal process was complicated. It took two years, but finally the court decided it was in Elaan's best interests to have Lynda as a parent as well.

So now Elaan legally has two mothers to love and adore and protect him. Two mothers to guide him through a difficult existence. Two mothers to make a perfectly delightful, if unconventional, family. He and Natasha live in one apartment and Lynda lives in the apartment directly above, in the same building. Lynda pops down in the mornings to see Elaan before school and comes around for dinner and bedtime stories in the evenings. Natasha and Lynda coordinate their teaching schedules so one or the other of them is always available, should Elaan need them during the day. They negotiate modern parenthood the same way any other set of parents would — only they happen to be friends, not romantically involved as social convention would have it.

Natasha and Lynda now have Elaan's modified birth certificate, which is emotionally significant for both of them. It makes their little family official and that's enormously gratifying. What we're able to call ourselves in relation to the people we love is really important, so for Lynda to be able to say she is her son's mother is a profoundly moving development. It makes things logistically easier, too, because Lynda is now allowed to make medical appointments for Elaan and liaise with his school, which she couldn't have done when her status was 'Elaan's mum's friend'. It also means they will have financial security for Elaan's future, including if anything should happen to either of them. Elaan's medical costs are huge and he is now entitled to two parents' pensions, which could literally, at some stage, be lifesaving for him. His physical condition remains precarious and neither parent is sure how long they will have little Elaan in their lives, but for however long that may be, they will be there for him — together.

I simply cannot think of a lovelier testament to the bond possible between two women. Two buddies, doing motherhood together. It's really affected the way I think about the future of family dynamics. I don't know if I want to have children — I'm at that delicate stage where I've spent nearly three decades assuming I would become a mother and now that the biological imperative is here, I'm scared and I have no idea what I want. I like the idea that perhaps by the time I get to it, there might be different combinations of people who love each other raising children together. Single motherhood is a brave and sometimes lonely choice. Natasha chose that path, but then gave birth to a severely disabled little boy whom she adored and fretted for at the same time. She would have loved him no matter what, cared for him no matter what. But having a close friend to co-parent with you is just such an unspeakably lovely revelation in a story that could otherwise have been so different. I spoke to Natasha and Lynda separately, and they both said the actual conversation — the 'I'd like to co-parent your child' one — was incredibly easy. The bond between Lynda and Elaan was so strong and so obvious, the move to make Lynda a co-mom was seamless. It's just an exceptionally charming story of female friendship and it makes me a little bit emotional, to be honest.

I love seeing our definition of family change to include more iterations of love. Why shouldn't two women (or two men) raise a child, whether they're romantically involved or not? A child deserves love and that's really all there is to it. Raising children is, from what I can tell, totally mad. It's the kind of beautiful chaos we voluntarily create in our own lives because we're compelled by something primal, by something in our blood and our ancestry. Having a friend by your side through all the broken sleep, tears, tantrums, desperate naps, heartache, worry, teenage angst and growing up would be wonderful and I can hardly see why a straight romantic partner would necessarily be any better qualified for the job. Natasha and Lynda are my current favourite poster women for female friendship. The way they've both negotiated being single, working mothers is seriously inspirational and I hope we start seeing more families like theirs in the future.

Now, we've just seen an exceptional example of family love enabled by feminism. It's a private, domestic manifestation of female friendship. There have also recently been some far more public demonstrations of female friendship. Now, as ever, I'd like to talk about Ms Taylor Swift. She is the most commercially valuable singer in the world right now, and it seems that part of her publicity agenda has been to promote the very idea of woman-to-woman friendship. She has invoked 'girl power' and for better or for worse, her very tall friends have become envoys of the cause. While the question of authenticity has lingered in the media over some of those relationships, you can't deny that Taylor 'Swifty' Swift is a staunch ambassador for female friendship.

Swift has a group of powerful, uber-famous women friends: Karlie Kloss, Blake Lively, Cara Delevingne, Selena Gomez, Ruby Rose, Gigi Hadid, Emma Stone, Lena Dunham, Lorde. It's also reported that she has maintained her friendship with her best friend Abigail, a pre-fame friend. Sure, Swift is sometimes reported as cutting and accumulating friends for publicity reasons, like many other celebrities. But I like to believe she's human as well as famous, and motivated by the same things we are. The need for intimacy, company and support, that kind of thing.

Whatever Swift's motives, she has essentially launched an advocacy campaign for female friendship. When she baked cookies with Karlie Kloss, walked barefoot on a beach with Lorde and threw Fourth of July parties for her 'squad', she started a cultural moment for female friendship. It's not something we usually talk about a lot, fixated as we are on romance — but since Swift's high-profile friendship rallies, we do. Swift has very publicly selected her 'squad' and celebrated what they mean to her on stage, in the media and on Instagram. Swift has made friendship (and love) into a type of performance art. It's not exactly my style, but then I'm not the world's most famous pop star either, and who knows how I'd behave if I were. Celebrity is a strange, foreign thing; you may as well have company through it.

Taylor Swift's squad might be the most exclusive clique on the planet. It's mainly made up of supermodels and actors, most of whom are white and wealthy. They often wear matching outfits and stand in choreographed positions for photographs. It would be easy, and probably mildly satisfying, to disregard the whole group as vacuous or staged or opportunistic. I might be naive, but I also think this group of women are a force for good.

What Swift shows us is that female friendship is one of the ways we communicate feminism, harking back to what Dr Klein has discovered in her research about the biological imperative for female solidarity in a man's world. Swift was converted to the cause of feminism by her own famous friend, *Girls* creator and star, Lena Dunham. Swift used to be one of those famous women who doesn't identify as a feminist — until she became friends with Dunham in 2014. She told *The Guardian* newspaper: 'As a teenager, I didn't understand that saying you're a feminist is just saying that you hope women and men will have equal rights and equal opportunities. What it seemed to me, the way it was phrased in culture, society, was that you hate men. And now I think a lot of girls have had a feminist awakening because they understand what the word means. For so long it's been made to seem like something where you'd picket against the opposite sex, whereas it's not about that at all. Becoming friends with Lena — without her preaching to me, but just seeing why she believes what she believes, why she says what she says, why she stands for what she stands for — has made me realise that I've been taking a feminist stance without actually saying so.'

I've spoken to women in their teens and early twenties particularly, who have had an entirely similar epiphany to Taylor Swift's. Some of those awakenings were *because* of Taylor Swift. For a lot of young women, feminism has had a PR problem for a long time, seen as this acerbic, unfashionable movement of women who hate men. Hopefully, with the exceptional impact of movements like the #MeToo campaign, in which women shared their stories of assault and harassment after more than 100 allegations were made against Hollywood producer Harvey Weinstein, there is more widespread pride in feminism now. Feminism, of course, goes so very far beyond Taylor Swift — in my opinion, her version of it is often perilously exclusive — but she has done good work in its rebranding, for she is a master of the makeover. If there are two things Ms Swift is exceptionally good at, it's break-up lyrics and publicity. She brought the latter to a cause that needs it, to recruit a new generation of girls. Sure, Swift isn't a perfect feminist. Nobody is. But she is now a prominent self-defined feminist and that matters. To get women to join the fight for equality, sometimes you have to speak to them in their own language. In this case, it's pop music and friendship.

The crossover of Swift's friendships and feminism reminds me of a particularly great article published in *New York Magazine*'s 'The Cut', by journalist Ann Friedman. It's about 'The Shine Theory', which is essentially the idea that you should befriend other women, rather than try to cut them down. You don't shine if I don't shine, we shine more brightly together, that kind of thing. If you live by The Shine Theory, you support other women by recruiting them as friends. Friedman wrote: 'I want the strongest, happiest, smartest women in my corner, pushing me to negotiate for more money, telling me to drop men who make me feel bad about myself, and responding to my outfit selfies from a place of love and stylishness, not competition and body-snarking.' It's essentially a mini thesis for feminism-via-friendship; Friedman is calling for women to surround themselves with the strongest possible allies in the fight for success, happiness and identity. She wrote: 'When you meet a woman who is intimidatingly witty, stylish, beautiful, and professionally accomplished, *befriend her.* Surrounding yourself with the best people doesn't make you look worse by comparison. It makes you better.'

That idea is at the heart of my argument for friendship as a transformative force. It argues for the deliberate cultivation of a strong friendship group with the explicit purpose of allegiance, support and shared brilliance. It's the ultimate way to spread and inhabit feminist ideas: one woman at a time, friend to friend, friendship group by friendship group until we meet in this glorious cross-stitch of womankind. Female friends are uniquely influential in each other's lives and they are in the perfect position to encourage feminist action. I'm talking about encouraging career ambition, calling out sexism and racism, reporting abuse, getting rid of toxic partners, knowing when to quit, caring for children, negotiating maternity leave, navigating love, ageing, looking after family and surviving. I'm talking about who will be by your side during one or many of the uniquely female experiences: getting pregnant, getting an abortion, getting your period, losing your period. And who will be there when you're blindsided by tragedy, paralysed by grief, bankrupt by hospital or disability costs, or you're told your life doesn't matter because of the colour of your skin, prosecuted, taunted, heartbroken, fired, destitute, homeless or lost. While men, politicians and church leaders believe they have a say in what we do with our bodies, how we manage our lives, what we teach our children, the worth of a life, or any other matter that directly relates to the experience of being female, we need each other for support. It's a survival tactic as much as a thing of great loveliness. Women fighting for women is one of the most powerful forces that exists on this planet of ours — it's why we wear T-shirts emblazoned with 'The future is female'.

For recent proof that female solidarity is formidable, just think of the extraordinary Women's Marches that happened across the world at the beginning of 2017. On 21 January, an estimated five million women (and their male allies) pounded the pavement together to protest against President of the United States, Donald Trump's alarming approach to women's rights, immigration and LGBTQI safety. The flagship protest was called Women's March on Washington, and half a million people turned up to (peacefully) storm the political capital of America. It was the biggest turnout for a protest since those against the Vietnam War in the '60s. Organisers estimate that 3.3–4.6 million American women protested against their new president that day, in the name of human rights.

In London, 5,894 kilometres away, I, and 99,999 other women, congregated outside the American Embassy so we could feel as though we were standing on common ground with our American sisters. Women around the world did the same thing, some in almighty numbers, others in smaller and sometimes clandestine groups because open political protest is not permitted in their country. Women turned up with their friends and colleagues in every corner of the world to show solidarity, and it was glorious. There were 673 protests worldwide, in the greatest demonstration of female anger in recent memory. Organisers in London expected roughly 30,000 people to show up in England's capital on an uncharacteristically sunny

Saturday, but it ended up being more than 100,000. The streets in central London were so crammed with incensed women, you could barely move. My flatmate and I got a bus (red, double-decker) into town, met some other badass women, took a selfie of our marching boots and set off to the beginning of the set route for the march — only to stand around for three full hours in a seething crowd of protestors about five blocks away because we literally couldn't fit into the square by the American Embassy. It was frustrating in the most wonderful, affirming way, like a beautiful traffic jam of revolutionaries.

You probably saw photographs of some of the signs women made and carried that day. Some of the best I saw included, 'Girls just want to have fundamental human rights'; 'This pussy grabs back'; 'I've seen smarter cabinets at IKEA'; 'So bad, even introverts are here'; 'I can't believe we're still protesting this'; 'Grab 'em by the patriarchy'; 'Diversity makes America great'; 'Put avocado on racism so white people will notice' and 'A woman's place is in the resistance'. And there was a baby with a sign around his neck that read: 'I love naps but I stay woke'. Which is why you have children: to raise them as tiny members of the resistance. But probably my favourite sign of the day was one that simply said: 'We are family. I got all my sisters with me'. Because that's what it felt like, having the sisterhood together.

But I can't talk about the Women's Marches without respectfully pointing out their flaws. There was some extremely valid criticism of these protests from black women, who argued this is the first time white women have come out in great numbers, when they should have been protesting alongside them at Black Lives Matter protests before now. Comedian Samantha Bee observed that all you needed to get white women out on the streets is to give them arts and crafts to do — because one of the trademarks of this protest was the bright pink 'pussy' hat, which is a DIY knitting project with political undertones. The absence of white women in the fight against racism is glaring and shameful. Feminism needs desperately, urgently, to be racially inclusive and I pray to Michelle Obama that the reaction to this protest has been a wake-up call for white feminists who only march when something directly affects them. The sisterhood is incomplete so long as we ignore or sideline some of our own.

What I'm trying to say is that the Women's March was magnificent, but we can do better. Millions of women got together around the world to send a clear message: 'We see you, Donald Trump, and we will not sit idly by while you take away our rights'. We loudly rejected the agenda of the misogynist-in-chief of America and that felt really, really good. Walking shoulder to shoulder with thousands of other women, yelling 'Hey ho, Donald Trump has got to go' in chorus, was extraordinary. But there's still work to be done — on the movement for women and the movement against Trump. We've reminded ourselves of the power we have when we get together, and that's wonderful. What we've got to do now is continue to fight, to go into political battle together, to have millions of female hearts beat as one. That's what female friendship is at its extreme, it's feminist solidarity that can genuinely change the world. Those marches were made up of friendship groups, lady-dates and family outings, all smaller circles of solidarity coming together. That's what we're working with here, when we do female friendship properly.

That's why I think female friendship needs a bit of a publicity overhaul. We're all plenty familiar with the myth that friendship between women can be snarky, petty or bitter. We probably witnessed some of it in high school. What we need now is to vehemently reject that sort of behaviour and instead lift each other up. Lift, but also criticise. The most productive friendships are the ones you can rely on for truth: encouragement and support when you need it, candid criticism when you deserve it. The only reason I believe my best girlfriends when they say something lovely is because I trust them to be honest about the ugly parts of life, too. I expect my dearest buddies to hold me accountable for anything stupid or bad I do, just as they cheer me on when I do something good. The same applies to feminism on a bigger scale — we are equally entitled to be celebrated and challenged. I do not believe it should be mandatory for women to support other women purely because they are female. That's reductive and dangerous: If we start thinking that way, I'd have to support Sarah Palin or Katie Hopkins based purely on anatomical similarities. No thank you. I reserve the right to disagree with other women and I am in no way suggesting a blanket rule of support among lady folk.

I am talking about strategic support for the women in our lives. It's the personal-life equivalent of the 'amplification' strategy used by President Obama's female aides. When

Obama came into office, two-thirds of his aides were male and the women on his team found it difficult to be heard in the boardroom, as so many of us do. Men were more likely to speak up, to claim ideas as their own and to take credit for being effective. So the women put a very simple but clever strategy in place: When one woman spoke during a meeting, another woman would repeat or echo what she had said to give it extra gravitas and to stop a man from speaking over her. They called it 'amplification' and it worked — President Obama reportedly noticed what they were doing, took their point and started to seek out the opinions of women and junior aides. It was a rather clever antidote to the invisibility some women feel at work. It's also how feminism spreads, via the amplification of certain ideas between women. Really, when we befriend someone, we're asking them to amplify our thoughts, fears and ideas. We're asking for an echo.

The other feminist thing we do in our female friendships is embrace imperfection. We allow ourselves to be fully developed characters in our own stories. I tell my WhatsApp group of girlfriends when I do something stupid, when I think I've hurt someone, when I worry that I've been awful, and when I've generally been a disaster of an adult human. I am the fullest version of myself with them. They know me in all my unashamed ridiculousness. They love me in moments of strength and in weakness — and I think that's crucially important. We are bombarded with the expectation of perfection from every angle, as women — from pop culture, magazines, books, TV shows, films and our extended families. Female friendships can be our respite from all of that. Together, we can be wicked and fallible and completely ourselves — and that's still a rebellious act.

Remember how revolutionary Lena Dunham's show *Girls* was when it premiered in 2012, and *Sex and the City* in 1998? The novelty there was that it actually dared to represent young (white) women realistically, and make friendship the focal point of their lives. The four central Girls characters, Hannah, Marnie, Jessa and Shoshanna, were written with a nuanced sort of realism we weren't used to: they're complex, unlikable, chaotic, changeable and fallible. They have sex and fall in and out of love, but that doesn't define them. They are allowed, as so many women in general before them were not, to define themselves. The show is an homage to female existence in all its great, aching messiness. It's evidence that we're starting to accept the full, inconvenient experience of being female.

Elsewhere in culture, we're seeing a surge of stories about women. The rabid popularity of Italian writer Elena Ferrante's 'Neapolitan' novels is proof that we crave deeper depictions of female friendship. The four books in the series tell the story of a lifelong friendship between two characters, Elena 'Lena' Greco and Raffaella 'Lila' Curello. Lena and Lila start their lives in Naples and remain, in one way or another, entangled, as though they cannot escape one another. Their friendship is as dark and vicious as any friendship could be, in so much as it is motivated by envy and spite as well as love. Right from the beginning, there's something combative about the way the girls interact, and they continue in this great, wild volatility. Lena worships and loathes Lila in almost equal measure and becomes utterly fixated on her. She is unable to work out who she is without comparing herself to Lila — fearing her entire life that people see her as 'Lila's pale shadow'. Lila is a brilliant, cantankerous thing; a bedraggled waif of a girl who grows into a tough, complicated woman. They live through poverty, abuse, crime, sexism, violence, love and tragedy, but not always as allies. It's more like Lena and Lila are bound to one another, unable in some fundamental way to truly exist without the other. The inevitability of their relationship is written into the DNA of both characters. In the first book, *My Brilliant Friend*, Lena says Lila is 'the only person I still felt was essential even though our lives had diverged'. Theirs is a bond that neither distance nor time can break. It's a more formative relationship than any marriage, romance or affair, any child, any job, any family member. It's the ultimate example of a torrid female friendship; one that touches every element of two existences.

The Lena-Lila connection began as many childhood best friendships do, with a closeness that seems to exclude everyone else on the planet. In the first book, Lena says: 'We were twelve years old, but we walked along the hot streets of the neighbourhood, amid the dust and flies that the occasional old trucks stirred up as they passed, like two old ladies taking the measure of lives of disappointment, clinging tightly to each other. No one understood us, only we two — I thought — understood one another.' I love that Ferrante compares twelve-year-olds to old ladies — it's the perfect way to capture that restless maturity some children reach right before adolescence. Lena and Lila were always ahead of their peers in that sense, always better with language and better at school than the other girls, always a step or several ahead of the boys. Together they have this lovely, languid maturity as children and then, in some ways, a stubborn childishness in their adulthood. Friendship has a way of stretching age and defying time like that. Intense friendship has a way of lifting two or more of you out of context: if you've known each other forever, you can regress to childish behaviour in moments, or slip into old habits and get drunk with the same girls you did at 21. In the same way childhood and teenage friends drag each other to each birthday like a race to grow up, old friends can keep you young. That's what happened with Lena and Lila; they were girls who wanted desperately to be women and then, when they became old enough, they clung to jealousy and disagreement like children unprepared for what the world can do to you.

The type of friendship Lena and Lila have is rare, in real life (though it's worth noting that there are rumours these books were autobiographical). It's too intense to happen all the time; it's utterly life-defining and consuming. But the very depiction of it by Ferrante is revolutionary in literature because it's a fully developed, rich, viscous, infuriating relationship between two female human beings. Truly, how often do we get that in our stories? Barely ever. Female friendship has, until recently, been too threatening to the patriarchy to appear with any prominence in pop culture. Its emergence as a major cultural force — in the visibility of Taylor Swift's squad in every major media outlet in the world, on the television and in the writing of Elena Ferrante — is a feminist triumph. It gives currency and validation to a hyper-female incarnation of friendship that's previously been dismissed or underestimated. But we cannot truly understand the potential of female friendship to unite and inspire and ignite without acknowledging the knotty, dark side of it. The thorny, bitter, tempestuous parts of some friendships that can tear apart two people rather than build them up.

Again, Taylor Swift is relevant. For all her glossy Instagramworthy friendships with women, there's one that darkens her reputation as Best BFF Ever. It's her allegedly bitter relationship with Ms Katy Perry. If you're not *au fait* with the ups and downs of celebrity friendships, Swift and Perry used to be very close, but then Perry allegedly 'stole' one of Swift's back-up dancers — an act of betrayal from which the friendship never recovered. Then, during her '1989' world tour, Swift invited many famous people up on stage with her except Perry. She also, allegedly, wrote the song 'Bad Blood' about their spat. Swift made a music video for the song starring all her real-life friends as hot warriors in a fight against an unnamed brunette nemesis speculated to be Perry, essentially a revenge fantasy. Katy Perry released a song called 'Swish Swish Bish', widely reported in the media to be in response to 'Bad Blood'.

Tabloid speculation about Swift and Perry is split: Either they genuinely had a fallout, like normal human beings, or in the lyrics to 'Bad Blood' Swift has shrewdly slandered her fiercest competition in the pop industry. If Swift truthfully felt as though Perry was a bad friend, then she has successfully excised a toxic friendship from her life. On the other hand, she may have used the friendship of other women for the purpose of excluding Perry. We simply may never know. Perry, for her part, has tweeted that she would be open to collaborating with Swift, on the condition she is given an apology.

The Swift–Perry friendship saga makes international headlines because tabloid media have always loved a good, old-fashioned fight between women and will take any opportunity to pit them against one another. It's also newsworthy because it hints at a darker side to femininity, to celebrity, to female friendship. Female friendship, like any type of relationship, is not perfect and there's little point pretending it is. Women (even Swift and Perry) are more than entitled to have dark and disastrous friendships — in real life as they are in fiction.

New York Magazine published a terrific essay on intense female friendship, called 'I'm Having a Friendship Affair'. In it, author Kim Brooks writes about 'the intensely obsessive, deeply meaningful, occasionally undermining, marriage-threatening, slightly pathological platonic intimacy that can happen between women'. She recounts the time she met a slightly younger writer at a conference and became instantly devoted to her in an endearingly deranged sort of way. They were the only two English-speaking writers at the conference and they got on fiercely, drank together, shared their deepest fears and became inseparable. When the conference ended, they kept in contact; such constant contact that Kim's husband suspected she was having an affair. Even Kim thought at one point that perhaps she was in love with this woman she'd just met — that's how intense the connection was. They emailed, texted, spoke on the phone and divulged all sorts of secrets they hadn't told anyone else in their lives. They planned trips away from their normal, adult lives and basically used each other for that glorious escapism a new relationship can give you. It was, as Kim called it, a friendship affair. And like Lena and Lila's relationship, like Rebecca and Nina's, Kim and her platonic partner seemed to defy age together. They became like teenage best friends, bound together in an exclusive bond so profound it felt like romantic love.

But then Kim and her new friend had a falling out. It was small, but it was devastating. Kim couldn't eat or sleep, she was so distraught. She couldn't believe her precious friendship might be toxic or fallible. Kim and her friend more or less patched things up but their one disagreement had fractured what they had. 'There was a slight undercurrent of hostility that hadn't been there before,' Kim wrote; 'a frightening knowledge that we could hurt each other as expertly as we could raise each other up.'

And that, to me, is the paradox at the very heart of female friendship: We can hurt each other as expertly as we can raise each other up. We can love and teach one another — and we can just as easily tear each other down. No matter how much time we spend cultivating shiny, happy, supportive friendships, we can all be capable of a Swift–Perry style conflict. Female friendships are unique and remarkable, but they're also just human relationships — and that makes them vulnerable, changeable and imperfect. It makes them fascinating and powerful. Whether we're trying to get by in the RAF, working for the President of the United States, writing a TV show called

Girls, reading a book about acerbic best friends in Naples, or smashing it in the pop music industry, female friendships are essential. They're our greatest refuge, our greatest challenge and our greatest vehicles for feminist action. They're also, quite simply, rather lovely.

I couldn't live without the friendship of women. I am eternally, feverishly grateful for my girlfriends and convinced the world is a better place when we work together. Here's to female friendship — the mess, the exquisiteness, the power and the transformative potential of it.

CHAPTER FOUR

Bromance and guy love

LET'S BEGIN WITH THE ULTIMATE in male friendship, shall we? That blessed holy grail of brotherhood: the bromance. A bromance is a very close, non-sexual relationship between two men, probably equivalent to a woman's BFF (Best Friend Forever) in that it's equal parts earnest and performative. It's a psychosocial bond between two guys that matches a romantic relationship in almost every way except the sexual interaction. There's physical affection, fierce loyalty, obvious closeness and a tendency to be seen everywhere together, like a two-for-one deal. It usually requires the participating bros to be shameless about their love for one another. The bromance is the most important relationship in each bro's life and there's often the implication that they compromise on female affection for this mightiest of man bonds. It is understood, by now, that the bromance is a safe space for men to be close — without any inference or rumour that they could be gay.

When I asked online for good stories of male friendship, a man called Keith got in touch to tell me his bromance with his mate Mike is the greatest bromance I would ever read or hear about, ever. 'You will never find a better story than ours,' he promised. Keith and Mike talked with me about their bromance over beers at the pub, which, by the way, they squeeze in at least once a week between work and looking after their kids. They live on the same street so it's pretty easy to set up. (Side note: This is the ultimate friendship dream, isn't it? Being grown adults with families and living on the same street so you're always a short trot away from gossip, binge-watching Netflix together, shared dinners, a cheeky afternoon wine and getting the kids to play together. I frequently send advertisements for castles, mews houses and conjoined holiday homes to my friends as extremely unsubtle hints that I consider co-habitation of some sort to be in our future.)

It turns out Mike and Keith's bromance is pretty normal (and beautiful, in its way). Their relationship revolves around being there for each other through rough times, drinking, playing sport, talking about sport, getting in trouble with their partners for spending too much time with each other and occasionally falling asleep on the beach in each other's arms. But what I particularly like is the competitive enthusiasm with which they talk about their friendship. Because that's what a self-identifying bromance is to me: brash, loving, and strangely competitive about intimacy. It's as though by effusively calling their friendship a bromance — you can't spell bromance without 'romance' — they pre-empt anyone calling them gay for being so close. It's performative closeness to ward off any accusations of being too close — how can anyone else say they're too close if they get in first and claim to be the closest two male friends have ever been? The intimacy is absolutely real, I've no doubt. Guys like this are close, real close. But I think the bromance moniker is intriguing because it somehow manages to imply both gentleness and hyper-masculinity. It seems to have become this lovely, useful label that enables male closeness between men who still want you to know they sleep with women. It's an identity marker that men use to both soften and reinforce their archetypal manliness.

The term bromance was apparently coined by a skating magazine in the 1990s to describe dudes who skate together a lot. As with any good social trend, celebrities have embraced it: Brad Pitt and George Clooney are bromantic, and so are Matt Damon and Ben Affleck, Owen Wilson and Ben Stiller, Sir Ian McKellen and Sir Patrick Stewart. These celebrities work together, go out together and say complimentary things about one another in the press. Such high-profile alliances are endearing as well as commercially savvy, with both members of the famous bromance benefitting from an increase in his stock by virtue of his closeness to another famous dude. The Pitt–Clooney friendship has been going many years and it makes any movie they're both in all the more bankable. The *Ocean's Eleven* franchise is the perfect example because Pitt and Clooney's real-life friendship makes their fictional one more appealing. When Damon and Affleck became famous after appearing together in *Good Will Hunting*, they emerged as Hollywood's favourite pair of talented buddies. They played best mates in the movie they wrote together and their bromantic connection became the currency of their fame. They've since forged separate career paths, but the beginnings of their fame were very much rooted in that friendship (two stars are better than one). Wilson and Stiller's collaboration in films like *Zoolander*, *Starsky and Hutch*, *The Royal Tenenbaums*, *Meet the Fockers* and *Night at the Museum* has made them an enormously successful double act. Their real-life friendship makes their professional working relationship all the more powerful because their combined comedic value is arguably higher than either could ever hope to achieve alone. We love to imagine actors are not really acting; that we're witnessing their real relationships on screen under a very thin guise. Don't even get me started on The Sirs, Ian McKellen and Patrick Stewart — they are so effusively lovely about one another on social media, in their matching bowler hats, that I just wish they were my honorary celebrity grandfathers. The pair appeared in *Waiting for Godot* and *No Man's Land* together, as well as the *X-Men* movies. As seen on Twitter and Instagram, they travel together, drink beers down the pub, cook risotto for each other, celebrate gay pride with glitter, go jogging, regularly hold hands on the red carpet and have even kissed on stage. I've never seen Patrick Stewart in a film or play, but I like him enormously based purely on his friendship with Ian 'Gandalf' McKellen. They double their fandom by hanging out together and seem to truly celebrate each other's successes. It's a beautiful validation of love between two men.

We've even seen the bromance narrative creep into politics. Remember that time two best mates ran the free world together? President Barack Obama took his buddy Joe Biden into office as Vice President in 2009. They spent a decent chunk of the next eight years parading their bromance for the public — and it was rather beautifully captured on film by White House photographer Pete Souza. The official photographs we have from those years show us a few different incarnations of Obama: the romantic husband, the good father, the great American. But perhaps the most adored version is best-mate Obama, walking shoulder to shoulder with Joe Biden. We have photographs of the two men giggling over burgers and milkshakes, picking up ice-cream cones on the campaign trail, watching college basketball in Washington, embracing at the lectern, wearing matching ties and sprinting together towards the Oval Office on Important National Business. There are photographs of Obama and Biden whispering sweet official nothings to one another during important meetings, and you can't help but yearn to know what they're saying. Were they conferring on matters of national security, or working out what to order for lunch?

In 2016, the people of the Internet did the only thing they could do with their curiosity about the presidential bromance: they made Obama and Biden into a meme. That's when people started annotating official photographs of the pair with imagined dialogue, usually making Biden out to be a sweet, devoted idiot to Obama's straight man. The premise of the memes was that Biden wanted to interrupt one or another important presidential thing to order food, play pranks or take a joyride on Air Force One. When President Donald Trump was elected, the Obama-Biden bromance memes started to play on the sadness of them leaving office. The memes started imagining Biden was playing tricks on Trump before he left the White House: ordering 500 pizzas for the day of his arrival, taking all the batteries out of the remotes, gluing a drawer in the Oval Office shut with the label 'secret Muslim agenda' and leaving a fake birth certificate in the President's desk for Trump to find. The captions were always put with photographs of Obama and Biden laughing, whispering, or sitting close together.

These memes were magnificent little jokes at a time when we needed them most. They were also a seriously interesting form of political expression. Now, a cynic may say Obama and Biden concocted their best friendship to soften their public image and make them more likeable. A cynic may say the release of chummy photographs from the White House was a deliberate effort to make us feel affection for one of the most powerful, potentially dangerous men in the world. A cynic may have a point, but believing in the bromance is so much more fun.

Obama and Biden often played into the bromance narrative themselves, either because they realised how powerful it was and how well it played, or because it's completely, gloriously genuine. Perhaps the most infamous instance of bro love was a tweet from Biden to Obama on his birthday: 'Happy 55th, Barack! A brother to me, a best friend forever', with a picture of two intertwined friendship bracelets with their names on them. The photo is actually a still from a Buzzfeed video about voting; the joke here is all Biden's. I'm very much down with both his sense of humour and his implication that he'd be cool wearing a bracelet given to him by another man.

Then there was that time Obama surprised Biden with the Presidential Medal of Freedom just days before the end of his presidency. Biden cried as Obama laid the medal around his neck; we all cried. Sure, it was the highest official recognition for work in the American public service, but it was also a tender public moment between two men. How often do we see men cry? How often do we see them cry at work? How often do we see them cry during a ceremony of national significance? Imagine, for a moment, watching that as a young man. If the Vice President of the United States of America can sob quietly as he accepts a Medal of Freedom from his best mate who happens to be President, then why can't we all? It was a poignant moment — and exactly the kind of thing young boys need to see. Not just young boys, actually. We could all do with this gentle subversion of stereotypical male stoicism.

Obama left the Oval Office with a 60-point approval rating, making him the third most-popular president to do so (Bill Clinton and Ronald Regan were the top two). The ink may still be drying on the first draft of the official history covering his years in office, but part of his legacy will surely be his friendship with Biden. It's one of the most memorable stories that emerged from Obama's White House — not to mention, for my purposes here, a rather lovely endorsement of close male friendship. It is fascinating that this story of friendship between a president and his running mate should resonate so strongly. It is a delightful thought, that these two men truly admired one another, confided in one another, and enjoyed spending time together while they did two of the most sombre jobs in the world. We loved this story; we helped write this story. We, the people, took photographic evidence of the Obama–Biden friendship and wrote our own buddy comedy, set in the White House. If it was a movie or an HBO series, critics would describe it as *House of Cards* meets *Dude, Where's My Car?* The credits would open with a close-up of one man doing the other's tie while a Jay-Z remix of the American national anthem plays. It'd be a hit because people are sick for both politics and love stories between two heterosexual men. And what is a bromance, if not a type of love story?

Bromance even has its own genre in Hollywood. Judd Apatow started a wave of bromantic comedies with his films *Knocked Up, Superbad, The 40-Year-Old Virgin* and *Talladega Nights*. He recruited Paul Rudd, Steve Carrell, Jonah Hill and Seth Rogen as his stars and rebranded the rom-com for men. Instead of making a heterosexual couple the focus of his films, Apatow put a pair of male buddies front and centre. There's straight sex and love in these movies, but it's totally sidelined by the bromance between dudes. There's usually some element of male friends banding together to resist the realities of growing up, which (in Apatow's imagining) involves marrying a hot woman and making babies. Apatow's men are juvenile and boisterous, trying to avoid the inevitability of being tamed or tied down by monogamy. Apatow's women are usually hyper-feminine stereotypes with very little depth or nuance, either because he can't write female characters with the same comedic dexterity as male ones, or because they're all beside the point. The point of the brom-com is to celebrate male friendship in all its apparently garish, filthy glory.

Possibly the greatest example of the brom-com is a 2009 film called *I Love You, Man*. It's not actually one of Apatow's, but I think it must have been heavily inspired by his spate of bromantic comedies. It stars Paul Rudd as Peter, a sweet-natured real estate agent who's just asked his girlfriend Zooey (played by Rashida Jones) to marry him. She celebrates their engagement with her girlfriends, but Peter doesn't actually have any friends with whom to celebrate. There's a scene early in the film where Peter overhears Zooey and her girlfriends talking about how awkward it is that he doesn't have friends of his own. And so Peter sets out to find himself a best man for the wedding. He goes on a few disastrous man-dates before he meets a guy called Sidney (played by Jason Segal) at an open-house inspection and they exchange numbers. They become genuine best mates, until — plot twist — the friendship starts to endanger Peter's relationship with Zooey. The film seems to yell a dilemma into lounge rooms around the world: can a guy have a best mate *and* a girlfriend? Does the human male have the emotional capacity to maintain both bromance and romance? By the end of this movie, the answer seems to be yes, he can. But I wonder at the question having to be asked at all. Do men really have to choose between a woman and their bros? Are they not capable of having both?

The idea that male bonding can't truly take place with female presence or approval is a recurrent theme in bromance films. Think of *The Hangover* movies, where a group of male friends go on a stag night, lose all control and end up living out every cliché of the debauched stag night adventure we've ever imagined. There's a distinct message that men possess some great, infinite mischief and it's only a matter of time before a woman comes along to quell it. In those movies, it's like real life only exists when a wife or girlfriend is present. Without her, it's just hedonism and brotherhood. Without her, it's unfiltered masculinity. Without her, male friendship can really get down to business. Which is interesting because, more typically, men demonstrate their heterosexuality by pursuing a woman. Here, it's all about male bonding as the ultimate display of manliness. This suggests heterosexual men could be shedding the insecurity that spending time with other men might make them seem gay (it goes without saying that there is nothing wrong with being gay — it is my great wish that we get to a place in society where it is no longer an insult or a fear to be called gay). That's been a well-documented fear for some straight men, and certainly an inhibitor of close male friendship in Western societies (in some other cultures, it is more acceptable for men to show affection for one another). Male friendship, in predominant pop culture as in real life, seems to have come with a disclaimer: 'nothing gay about it, though'.

Perhaps a gentler version of the bromance is the friendship between J.D. and Turk on the TV show *Scrubs*. J.D. and Turk met in college and then, as doctors in the same hospital, they become inseparable. They feel the sort of infatuation that's usually reserved for love, and their friendship has every element of a romantic relationship but the sex. They share their dreams and feelings, spend quality time together, canoodle, high-five and even have a man-date every week called Steak Night. It's one of the purest examples of guy love in pop culture, made even better by the rumour that the actors who play J.D. and Turk, Zach Braff and Donald Faison, are best friends off-screen too. In the show, Turk is married and J.D. is in and out of relationships with women, but the men are platonic life partners through it all. As shameless as they are about their love for each other, even they had to have a, 'nah but we're not gay' disclaimer. They play around with that in season six, episode six, with a song called 'Guy Love'. It's about how J.D. and Turk are closer than a married couple, have matching bracelets and will stand by each other for the rest of their lives. But, predictably, the disclaimer: 'but in a totally manly way'.

The thing about J.D. and Turk's friendship is that it doesn't actually threaten or diminish their manliness. It's obvious they're two straight guys engaging in some sweet, sweet guy love. It's a beautiful thing, and I wonder if it's meant to be aspirational for men watching *Scrubs*. Maybe this kind of platonic infatuation between two men, especially the performative element of it, is rare. Maybe it's more common for men to have trouble disclosing their affection for other men. Maybe the J.D. and Turk bromance is a deliberately exaggerated TV relationship designed to highlight the lack of demonstrable intimacy between men. The tenderness is hyperbolic and endearing — so much so that this becomes the central relationship of the entire show. If J.D. is the main protagonist, the one we follow through the plot, then Turk is his main love interest. Sure, J.D. falls in love with women, but the one constant in his life is Turk. Their whole relationship seems to come with a wink and an affirmation: 'hey, guys, it's okay to be super tight with another guy, it won't interfere with your sexuality — in fact, it could be the manliest thing you do'. Being cosy and loving with your best mate is probably a sign of comfort with your sexuality, anyway. That's what J.D. and Turk are trying to convey: that friendship can be masculine and emotional candour can be a sign of strength.

That's true, obviously, but it hasn't stopped people from assuming other pairs of fictional best mates are gay. Think of some fictional best friends, and the way we've projected gay romantic fantasies onto them — either for fun or because we're so confused by the sight of male friendship, we have to appropriate it into love. Sherlock Holmes and Dr John Watson exemplify this cultural habit of making gay men of good friends. In Sir Conan Doyle's serials about the crime-solving duo, he has them sharing a flat together in Baker Street, London. It was perfectly common in Victorian times for men to live together for companionship and affordability, but, even then, audiences read more into the relationship. There's been speculation ever since the original stories were published that Sherlock and Watson were more than flat mates, and that's only intensified since Benedict Cumberbatch's cheekbones got involved.

And that brings me to the cultural trend known as 'shipping'. The term comes from the word 'relationship': to 'ship' is to wish that two characters in a fictional story were involved in a romantic relationship. Fans usually write fan-fiction or make art depicting their chosen pair in a romantic or sexual position, and often petition the creators of their chosen story to actually write the romance they want. You can technically ship anyone, whether they're straight, gay or otherwise; it's all a fantasy. People even ship Pokémon characters. The shipped couple is usually given a composite name of their two names — so John Watson and Sherlock Holmes become 'JohnLock'. Right from the beginning of the BBC series *Sherlock*, with Benedict Cumberbatch as Sherlock and Martin Freeman as Watson, fans ardently shipped JohnLock. When Sherlock faked his own death, they saw Watson in mourning as a grief-stricken lover, standing by the gravestone of his beloved. When Sherlock returned, never having died, they saw Watson's anger as the reaction of a betrayed lover. Whatever Sherlock and Watson did, whatever gesture of friendship they shared, it was translated into the behaviour of love.

Then the finale of season four aired: the one with *the hug*. Watson is hallucinating conversations with his recently dead wife, Mary. Throughout the episode, Mary refers to Sherlock as 'the man we both love' and tells Watson to 'get the hell on with it'. Fans who ship JohnLock treated both phrases as the ultimate proof that Sherlock and Watson are romantically interested in each other. They interpreted 'the man we both love' in the romantic sense and took Mary's 'get the hell on with it' to mean getting the hell on with being together because life is short. People tweeted things like 'JOHNLOCK CONFIRMED' and 'This is the best day of my life #johnlock'. (A friend of mine 'lost the ability to breathe for several seconds' and would like to point out that Watson's and Sherlock's rooms in the Baker

Street flat are joined by a bathroom, so discreet access during a sleepover would not be a logistical problem.) Then, in the final scene, Watson is crying. Sherlock approaches him and, in a most uncharacteristic move, embraces him. It's a tender hug, with Watson's head on Sherlock's chest as he comforts him. There's a little light neck-stroking going on. Depending on your vantage point and perhaps your comfort level with male intimacy, it's either an exquisitely sad moment between two dear friends, or an embrace between would-be lovers.

Rumour has it season four may have been the last for *Sherlock*, so we may never get closure on the possibility of romance between our favourite sociopathic detective and his mate, the doctor. There are reams of fan-fiction online for anyone wanting to fantasise about that relationship — and, as an aside, a truly magnificent number of people who are very angry when they visit the Sherlock Museum in London and discover Sherlock Holmes was not a real person who actually existed.

Sherlock and Watson are not the only fictional blokes to get shipped into a hypothetical gay romance. Recently it also happened to two of J.K. Rowling's characters (it always happens to her characters, to be fair; a lot of people online ship Harry Potter and Draco Malfoy, too). Rowling gave a playwright called Jack Thorne the rather extraordinary task of writing Harry Potter and his contemporaries into a script, which was developed into a West End play. *Harry Potter and the Cursed Child* is the eighth Harry Potter story, set 19 years after the Battle of Hogwarts. Harry, Hermione and

Ron are middle-aged and the story revolves mainly around Harry's middle child, Albus Severus Potter, and his unlikely best mate, Scorpius Malfoy (Draco Malfoy's son). Quite apart from anything magical, the play is really an extremely moving depiction of adolescent friendship between two boys. Albus and Scorpius meet on the Hogwarts Express on their first trip to the wizarding school and, like teenagers do, they latch onto one another fiercely in one of those intense best friendships built on mutual insecurities. When the book version of the script was released in 2016, readers around the world started shipping Scorpius and Albus (their shipping name is Scorbus). Countless people who saw the play in London commented online that the story could just as easily be about two gay teenagers in love. Again, readers made homosexual subplots of their own, spinning romance out of friendship.

This propensity of ours to cast men as gay lovers says, to me, that we value romantic love above all other kinds. The most popular plotline in fiction is romance, and we will demand it even where it's absent. Profound same-sex friendship doesn't seem to have quite the same commercial appeal, which is perhaps why showrunners introduce an element of sexual ambiguity between their characters. The idea that Sherlock Holmes could be a repressed gay man adds another layer of drama to the stories. The notion that Harry Potter's son may be secretly in love with Draco Malfoy's is a superb plot twist for a Harry Potter fan. But the overwhelming fan reaction to both these male relationships suggests that we, as an audience, don't have much time for platonic friendship. If the creators of a series won't give us explicit sexual interaction between two beloved characters, we'll make it up ourselves. It's complicated: if we're so keen on imagining gay love between men, why aren't there more shows written about open gay relationships? Why is it that we are so hungry for the suggestion of flirtation, rather than the real thing? Could it be that we are still, as a society, conflicted about what modern masculinity looks like — so much so that we blur the lines of fictional characters' sexuality?

We 'ship' real-life human beings, too. This propensity of ours extends to celebrities as well as fictional characters. My personal favourite contemporary example of real-life shipping is Harry Styles and Louis Tomlinson, former members of the boy band One Direction. Their shipping name is Larry Stylinson. Great swathes of the band's young female fans fantasise about a secret gay romance between the boys. The sheer volume of Larry Stylinson erotica available online is astonishing. There are countless articles and Tumblr posts compiling 'evidence' of the boys' alleged trysts, where fans interpret every gesture, every smile and every moment of fleeting eye contact as proof of their love. Boy bands are inherently homoerotic to begin with — when they sing the lyrics of their love songs together, it's easy to imagine they are singing to and about each other. Their closeness as a troupe is a huge part of their appeal, and so they take every opportunity to demonstrate the intimacy between them. Friendship between the 1D boys was a huge and very important part of their marketing campaign, and what made them one of the most lucrative music acts of all time. Their banter on stage was often cheeky, borderline flirtatious (I would know; I've been to three of their concerts). Sometimes they'd egg each other on to get shirtless or dance solo, and each of these moments has been enthusiastically drawn into a great big gay narrative. Their matching, peppy aesthetic and mostly wholesome British vibe just makes the secret gay conspiracy theory all the more tantalising for fans. The idea is that Harry Styles and Louis Tomlinson have to hide their love because the world wouldn't be ready for such a high-profile gay romance. And maybe that's accurate; maybe the world at large isn't ready. Teenage girls are progressive and adoring, and imagining their beloved boys in a secret romance is, strangely enough, a safe way for them to play with their own sexuality. They'd be ready for the romance — as it is, they're practically salivating at the prospect that Harry and Louis could one day come out. In truth, it's all a fantasy, there's nothing to suggest Harry and Louis are romantically involved and, in fact, they have both had several well-documented female love interests. But their homoerotic shipping is further evidence that when we see a prominent male–male friendship, we just can't resist projecting romance onto it, rather than confronting the very real camaraderie between mates.

We tend not to know what to make of intimacy between dudes in our own lives, too. But from what I have observed, real mateship absolutely exists between guys. I don't mean to invoke any sort of *Men are from Mars, Women are from Venus* rhetoric, but I find that men and women do friendship in some starkly different ways. The way male friendship operates is sometimes baffling to me; the insults, the bravado, the endless *Family Guy* quotes bandied about between them. Outside of the movies and celebrity, men usually do require a male-only environment to truly bond. Just as women need their wine bars, cafés and bedroom floors to chat and gossip and confide, men need their lounge rooms, basketball courts and pubs to co-exist in. Obviously, I'm generalising wildly for clarity here; there are plenty of women who play sport and plenty of men who like to catch up over coffee. I'm speaking in stereotypes so we can pick out the differences between male and female friendship more easily. The main difference, as I see it, is the format. Lady-folk share emotions, ideas and concerns to get close to one another; men-folk build loyalty by hanging out together, doing things. Female friendship is a lot more communicative; male friendship is more activities based. That tends to make female friendships more brittle, too. When they break, they break catastrophically and the fallout is like the end of a romantic relationship. Something that is built out of intimacy is easier to destroy than something founded on loyalty.

It's loyalty that seems to define male friendship. Now, as you may know, I am a woman. There is no way I can truly get inside a male–male friendship, see its inner workings and report back on its secrets. If I want to understand male friendship, the only thing for it is to talk to men about theirs. I spoke to men in my own life and strangers online to try and work out how male friendship works. Pairs of best male friends told me how they'd met and why they became friends — mostly it was childhood, school or university, and more often than not based on proximity, chance or a shared hobby. They lived in the same suburb and caught the same bus to school, they were sat next to each other in the first year of high school, or they were both just mad for cricket. What seems to sustain a male friendship is more interesting to me. Where my friendships with women have always been about exchanging emotional intel and reiterating support for one another, these male friendships seem to be based on well-intended ridicule, physical activity and the act of doing something stupid or outlandish. When asked for his most significant friendship memory, one guy told me joyously about the time he and his mate dressed up in full tiger outfits to go to a football game, for no reason at all other than the solidarity between them, and for a laugh. My boyfriend recently went to the rugby with his two best mates and for some reason they imposed a compulsory dress code: wear the worst taste shirt you own, preferably with shorts of a clashing pattern. That explains the short-sleeved, pizza-print shirt in my boyfriend's wardrobe (should it mysteriously go missing, it wasn't me). A number of men I spoke to online listed among their formative friendship memories times when they had dressed up with a mate or played a prank on someone else with their best mate. Women do this, too — fancy dress is a powerful unifier and friendship is always buoyed by a sense of fun — but these occasions seemed to have particular emotional significance for the dudes who lived them. There was a lot of rugby, cricket, football, badminton, running, volleyball and basketball involved in these friendships too, either playing the sport together or watching it at the pub or at home. But it's not all macho outings. These outings are their own form of mateship, obviously, but they don't always have to be so macho.

Speaking to friends Neal and Sertan about their friendship moved me the most. There is an obvious and touching camaraderie between them that reminds me of some of my own favourite friendships. They met through being experimentally funny at university: Sertan was auditioning for the Arts Revue at the University of Sydney, which Neal was directing. They became mates and decided to perform improv together as a pair. If you've ever done or seen improvised comedy (*Whose Line Is It Anyway?* is a good telly example), you'll know it's basically high-pressure friendship on stage; it's entirely based on trust, synchronicity and generosity. You cannot be funny together on stage if you're selfish, untrusting or inflexible. Live comedy like the kind Sertan and Neal do is a beautiful, if slightly mad, place for a friendship to develop. The whole idea is that one person sends an idea out into the performance space — a line of dialogue, a gesture, a one-liner — and the other person has to pick it up and run with it, adding to it, developing it, making sense of chaos. Truly great improvised comedy is like a waltz between mates who know each other well enough to anticipate what the other person might say or do, and know how to fall in line with it. I've seen Neal and Sertan perform together and they do exactly that. Their innings of competitive improv are always slightly surreal, but always made possible by cooperation and mutual respect. This is why so many comedians — Amy Poehler and Tina Fey, Will Ferrell and Kristen Wiig — made such close friends in theatre groups. The feeling of danger that comes from improvisation helps people bond, not to mention the fact that entire friendships can survive on a shared sense of humour.

Choosing your improv partner *is* choosing a friend; if you do it right, you're able to speak without sound. Friendship is its own comedy double act (think of Ant and Dec in the UK or Hamish and Andy in Australia, whose entire careers depend on their bromances). What could be a more joyous friendship workout than making other people laugh simply by interacting in public?

Neal and Sertan have a beautiful friendship off stage too and it's not all competitive hilarity. They might call each other 'weirdo' and 'dick' a lot throughout their chat with me — insults seem to be a very male expression of affection — but there's clearly a profound love between them. Sertan says Neal helped him cure his stage fright by making him feel comfortable on stage, and I get the impression he's done that in real life, too. Sertan was sexually abused as a child and when he told his parents, they didn't react how he really needed them to. It was the first time he realised he couldn't depend on his parents for every emotional need, and so he went to Neal. Neal was the next person he told about the abuse, and though Neal was obviously confronted and upset, he was able to react with compassion and respect. He understood the gravity of Sertan's revelation and tactfully supported him, which enabled Sertan to talk about it more over the years and with other people in his life. Neal says that in comparison to Sertan, he's lived an idyllic, sheltered life, but that whenever he's needed him for a comparatively trivial matter, Sertan has always been there for him. It's like these two have given each other vouchers for emotional support, which they are able to cash in for reassurance at any time. It's a profoundly lovely thing to witness.

It has to be said, Neal and Sertan have the sort of companionship we might often unfairly ascribe mostly to women: they keep each other's secrets, tell each other everything, and rely upon each other for emotional support and validation. It's the sort of closeness I wish more men would admit to, or actively cultivate. There's an ease and a comfort between the two men that anyone would be lucky to have in their lives. They consider one another family, and they have done for years. They speak every day and they've lived together for four years. As Sertan is quick to claim, they're like Adama and Tigh from *Battlestar Galactica* or Bartlett and Leo from *West Wing*. Or, Neal adds, like House and Wilson from *House*. Which is to say, they're tight.

So, I've seen real-life examples of male closeness, which proves to me that intimacy between two men is entirely possible. And yet, some experts claim members of the male population continue to suffer from an intimacy deficiency. Professor Niobe Way — a Professor of Applied Psychology at New York University — for example, says there is a 'crisis of connection' among boys and men. She has been talking to teenage boys about their lives and their feelings for nearly 30 years. Professor Way started out her professional life in the '80s as a school counsellor. Boys would visit her office to talk about their very personal lives. One of the most recurrent themes in those sessions was friendship and, often, how much these boys wanted friendship — proper, meaningful, deep, sincere friendship, not just playground banter. Over the past three decades, Professor Way has interviewed hundreds and hundreds of boys on their psychological development for her research and she is adamant they're trying to tell us something shocking: that boys need as much intimacy and emotional connection as girls do, and they're simply not getting it. As Professor Way tells it, we are all born emotionally hungry. In childhood and adolescence, we particularly crave the emotional closeness that girls are famous for having, and boys are infamous for rejecting in favour of banter about sport, or whatever. Professor Way says that's a fallacy: actually, boys secretly want what girls seem to manage so easily, and they have an equal need to connect emotionally with their peers, but that becomes harder as they begin to get socially conditioned as men. She argues boys do have those delicate, beautiful, intimate best friendships as children and young teenagers, but as they get closer to adulthood, they're told connections like that are feminine and so they start to fear being called gay for having too close a friendship with another guy. That fear is so consuming, they sacrifice friendship intimacy with other guys and make their friendships more casual and more centred on manly banter than emotional disclosure. The disconnect between what these boys want and what they end up cultivating as men is extremely damaging. According to Professor Way, it's the resultant loneliness, isolation and confusion that leads to things like suicide, mass murder and violence. When a heinous crime is committed by a lone man, we always say we didn't see it coming, that the guy seemed so normal, that perhaps he's mentally ill or an extremist. But what if violence and criminal behaviour is a worst-case scenario reaction to the systemic undermining of social connection for young men? What if these seemingly inexplicable atrocities can be partially explained by the lack of intimacy in men's lives as they grow up? Young men are allegedly having some of their most important, formative relationships severed at the fragile age of impending adulthood, and that can affect them dramatically.

Professor Way returns to one phrase in particular that was uttered by a 16-year-old boy one time, in her confidence. 'It might be nice to be a girl,' he said, 'because then I wouldn't have to be emotionless'. She repeats this sentence to me several times in her American drawl, each time more emphatically. She is still, after this long, shocked by the things she uncovers in her own research. She is still astounded by the things young boys tell her about themselves and the world. She says that this 16-year-old boy's idea that he has to be emotionless because he's a boy is echoed again and again by other boys, all of whom think stoicism is a requisite part of their identities as they get older. Professor Way believes boys know the problem of their own lack of intimacy, but they also know the solution — and they're trying to tell us what it is. She explains with an anecdote.

Professor Way works at a school in the Lower East Side in New York, where the boys are 12 or 13 years old and mostly black, Latino or Asian-American, usually from working-class immigrant families. She spends time in an English class, where she talks to the boys about friendship and identity. She starts with a very simple exercise: she asks the boys to recite a quote from the opening page of her book, *Deep Secrets: Boys' Friendship and the Crisis of Connection*. The quote is from a boy around their age and it's about how much he loves his best friend. He says he couldn't live without his friend and that he knows him so well, he doesn't even have to express it. When it's read aloud to the class, all the boys start laughing. 'Why are you laughing?' Professor Way asks, knowing exactly why but wanting to coax the boys into some self-awareness. They keep laughing and then, finally, one boy pipes up: 'Well, this guy sounds gay, miss.' Professor Way starts off by saying she has no idea what this boy's sexual orientation is because that's not the point of her studies. Then she tells this classroom of boys a simple fact: 85 per cent of all the boys she's interviewed over three decades of research sound exactly like this one at some stage in adolescence. There's silence in the room, then one boy says 'For real?' and she says 'For real. That's what teenage boys sound like.' 'Do you know what happens next?' she asks me. I hold my breath. 'Within a second, I tell you it was under a minute, I have boys all raising their hands wanting to tell stories like the boy on the first page of my book. When they first hear the emotional quote about friendship, they see it through a cultural lens and read it as "gay". All I did was normalise it and they're ready to talk.' So, boys simply need to hear that real friendship is perfectly normal and they're ready to divulge their own needs and experiences. It could be as simple, or as complex, as changing the way we speak about intimacy between two boys.

This makes me immeasurably sad. Teenagers are so impressionable; they're right in the middle of working out who they're going to be. Young girls have their own problems at this stage of life, and I feel like I know them well, having lived them or observed them. I've spent less time thinking about what young boys might face at that age, and it's devastating to think that just when they need social reassurance the most, it could be taken from them by a society that demands manly stoicism above the right to be vulnerable. Because I think that's what we're talking about here: boys are frightened to be vulnerable with their mates. They're scared to talk about or get too close to another guy in a conventionally feminine way because they'll be mocked for being gay. The fact that appearing gay can still be used as an insult or a slight is deeply upsetting — we've made a grave cultural error here, doling out value judgments about certain incarnations of love. Everyone deserves the right to adore another human being, and that includes straight men who love each other as friends. It is disturbing how virulently we have judged, banned and mocked certain types of love between combinations of people. And that homophobia is so pervasive in our culture, it can taint young boys just trying to connect with the people around them.

It isn't just Professor Way who speaks about this fear of being gay among men. Dr Geoffrey Greif — Professor at the University of Maryland School of Social Work — writes about it, too, in his book *Buddy System: Understanding Male Friendships*. Greif interviewed hundreds of people and says about a quarter of the men he spoke to worried aloud about coming across as gay in a friendship situation. He met a guy in his mid-thirties on an aeroplane whose first question when he found out what Dr Greif does for a living was, 'How do

I make friends without seeming gay?' According to Greif's findings, that miserable teenage fear of seeming gay travels into adulthood, especially as men struggle to make new buddies in their twenties, thirties, forties and beyond. Dr Greif agrees with Professor Way that men tend to struggle making and maintaining friendships as they age — he says a lot of men feel like they have to know someone a long time to qualify as their friend and that they lack the skills or the confidence to make new friends as they age. Greif says men are simply not taught to initiate a bond, pick up the phone and organise a get-together or, scariest of all, follow up that first conversation with another one. That explains the onslaught of middle-aged male loneliness, when men sometimes find themselves left with one meaningful close relationship: the one with their spouse. Both research and my own conversations with people reveal that once they're married, men tend to shut down some of their extra-marital friendships as though there's some sort of unspoken rule that they can't have both a marriage with a woman and friendships with people outside of that. Women tend not to do that, they tend to hold onto friendships throughout their marriage and invest time and emotion in them for the duration of their lives. Lifelong friendship is not an easy feat, but women appear to be far more adept at it, perhaps because their upbringings equip them with the requisite emotional skills to do so.

Dr Greif doesn't agree with Professor Way's thesis that men's friendships are in any way deficient, though. He does not think there is a 'crisis of connection'. He thinks Professor Way is looking at things from a female perspective, judging male friendships through a female lens and expecting the same levels of intimacy across sexes. He says some men yearn for closer, more intimate and traditionally feminine friendships, but most men are perfectly content with the level of emotional disclosure they currently have with their mates. They'd be uncomfortable having the level of intimacy female friends have, and they're perfectly delighted to escape from that intensity by hanging out with other men. They have their jokes and their gestures and their unwavering loyalty, and they're sweet with that. Dr Greif believes men do friendship differently — and that's okay. They have friendships based on activities and doing things together, where women's friendships are based on talking and exchanging information. Men are shoulder to shoulder against the world; women are face to face. Men, archetypally speaking, bond over a specific thing they can watch or engage in, like sport. Women, generalising wildly here, are more likely to directly focus on each other, perhaps sitting across the table with a glass of Pinot Grigio. As far as gender comparisons go, the difference in friendship style between stereotypical men and women can be baffling.

Here's an example of the exasperation some women feel when they realise how male friendship works. Man goes to his mate's house to watch a sports event. Men drink beer and hang out. Man returns home to wife later that night and wife asks how the mate is doing after his recent split with his partner. Man says it never came up, so he doesn't know. Wife despairs at men's limited capacity to connect and wonders how they could possibly have spent hours together without the topic of the mate's crumbling marriage coming up in conversation. Wife asks what they actually talked about, if not something that important. Man shrugs shoulders in masculine gesture of nonchalance: he was just happy watching the game and he reckons his mate would come to him if he really needed to talk about the break-up. Woman tells her girlfriend about this the next time they meet for brunch. They roll their eyes and reiterate that they know every detail of the mate's break-up already, including the time, date and place the relationship started to disintegrate and who said what to whom — they heard it from the mate's wife last week. It's their evolutionary prerogative to gossip about other people and emotional disclosure is the currency of their friendship — it's just how women operate.

Male friendship might seem shallow in comparison to the deep connections women tend to build out of secrets and confessions and confidences. It might seem perfunctory, with minimal effort required to maintain it. It might seem, let's be honest, inferior to what women have. But are we doing as Dr Greif says: expecting male friendships to comply with the standards we set for female friendship? I look at the friendships I have with women — we mean everything to each other, we couldn't live without each other, we lift each other up and talk about one another with such hyperbole you couldn't be blamed for thinking we're all polygamists madly in love. We speak as often as possible, no matter what platform it's on. We invade each other's privacy as a matter of routine and keep barely any secrets between us. And we're incredibly loving towards one another. It's all 'love you' and 'xxx' and dancing lady emoji. Then

I look at the friendships between the men around me — they tend to be all about innuendo, action, gestures of loyalty, jokes, mockery and bravado. There's an unspoken understanding that if it was required, some sort of support would be deployed, but they don't feel the need to reiterate it all the time like women do, or offer it on every occasion it might be necessary. Male friendship doesn't seem to be effusive or expressive in the same way as female friendship, and that could well go all the way to our evolutionary instincts as early human beings. Men would go out and hunt together, women would stay at home and bond for social protection. Perhaps the way we conduct friendship now is a remnant of those very early foraging days.

But, then, if you'll allow me to undermine everything I've just said, maybe it's totally unhelpful to talk about friendship in gendered terms. Perhaps it's a ridiculous thing to do, to force something as malleable and unique as friendship onto a spectrum of gender. Maybe it's considerably more helpful to think about friendship existing on a spectrum of intimacy: there are close friendships and there are more objectively distant ones, but both men and women are capable of both. The connection between two human beings is so wholly idiosyncratic, it seems almost absurd to insist they would follow gendered patterns. Men should have the right to intimate friendships if they want them, hang the traditional mores of masculinity. Equally, women are capable of casual, loyalty-based friendships and should be allowed to cherish them as little or as much as they like.

CHAPTER FIVE

Can men and women ever be just mates?

CAN MEN AND WOMEN truly ever be platonic friends? Ooph. It's a big, complex question — one that couldn't even be comprehensively answered in 10 whole seasons of the TV show *Friends*. My optimistic answer is yes. Yes, but with a caveat: it is likely that at some stage in your friendship, you will have to address the prospect of romance or sex. Even if you, the actual individuals involved in the friendship, can make it through years without hooking up, society will ultimately demand to know the exact nature of your relationship. You can protest as much as you like — 'but he's like a brother to me', 'I just don't think about her that way', 'we're genuinely just mates' — but eventually someone in your lives will want to know why you haven't bumped uglies. And let's be honest, by that stage you've either already thought about it, or done it. At the very least, you assessed your buddy as a possible romantic partner and/or shag when you first met them. It's what we've been programmed to do, as a species (always blame evolution). Even if you dismiss them as a sexual prospect straightaway, you end up spending all this time together and if you're the right sexual orientation, you're single and they're single, a little 'what if' will creep in at some stage. Our social conditioning to think of humanity as an almighty pool of romantic possibilities is extremely strong; a platonic friendship is basically an act of rebellion between two beautiful renegades who don't need an evolutionary reason to hang out.

This chapter, like all the others, required me to talk to scientists, psychologists, my mates and strangers from the Internet. Obviously it was also mandatory for me to watch *When Harry Met Sally*. For the time being, I've focused on heterosexual pairings of opposite-sex friends because I wanted to investigate whether sexual attraction interferes with friendship, but I want to make special mention of the beauteous love between other combinations of people, too. One of the reasons straight men and women have such trouble being friends is there's a level of potential threat there, like the sexual possibility between them affects the authenticity of a friendship and even, in some cases, can make someone feel unsafe (see: the anger with which the term 'friend zone' is used by men to punish the women who made the perfectly reasonable decision not to sleep with them for an indication of how charged the friendship-or-intimacy dilemma can be). Whereas, between a woman and a gay man for instance, there's often a sense of peace because that sexual possibility simply isn't present. The friendship is left to grow on its own terms, quite liberated from any consideration of sexy times. Instead, there's an implicit trust there, a sense of kindred safety. The same, I assume, is true of the friendships between gay women and straight men, or straight women and gay women, or gay men and straight men. Where there is no prospect of mutual sexual attraction, it can be easier to nuzzle into a new friendship and stay there. Not to mention there's a sweet sort of alliance between people who don't fall into the straight male category because there is the shorthand of knowing what subjugation feels like. I will love my darling gay friend Andre forever and a day and we definitely talk about sexuality, as well as every other facet of our lives, but it's simply never been something that's impeded or defined our friendship. We have been free to build our friendship on things like love, our lifelong allegiance to Britney Spears, takeaway Thai food, pink fizzer sweets, travel, advice, lying in the sun, cocktails, sleepovers, movie marathons and whispered (or WhatsApped) confidences. We are free from the complications that might arise from me, say, trying to be friends with a straight guy I kissed once.

For this chapter, I spoke to a number of surprisingly willing participants and they generously offered me a glimpse into their psyches — and for that I am extremely grateful. But I hardly thought it was fair for me to get away scot-free in the course of my own research. They say you must suffer for your art, and so I decided to interview one of my best straight male friends about whether we've ever fancied each other — knowing full well that we have.

It's the kind of conversation that should happen over several wines. It's not generally advisable to discuss matters of the heart/loins with one of your oldest mates without some sort of Dutch courage. But, as it is, my friend Bernard (I let him choose his own pseudonym and he identifies with Dylan Moran's drunk Irish alter-ego, Bernard Black) lives 13,500 kilometres away from me and the time difference is 11 hours, so it's breakfast time for me when we Skype. He, being the guest in this interview and it being night time where he is, is allowed to drink a big old glass of red. I'm not allowed any such social lubricant, which makes me a little nervous, to be honest. We're extremely open with one another, Bernard and I, but we've never sat down to discuss the nature of our friendship before. If you'll excuse our delusions of nobility for a second, we did it for every man and woman who's ever had to defend or question their platonic friendship.

So I start our conversation by pointing out that Bernard and I have been friends for 16 years. We've been friends longer than we haven't been friends, I say, with the sort of pride most people reserve for professional achievements or lifetime milestones. He's not surprised; my friendship style is heavy on nostalgia and I like to frequently remind people how long we've been hanging out. He's probably had a relatively recent update. But it does, for the purposes of our story, take us back to the age of 13. Bernard was a total cherub, as I remember: chubby with a Celtic afro and a lovely intellect, sucking on a joint at every possible moment and managing that teenage shyness that tries its hand at bravado in the company of the opposite sex. His first date was with a friend of mine, and she turned up at the movies with an entourage of at least eight girlfriends. These were not sophisticated times for romance. Bernard and

I both went to single-sex schools, so we accumulated friends of the opposite sex by chance and liaised almost exclusively through MSN Messenger. At the time, I was seeing my very first boyfriend, whose main attraction was the fact that he was on his school debating team, like me. We flirted via predictive text on our Nokia 3310s as only high-school debaters could: with a deeply unsexy but very logical banter that bordered on being argumentative. Bernard, as he tells me now, couldn't understand why I had chosen to feverishly make out with this debater guy instead of him. Bernard wanted a relationship with me, which I find really interesting because I've never really thought of Bernard as a relationship kind of guy. I think his criteria for a teenage crush was fairly basic at the time: I could maintain a satisfactory level of banter with him at parties and I wasn't hideous to look at. It sounds as though he chose me relatively arbitrarily as an adolescent fantasy, or a way of testing out what it might be like to be with a girl without the bother of actually having a relationship.

For my part, I thought of Bernard as a close friend. He was funny and smart and I enjoyed having him as my confidant. I liked being in his company. He was, for many years, my authority on the male perspective, in that sweet way young people think talking to a couple of guys might provide insight into the entire experience of masculinity. I followed up my debater with my next boyfriend, a childhood best friend who had such cool taste in music and movies that I lied to him about every piece of pop culture I'd ever consumed. Bernard was still there, on the periphery, as a friend. It suited me to tell myself he didn't have feelings for me because that way I got to keep him as a buddy.

By the final year of school, though, something changed. We were both single and Bernard had started wearing tank tops. I'd had my braces taken off and tentatively started feeling like a woman. He started looking like a man (he would continue, for some years, to behave like a boy). I noticed his biceps / plausibility as a romantic partner and we started being more flirtatious with each other. We ended up kissing one night — and we agree now that alcohol must have been involved in the incident. Neither of us had the kind of confidence required to touch lips with another person while sober, particularly someone you've called a buddy for years. As we confirm in this Skype call, it happened on a sofa at a house party, while the host was in the bathtub with a friend of Bernard's. It was right in front of all of our friends and I'm pretty sure there was even someone sitting next to us on the sofa. We had no standards or illusions of privacy; we just made out in that awkwardly exhibitionist way teenagers do when they're too young or too shy to actually get a room to kiss in. Later, Bernard would say that kissing me was 'like putting my face into a festering wet mop'. He doesn't remember saying it and insists it would have been his way of diffusing the tension between us. I must have retaliated; I think I told him that kissing him was like 'making out with a sweat patch'. That was our way of making things normal again.

For three days after the kiss, we didn't know what to do. Were we meant to date now? Could we pretend it didn't happen? Did this mean we liked each other? For Bernard, it was what he'd wanted for a long time. For me, it was a new prospect with an old friend. But something was getting in the way: our friendship. As Bernard tells me, he'd spent years wanting to be with me, then when he got me, he didn't know what to do next. I had no idea either. We kind-of wordlessly agreed not to do anything about it. It went unsaid (until this call), but we actually preferred our friendship to whatever future kisses we could have had. We'd become really close, we were allies, we shared secrets and we talked about everything and anything. Our friendship had become too important to risk on a possible romance. Bernard was not used to being in relationships and assumed, probably quite accurately, that I was prone to getting into quite serious ones despite my age. There was one particularly enthusiastic hug on a main road in Sydney many years later that made me think, 'Is there something here?' but apart from that Bernard and I never really entertained the idea of being together again. Not least because, by this stage, we'd spent too many years being honest with each other about what we wanted in a relationship and our expectations did not match, oh no, not at all. We drunkenly agreed to get married if we happen to be the last two unmarried people we know, and that agreement stands, disastrous as it could be. Other than that, any attraction between us just naturally disappeared and where it once was, now there's just this lovely, close friendship. If anything, we know each other too well now to think of each other romantically. I know all his sordid stories and he knows mine. We've become close enough to rule each other out as romantic or sexual options. We know exactly what the other person would be like in a relationship and we politely decline, thank you very much.

As it turns out, that's actually a pretty standard trajectory for a platonic friendship. There are a few academics who study this kind of friendship, and I tracked them down. First, I spoke to Dr Heidi Reeder from Boise State University in the United States, after reading her paper, 'I Like You ... as a Friend: The Role of Attraction in Cross-sex Friendship' in the *Journal of Social and Personal Relationships*. Reeder interviewed 20 sets of male–female best mates to find out how they felt about each other, then followed that by giving 231 college students a questionnaire about their close platonic friendships. She identified four different types of attraction between these pairs of people: romantic attraction, friendship attraction, objective sexual attraction and subjective sexual attraction. Romantic attraction is self-explanatory. Friendship attraction is obvious. Objective sexual attraction is covered by the phrase 'I can see how other people would find him cute, but I'm not personally attracted to him' or 'I think she's beautiful, but I just don't feel anything sexual towards her'. It's the acknowledgment that someone might be objectively attractive, but they just don't do it for you. Subjective sexual attraction is when you are specifically, actively attracted to that person. Bernard and I have, at various times, felt all four types of attraction but we've finally settled into the most convenient combination: objective sexual attraction and friendship attraction (I acknowledge that Bernard does not aesthetically offend me and suspect some women find him quite attractive — I'm just not one of them. He, similarly, admits I am not repulsive, but does not personally fancy me).

The results of Dr Reeder's research are very satisfying in the sense that, when you hear what they are, you feel as though you already knew them to be true. Forty per cent of her subjects said they became less sexually attracted to their friend over time, which certainly makes things easier. That tends to happen in romantic relationships too; that first flash of intense sexual attraction settles into something more comfortable and familiar. Only 20 per cent of the study said they got more sexually attracted to their friend over time, which is a bit awkward, but not insurmountable if it's not reciprocated. Thirty-nine per cent of people said romantic attraction towards their mate decreased; only 8.7 per cent said it increased.

Dr Reeder says a whopping majority of the people she spoke to made a real point of being clear they didn't want their friendship to become romantic. A number of them gleefully pointed out the flaws in their friend that they thought made them undesirable as a romantic partner, and I particularly love that. It supports my theory that the better we get to know someone in a friendship capacity, the less likely we are to think of them as a prospective partner — because we know too much. What makes an unsuitable partner can make a fabulous friend, and I love that our flaws belong somewhere. Bernard, for example, is mischievous and wild in a way that makes him great fun as a friend, but my idea of a total nightmare to date. Similarly, I bet he's seen sides to my personality or quirks in my behaviour that make me undateable to him — and that's the glory of friendship. Where we might start out trying to impress our romantic partners with all the loveliest elements of who we are, there's something less filtered about friendship. We're free to be our full revolting selves earlier on, and I think we all need that safe space to be fallible and weird.

Also, with regards to cross-sex friendships, I feel it's often difficult to move someone between the genres of relationship in your life: once they're a friend, they're likely to stay a friend. We have mental categories for people and despite what romantic comedies would have us believe, it's not easy to mess up our internal filing system. The exception to that rule is all the married couples who say they started out as best friends, but I'm inclined to think their backstory is more complex than a wedding or engagement party speech will tell. They've been through different forms of attraction, too, they just happened to land on romantic attraction at the same time.

And now we get to the good bit in the argument for cross-sex friendship: 71 per cent of Dr Reeder's study group said friendship attraction got stronger over time. Only 18 per cent said their friendship attraction faded and that seems to largely be covered by people who don't actually like one another and should probably stop hanging out. So, like what happened with me and Bernard, sexual attraction seems to diminish as friendship attraction strengthens. Time tends to dull romantic attraction and platonic affection ultimately replaces it. Which sounds as though it is entirely possible for men and women to be friends without having some kind of ulterior sexual agenda.

Either they weren't attracted to each other in the first place, or they just have to try something sexual and move on, or wait it out until the attraction naturally dissipates. Dr Reeder says friendships are a safe space where men and women can see one another as 'not just mates or objects, but comrades and pals'. I like this very much. As a society we've always spoken about romantic love as being 'more than just friends' and I've always taken issue with that hierarchy of emotional connection. Cross-sex friendships can be important and elucidating. They're also a product of increasing equality between the sexes.

But before we get to feminism, I'd like to talk about the sex thing for a little longer. It is a relief to me to find that sexual attraction wanes over time, because that does enable platonic friendship. But what of the people who don't wait for the disappearance of chemistry? What of the ones who act on their initial attraction? That is, what happens when friends actually have sex? In a Penn State University study of 300 college students, 41 per cent admitted to having sex with a friend. Of that saucy group, 56 per cent said the relationship did not become romantic, which hints at that other relationship I haven't mentioned yet: Friends with Benefits. There are certain people who are capable of being friends and having sex without it developing into a romantic relationship or a soul-crushing mismatch of feelings. I'm personally extremely sceptical of the Friends with Benefits arrangement because, to me, friendship and sexual chemistry make a romantic connection, and the decision to have sex but remain friends seems like a way of copping out of an actual relationship. That, and I'm just not convinced you can truly go back to being buddies after you've seen each other naked.

But, I could be wrong. In that same study, 67 per cent of people said sex improved the quality of their friendship. Sixty-seven per cent! Even the researchers were shocked by that result. It leaves me flummoxed because it goes against everything we think we know about the way this kind of friendship works. How many times have you heard of people abstaining from sex with a friend because they didn't want to risk losing the friendship? What if, all along, the answer has been to shag and then get on with our lives? Maybe it really does make for better friendship if you've eliminated the sexual prospect and therefore any tension between you. Perhaps that's why it's possible to be friends with an ex. There's another controversial incarnation of friendship that I believe in — friendship with an ex. I've made it a strong policy in my life to be friends with ex-boyfriends and with the exception of a few who didn't really mean enough to keep around, I genuinely have remained friends with the people I once loved. It's something I'm quite proud of, to be honest, like it's an achievement to salvage something from a broken relationship. That doesn't work for everyone — I think where there is still anger or resentment or even proper love, it may not be possible to stay buddies with someone who once had your heart. As my dad would say, 'Matters of the heart, sweetheart, there's nothing like them.'

I continue to find it fascinating that people tend to take a strong stance on the matter of friendship between men and women. Most people I've spoken to about the subject are vehement about their position either way, and I'm yet to speak to someone with a tepid view on the issue. It's funny, really, that a particular type of friendship is something we believe in, or not.

My stepmother doesn't believe in friendship between men and women. Just flat-out, straight up doesn't think it's a legitimate thing. She says inevitably one person will have feelings of a romantic or sexual nature towards the other and that will disqualify them from being friends. She's not alone — a lot of people are very hardline on this topic. They tend to be the same people who say you can't be friends with an ex and they do *not* like it when I put a personal joke on their boyfriend Charlie's Facebook wall. The non-believers are essentially saying sexual attraction cancels out friendship and romantic fantasy makes it void. Wherever saucy fantasies lie, there can be no friendship.

But what if sexual attraction doesn't preclude friendship? What if two people have mismatched desire for each other but are nonetheless loyal, kind and supportive of one another? Are they not friends? People in love are allowed to be friends, so we can't say that friendship and attraction are mutually exclusive. We just, for whatever reason, get very caught up on this idea that you can't fancy someone and be friends with them at the same time. Which, to me, seems limiting. I've fancied friends before, but staying 'just friends' with them has been a matter of circumstance, choice and discipline. Maybe they've been in a relationship, maybe I have been, maybe they're wildly undesirable as an actual partner, but happen to be quite cute. Like monogamy is a conscious choice in a relationship, friendship can be something you opt into with a certain person. It's another story altogether if one person is hopelessly in love with the other and it's not reciprocated; I'm just talking about chemistry between two people. I could give you a list right now of people who have fancied each other and still had functional friendships, but I'd have to give them pseudonyms and that'd take the fun out of it a bit. My point is, why are we so insistent that attraction and friendship can't co-exist? Why do we keep asking the question, 'Can men and women be friends?' when there's evidence all around us that they can be?

Perhaps it's because we haven't had much time to think about the concept of male–female friendship. In the grand scope of existence, I mean. Friendship between a man and a woman is a relatively new phenomenon. For 99 per cent of human history — or, until 10,000 years ago — we were nomadic foragers fighting to survive. Primitive women hung out with their family and the man who impregnated them, and that was it — girlfriend had neither the time nor the instinct to befriend men just for the fun of it. Since then we've been segregated by sex in just about any historical context you care to name. Same-sex friendships have always been the primary type of friendship because, at first, we needed to make those connections to survive and later because social protocol said we had to. Practically speaking, where exactly would a lady in ancient times have met a prospective male friend? Could a medieval lass have escaped the restrictions on her gender long enough to make buddies with a man who was not a suitor? Would it have been proper for an unmarried man and woman to just hang out with one another in Victorian times? The very idea of friendship between a man and a woman throughout history is either laughable or dangerous. Indeed, in some cultures, it still is.

As recently as the 1950s, it would have been rare for a woman to have a friendly relationship with a man. Now, 80 per cent of adults have or have had a close cross-sex friendship. The advent of these types of friendships is partly to do with logistics. Since women have had access to education, gone to university and ended up in the workplace, they've actually been physically in the same place as men, which makes it a hell of a lot easier to befriend some.

Feminism has created a favourable environment for friendship between men and women. Aristotle believed friends must be peers and that any imbalance of power negates the friendship because one person always has something to gain from the other. If old mate Aristotle believes friends must be equals, then he'd probably be quite surprised to discover men and women can be friends now. Our work on gender equality is far from done, but we have come a long way in terms of levelling out the disparity in social status between men and women. Now cross-sex friendships can start on somewhat even ground. And where things are not yet equal — with regards to the gender pay gap, the pension gap, the burden of motherhood, the underrepresentation of women in power positions and various industries, the unfair division of domestic work and childcare etc. — women should now be able to depend on their male friends to lend their weight to the fight. A man who doesn't actively want equality between the sexes ain't no friend at all, and while I believe feminism as a movement belongs to women, with this relatively modern phenomenon of male–female friendship, I'd hope we've gained some allies in the battle. I truly think we disseminate ideas most powerfully friend to friend, and I like to think of all the fabulous women passing on feminist ideals to their male buddies.

And that's the beauty of friendship between men and women: the glimpses you get into the other's existence. Having one lady buddy does not make a man an expert on feminine existence, but it sure as hell helps. A woman with a man pal doesn't have an authority on male experience, either. But I can only see that talking and hearing about different gendered experiences would breed compassion. Studies show that young boys behave entirely differently in a group of other boys to how they would in mixed company. With other boys their very maleness becomes exaggerated, they are more aggressive, more likely to take risks and generally more abrasive. Female company has a calming effect on boys, just as male company can have a galvanising effect on girls. Girls, left to their own devices, will chat, trade secrets and play games that generally amplify their gender roles. Growing up, we're mostly socialised to stick to our own gender for friendship, but as teenagers and adults we start collecting members of the opposite sex as friends, and that broadens out our social circles beautifully.

I did a call-out on Twitter for people who have good friends of the opposite sex, and got an impressive response. Stories of male–female besties trickled into my email inbox and Twitter newsfeed for days. Obviously, having people self-report their friendship with someone of the opposite gender means they inherently believe in that type of friendship, so I don't pretend my investigation into this matter was in any way quantitative or comprehensive. I simply chatted to a bunch of people about their friendships and it was a jolly lovely thing to do. Here's what I discovered. There are a few mitigating circumstances that tend to make friendship between a man and a woman easier. One is when the man or woman is gay, which takes the sexual possibility out of the equation. Another is when the guy and the girl have grown up together and it's more of a sibling relationship so the sex thing is totally off the cards and they just continue blissfully insulting one another like family members. And it seems to work between people who are determined to make it work. One man I spoke to — let's call him Ray — had very serious feelings for his friend — let's call her Rachel — when they first met at university, but she didn't reciprocate. In response, rather than abandoning the connection between them altogether, Ray became doggedly committed to keeping Rachel as a friend so she would still be in his life. 'When you get involved in a romance, you create more ways to lose a person,' he said. And although I suspect he may have been infatuated with Rachel for longer than he admitted to me or in fact told her, he is now in a relationship with someone else and continues to cherish the friendship. This leads me to believe that, where there is emotional transparency as opposed to clandestine love, there is the possibility for real friendship.

I should say, though, that at the very end of our conversation, Ray mentioned he still thinks about what it would be like to kiss Rachel. When they have a few drinks together, sometimes they talk about it. Does that still count as friendship? Or have they entered a weird grey zone with the sort of sexual ambiguity that would give Ray's girlfriend the jealous shivers? Does Ray still hope something will happen between them? I asked, he said no, I suspect yes. Perhaps he's no longer in love with her, perhaps there's simply some residual lust or even the frustration that he's been rejected in the past and to be with Rachel would be validation of some kind for him. That harks back to the most common argument we hear against the legitimacy of male–female friendship: that the man ultimately can't engage in a proper friendship with a woman because he can't control his sexual impulses.

If men are routinely accused of holding out hope for something sexual with their female friends, then women are just as often accused of keeping a man on standby in case they don't find a better romantic option. I spoke to women who said they'd happily marry their best mate, but only if they get to an arbitrary age like 35 or 40 and find themselves still single. I spoke to women who like to keep their flirtatious male friend around as a self-esteem boost, no matter what effect that might have on him. I spoke to people of both sexes who enjoyed the slight sexual tension in their friendship and actively wanted to preserve it. A study by evolutionary psychology professor April Bleske-Rechek found that men are more likely to believe their female friend is attracted to them and to generally be more cognisant of sexual tension between them. Whereas women who didn't 'feel that way' about their male friend assumed said friend was not attracted to them either, which certainly makes it easier for them to continue the friendship. It's almost as though women are defter with the concept of platonic friendship ... Or that we wilfully deny suspicions that a man is attracted to us so we can keep them on as friends. I may have been guilty of this in my time.

American comedian Chris Rock did a stand-up bit in the '90s about exactly this. He makes the argument that women get to have platonic friends, while men just have failed romantic prospects (as he puts it, 'women they haven't fucked yet'). He bemoans the existence of the 'friend zone' and suggests that women keep their male friends around just in case they can't find a better romantic partner — as back-up, rather than as legitimate friendships in their own right. If you'd like his phrasing on that one, too, he calls male friends, 'A dick in a glass case — in case of emergency, break glass.' I'll let you reminisce on your own experiences with male–female friendship and decide what kind of truth, if any, there is in Chris Rock's take on the matter.

So, if we're to believe the worst in everyone, men keep women as friends purely because they hope someday they'll let their guard down and deign to sleep with them. Meanwhile, women keep male friends around on the off chance they won't find a better romantic partner and, at a stage when they feel biologically desperate to settle down, they'll go for the buddy who's always been there. It's a pretty stark way of looking at things, but has some truth, in that inglorious way comedy tends to confront us with our own uncomfortable realities. We will get to the way pop culture treats male–female friendship in a moment, but first, a few words on this idea of the 'friend zone'.

The 'friend zone' is basically purgatory for a man who wants to shag a woman but ends up getting cast off as her buddy instead. Women can be put in the friend zone too, but culturally, men seem to have a more aggressive response to finding themselves there. There is no positive connotation to the phrase friend zone (even though it sounds like a frankly delightful place), and it's always said with an eye roll or an empathetic sigh. To be 'friend zoned' is to be rejected as a sexual prospect and for some people, that's the ultimate insult. For some men, friendship with a woman is the unforgivable rebuke. There's plenty of offensive literature by Pick Up Artists (PUAs) on the Internet, instructing men to basically trick a woman into taking him on as a sexual partner. A frightening number of 'how to get out of the friend zone' articles recommend wearing down the woman's confidence so she feels rejected, vulnerable and therefore interested, possibly enough to seek comfort in the form of sex. PUAs like the author of *The Game*, Neil Strauss, speak about the friend zone as if it is the worst possible outcome for a man, as though it is an affront to his masculinity and a sign of abject failure. It can be an extremely misogynistic conversation and I'd really rather not spend too much time repeating what men like him have to say. Suffice to say some men view women purely as sexual objects. To me, the friend zone is simply a figurative place people hang out in if a romantic relationship between a man and a woman is not possible, usually because one party just doesn't feel the chemistry. It's perfectly reasonable for a woman to decline a man's sexual advances and, frankly, he should be so lucky to end up in the friend zone at all. Friendship between a man and a woman, as we have covered, can be perfectly lovely and important.

And yet. Pop culture tells us again and again that friendship between men and women is impossible. Romantic comedies have to be the greatest culprits because they're specifically designed to make you see romance in everything, and perhaps the guiltiest rom-com is that rather fabulous Nora Ephron movie, *When Harry Met Sally.* It starts at the very moment when Harry Burns (Billy Crystal) first meets Sally Albright (Meg Ryan): it's 1977 and they drive together for 18 hours from college in Chicago to New York, where they are both, separately, going to start their adult lives. They squabble most of the way — about death and naivety, sex and honesty, love and work. There's chemistry there, if only the kind between a confident young man and the woman who has to tolerate his observations about life in a confined space. Harry is dating Sally's friend at the time, but tells Sally that, objectively speaking, Sally's an attractive woman. Sally takes this as a come-on and what follows is a now famous, acerbic little back-and-forth that perfectly sums up the main argument that men and women cannot be friends. Harry declares he and Sally can never be friends because, as it allegedly is with all men and women, his attraction to her cancels out their companionship. Sally is indignant, claiming to have several men friends without any sex being involved, and Harry informs her they all secretly want to have sex with her, essentially not making them friends at all, but lovers-in-waiting. Harry says it doesn't matter that the woman doesn't want to have sex with the man, that she just wants to be friends, because 'the sex thing' is already present and therefore the friendship is doomed from the start.

Despite Harry's take on things here, he and Sally do eventually become friends. The third time they meet (serendipitously of course because this is a romantic comedy), they actually like each other and decide to go on a series of friendship dates. They hang out all the time, speak on the phone (landline — it's the '80s), go out to dinner and visit museums in a sweet little montage of platonic friendship. Both their best same-sex friends can't understand why they're not together; why would you spend so much time with someone if there isn't a romantic pay-off? At this stage of the film, it could have been a delightful story about a platonic friendship 11 years in the making. It could have been a seriously great antidote to every other rom-com in the world. But, alas, no. Harry and Sally inevitably sleep together, he leaves quickly the next morning, she gets upset, they're paralysed by their sexy mistake and they fall out of friendship. The film, even then, could still have been about an imperfect friendship. Instead, in the home stretch of the plot, it transforms from a perfectly erudite little fable about friendship into a love story. Oh, it's lovely — this is Nora Ephron we're talking about here, of course it's lovely. It's got all the trademarks of a romantic classic: frantic running across New York streets at night time, our lovers' eyes meeting across the room at a glamorous party, the countdown to midnight on New Year's Eve perfectly coinciding with a proclamation of love. It's a great film, and Meg Ryan's hair deserved an Oscar for its supporting role. But Ephron missed a chance to be revolutionary when she decided to write those two friends into a romance. We could have had an extremely rare tale of platonic friendship; instead we got another rom-com with a happy ending. Sorry to be such a Grinch about it, but I do wish Harry and Sally hadn't ended up together. Their friendship was valid and moving as a standalone storyline, and it needn't have all been foreplay for a romantic relationship.

Fiction has almost always matchmade its opposite-sex protagonists, presumably because romance is the most bankable outcome. The explicit friends-ending-up-together narrative happens in *Cheers*, *The Office*, *Scrubs*, *He's Just Not That Into You*, *No Strings Attached*, *Some Kind of Wonderful*, *Friends with Benefits*, *Win a Date with Tad Hamilton*, *Clueless*, *Spider-Man*, *The Ugly Truth*, *One Day*, *Starter for Ten* and *Love, Rosie* ... to name a few. We're repeatedly being told our platonic friendships are not enough on their own; that they're failed romances or a missed chance at love. The implication is that we're all on a single-minded mission for romantic love and that any other story is not worth telling (the film and television rights to my 16-year friendship with Bernard are still available).

Just look at the statistics from the hit '90s sitcom, *Friends*: two-thirds of the main characters end up romantically involved with another Friend. On a show ostensibly about friendship, we end up with several neatly resolved romantic endings. We started out the series with six friends — three men, three women. As it turned out, that was the perfect formula to tease out the minutiae of life as twenty-something adults trying to work out who they are. As one of the most lucrative TV shows of all time, it's safe to say that it resonated. Over a decade, *Friends* played out just about every friendship scenario between its six main (conspicuously white, heteronormative) characters. We got the bromance between Joey and Chandler, the sibling relationship between Ross and Monica, the legacy friendship of Rachel and Monica, the college best-friendship of Ross and Chandler, the squad goals of the three girls, the bro code between the three boys, the friends-with-an-ex dilemma of Ross and Rachel, the unrequited love arc with Joey and Rachel, the slept-together-by-accident storyline with Monica and Chandler and the flirtatious but ultimately sexless friendship between Joey and Phoebe (and they may well have been paired off too, had Paul Rudd's contract not been extended because he was so fabulous as Phoebe's partner, Mike). The show lasted so damn long, the writers had to call on every possible incarnation of friendship to pad out the plot, and it was great telly. You won't find anyone who has watched that show more than me.

But ultimately, if we look at the way the series ended, the majority of Friends had to end up together to satisfy us. Ross was always in love with Rachel, and they fell in and out of love with one another throughout the series, so I can forgive that one. It was one of television's greatest will-they-or-won't-they storylines and the messiness of their decision to have a baby and live together as friends for a while was surprisingly radical. But Monica and Chandler's marriage was one of narrative convenience. Their romance was never plausible and their ending up together seemed to have been motivated more by what the writers thought people would rally behind than what would have made the most interesting story. Ideally, those two would have slept together drunkenly that one time and spent the remainder of the show making callback jokes to a very real, inherently funny scenario between friends. As it was, Monica ended up proposing unconvincingly to a fairly mediocre man with whom she was barely compatible (rather than marrying the loves of her life, Richard and his moustache). It was a plot device that put obvious romance before genuine friendship, and to me that seemed like a cowardly move on the part of the show's creators. And if not cowardly, boring, which is almost worse.

That was eons ago in television years, though. More recently, we've actually had some rather sweet depictions of male–female friendship on TV, which might hint at our increasing acceptance of that kind of friendship. A couple of the best come courtesy of two television-dwelling goddesses of the highest order, Amy Poehler and Tina Fey. Amy Poehler starred on a show called *Parks and Recreation* as Leslie Knope, glorious feminist queen and possibly the most enthusiastic local government employee to ever fictionally exist. She and her boss, a mustachioed man named Ron Swanson (played by Nick Offerman), are extremely close friends. There are no clues in either character's personality that would suggest they might make good or even believable friends. She's a ray of sunshine, he's a cantankerous grouch. She's a romantic, he's a cynic. She likes waffles, he likes bacon. And yet, they develop a genuine friendship. There are moments of loyalty and solidarity between Leslie Knope and Ron Swanson that could make a person cry, they're so good. They are capable of that urban myth: genuine, dependable and purely platonic friendship in spite of their biological differences.

When Leslie gets married, she asks Ron to walk her down the aisle. Ron is a manly man, a man of woodwork and meat products, a man of few words and even fewer emotional revelations, and yet, on the day of Leslie's wedding, he makes possibly the longest sentimental monologue of his life: 'You are a wonderful person. Your friendship means a lot to me. And you look very beautiful.' Her response? 'Okay, weirdo.' They care about each other deeply but their most common way of expressing it is through insults, jokes and gestures. Which is typical, I find, of friendship with men. Compare that to the way Leslie treats her female BFF, Ann Perkins (played by Rashida Jones) and you have a neat demonstration of the difference between female–female friendship and male–female friendship. With Ann, it's all compliments ('Ann, you poetic and noble land-mermaid'), support ('I believe in you, Ann') and catchphrases about female solidarity ('Uteruses before duderuses,' 'Ovaries before brovaries'). Ann amplifies Leslie's femininity, where Ron brings out her brusquer, more traditionally masculine side. Leslie Knope has got her friendship situation sorted because she's got both.

Meanwhile, Fey starred on a show called *30 Rock*, as the head writer on a comedy sketch show based very much on

Saturday Night Live. Her character, Liz Lemon, strikes up an unlikely but strangely authentic friendship with her boss, Jack Donaghy (played by Alec Baldwin). She's a scrappy but talented career woman who lives in functional but endearing disarray; he's a glossy, conservative mercenary who should logically be her nemesis. There is no obvious reason for them to get on. In fact, nothing about them is conducive to good, healthy friendship: there's a power imbalance because he's her boss, they're opposed on virtually every political issue, they come from different backgrounds, they have no friends, interests or hobbies in common — and then there's the matter of their being opposite sexes. And yet, they get each other, defend each other and need each other. Jack toughens up Liz's resolve in life and Liz softens Jack's misogyny. They find a way to be affectionate with each other in an asexual way (Liz: 'It's the hug plane coming in for a landing'; Jack: 'Cleared for landing') and have their own way of defining the terms of their relationship (Jack: 'Our relationship is purely platonic, if Plato had an elderly, shut-in aunt'). They make each other better people and if that's not a good rationale for male–female friendship, I don't know what is.

Thankfully, Liz and Jack never hook up because that would be, frankly, ludicrous. Sure, they have technically touched lips one time, shared a bed and accidentally got married on a yacht because they misunderstood what a French man was saying, but there was never any real romance. It's hinted at a few times, then vehemently rejected as a possibility. The writers of the show were too busy paying tribute to that strange, beautiful thing that can happen between a woman and a man when the time and circumstances are just right: friendship. Finally, blissfully, we are getting stories about male and female characters that realise the comedic potential of a platonic friendship.

And that, to me, is one of the most important traits of friendship between a man and a woman: comedy. My friendship with Bernard, now that we're comfortably platonic, is a lot more brash than my friendships with women. We insult each other, tease each other and laugh openly at the other person's life choices. If you could see what friendships were made of, ours would be a mishmash of personal jokes, high-school memories, shared history and gossip. We'll openly criticise each other in a way that I just don't do with women, because laughter isn't the main currency of my female friendships. By the standards of any other relationship, I'm quite mean to old Bernard, and he can be to me. But it makes us laugh, and it works. I think it's because we find each other ridiculous, in that way you sometimes just do not understand the opposite sex. It's a perpetual eye roll. I also think we've quite deftly negotiated a compromise between a male and female version of friendship. He encourages me to interact with him in a more traditionally masculine way, with a lower maintenance emotional connection than I have with women. Whereas I would bet that he's slightly more open about certain things with me and his other female friends than he is with some of his male buddies. That, and we're more likely to gossip over brunch than most pairs of men are. He toughens me up and I soften him — that may not be the case with every friendship, but it is with ours. It's a nice trade-off and now that we don't fancy one another, he can actually give me dating advice from a dude perspective, which can be, ah, somewhat enlightening.

So, can men and women ever truly be friends? It's a 'yes' from me. They can — but with probable complications. Let's face it, sexual chemistry is persuasive and some people find it difficult to tame. I'd also say not everyone is made for friendship with the opposite sex. There are some people who, for whatever reason, whether it be an inability to control their sexual impulses or a hapless affection for someone they just can't get past, are not destined to be proper friends with someone who arrived on this Earth with a different combination of chromosomes. Of course, if you don't believe in the concept of friendship between men and women, you're unlikely to practise any such friendships because it would be against your belief system. In some cultures, it's simply not safe or wise to do so. And then there are men who believe that friendship with a woman would somehow threaten or diminish their masculinity, and women who just can't tolerate male banter on a regular, voluntary basis. And that's fine, but I do think they are missing out on something rather great and wonderfully unromantic between two people society would most likely prefer to see end up together. Like I said, people who befriend the opposite sex are evolutionary rebels and I salute them. The moral of the story, in both pop culture and real life, is that not every Harry has to marry his Sally. Not every Monica has to settle for a Chandler. Sometimes they could just hang out and shoot the breeze, making each other's lives a bit more awesome without falling in love.

CHAPTER SIX

Work wives and 9-5 husbands

HAVE YOU EVER NOTICED how tiny John Travolta's beard is? It's really small. Like, very, very small. Or at least, it was around the year 2014. In fact, perhaps it doesn't even qualify as a beard; it's more an infinitesimal island of facial hair that set itself up on John Travolta's face and refused to leave. It can't have been an aesthetic decision, surely not. Perhaps it's hiding something, some sort of grotesque chin abnormality. Perhaps it's in a movie contract. Whatever it is, the discovery of John Travolta's tiny beard was perhaps the greatest moment of friendship celebration I've had in an office environment. It truly, truly broke me and a number of others. To this day, photographic proof of the tiny beard can still undo me. Circa 2014, my friend Rosie and I were browsing the Internet (it was our job to do so, at the time) and came across an article by a very funny Australian journalist called Nick Bond. Nick announced the debut of the tiny beard with a full photograph of John Travolta, in a suit, on the red carpet. What followed was a series of photos, each zoomed in slightly more than the last, until the final one, which was literally just the offending facial hair in question. Something about the simple genius of this article really tickled Rosie and me. We came very close to printing it out and wallpapering the entire office with it. For a start, we couldn't quite believe Nick Bond could get away with publishing increasingly zoomed in photographs of John Travolta's beard as a legitimate piece of journalism; we worshipped him for this act of pure silliness. To us, it was perfect. Rosie and I both often wrote about social issues and famous people for a living, and nothing pleased us more than this flagrant disregard for the rules of journalism. Of course the content was perfect, too; the dissemination of news like the fact that John Travolta had grown a tiny beard is actually the reason the Internet was invented in the first place. As far as celebrity journalism goes, it's got it all: intrigue, suspense, chin sweat. And then there was the twist: Rosie had been to a red carpet event in LA and actually had a photograph taken with John Travolta *and the tiny beard*. Her face was nearly touching the beard as they leaned in for a selfie. She brought the photo up on her laptop and by this stage, we were screaming. We were in such fits of giggles there was no chance of us doing any proper work all afternoon. We cried actual salty tears of happiness. Worse, if we're going to think about workplace productivity for a moment, is that it was contagious. Obviously people wanted to know what we thought was so funny, so the image of John Travolta's tiny beard was circulated around the office and we started dragging everyone into the joy of its discovery. When someone went to a meeting or the bathroom, we'd change their screen saver to a picture of The Beard. I don't think I've ever laughed so hard at anything in my life.

And that's what work friendship can be like: magnificent and funny and irreverent. It can make work a joy, and can literally change your entire attitude to getting up every morning and turning up at the same place every day. Good work friends are total game changers. Sure, they can be a huge distraction — whispering about your latest Tinder date as you mainline free cookies over the sink and dedicating entire email threads to Ryan Gosling's true feminist intentions are not, strictly speaking, what your boss would consider the best use of your time — but I'd argue everyone needs a certain level of escapism built into their corporate lives or they'd go mad. Work can be satisfying and fulfilling and all that lovely stuff, but it can also be hectic and painful and dull. We are in the middle of an epidemic of workplace stress and it's causing very serious mental health issues across many industries. What with the immersive experience of having a smartphone and an Internet connection, we are increasingly forgetting to switch off altogether, and more of us are allowing work to seep into every goddamn orifice of our lives. With that in mind, it's bloody nice to have a friend to share it with.

Having Rosie at work meant I always had a confidant, an advisor and a buddy. We could go get beef pho together down the road and swap secrets, talk about boys and debrief about work. We could check on each other when things got emotional, back each other up in meetings and big up each other's work. It was a genuine delight to have her as my work buddy, and we've kept that friendship going since we both left the job we were doing when we met. The friendship worked because we were both senior employees so there was no power disparity between us and we rarely went after the same stories so there was no envy or competition. We spent so much time together too; probably more than we spent with our families. She was, in the popular language of the cool people, my 'work wife'. People often refer to their closest friends at work as their 'work wife' or 'work husband', which probably hints at the fact that we see these people more often than the ones we choose to marry/sleep with/share residential space with/unconditionally adore. The coining of that phrase probably also has something to do with the level of emotional support that person provides. Work can be an extremely stressful place, and your work wife or husband is your sanctuary and your support. That is, if you've got a good one. Or maybe two.

A friend of mine — let's call her Ingrid — works in a high-pressure marketing job, in an industry that could easily be described as overtly masculine or male dominated. She is exceptional at what she does, a real prodigy. But outright conflict and the subtler politics of jimmying egos and clashing motives are inevitable in any workplace and that sometimes threatens to take over her job. Navigating the ins and outs, ups and downs, backwards and forwards of people's intentions and ambitions can be a full-time job in itself, if you're not careful. And so Ingrid has recruited a duo of best friends — it's a polygamous work marriage — to support her throughout all that. They met doing a problem-solving task and got on so well as a trio, they became close. They talked at work, got lunch and eventually started going for walks and catch-ups on the weekends. They've discovered something rather beautiful, and perhaps rare: they seem to take turns building one person up and making them believe in themselves. When Ingrid had to write a 'big scary email' to her boss, her friends helped her draft it. When one of the others had to be assertive with someone senior to her, they practised her speech together. And when the other had to re-negotiate her position, all three role-played the scenario until she felt confident enough to do it for real. They call each other when they can't solve a work problem, share funny things on WhatsApp and offer each other genuine emotional support. They make each other better at their jobs because they crowd source the parts that overwhelm or intimidate them. They lift each other up.

Friendship like this in the office is an obvious morale boost. Having work mates can, at least, put you in a good mood and at best, completely change the way you approach your work life. This isn't just anecdotal, either. Studies show that having just one close friend at work improves mood, attention span and perhaps more surprisingly, productivity. Work spouses can make us more focused, more loyal and more passionate. A well-known 1999 Gallup Poll found that those who had a friend at work were 43 per cent more likely to report they had received praise and recognition for their work in the past week. The objective of the poll was to identify what companies with high levels of the following are doing right: employee retention, customer metrics, productivity and profitability. The guy who devised the survey questions was almost laughed out of the office when he suggested they ask how strongly people identify with the statement, 'I have a best friend at work' but his insistence on including friendship as a metric of corporate success was validated. People with strong work friendships were 37 per cent more likely to report that someone at work has encouraged their development, 27 per cent more likely to report that the mission of their company makes them feel like their work is important and 27 per cent more likely to report that they feel like their opinions matter. All of which is to say, unequivocally, that friendship in the workplace is an important thing. Not just to keep employees happy, but to make them better at their jobs. Research consistently and overwhelmingly suggests that people with at least one strong work friendship perform better, think more creatively, show more initiative and get better results. They get sick less often, have fewer accidents and change jobs less frequently. Managers and bosses all over the world should and do take notice of this research; why else do you think Google bought so many brightly coloured bean bags for their meeting rooms, why else does every start-up and creative agency have a ping pong table? We are becoming increasingly aware that friendship (or at the very least, a congenial atmosphere made up of comfortable, garish furniture and indoor sports) is essential to success, quite contrary to the rather dismal urban myth that the greatest achievers among us are loners.

The importance of workplace camaraderie became obvious to me when I worked at *Cosmopolitan* magazine in Australia. When I started there as features editor, I had my own office.

It was the first time I had my own four walls at work, and it made me feel extremely important. I had space for armchairs so my team could congregate for meetings, and when nobody was looking I could put my cherished turquoise high-heel sneakers up on the desk as I was editing articles. I covered the walls with torn-out pages from magazines: Amy Poehler, Tina Fey, Nicole Kidman, Jennifer Lawrence, Emma Stone, Kerry Washington and Feminist Ryan Gosling. My predecessor had wallpapered an entire cabinet with vintage *Cosmo* covers: Christina Aguilera, Britney Spears, Jennifer Lopez. It was my little sanctuary, my little den of inspiration, and at first, I loved it. It was quiet when I needed to read or think or write. It was peaceful. But then I started to notice that if I wanted actual human interaction, I had to venture out of my four walls or invent a reason to invite someone in. I'd hear little snippets of banter as people walked by my door, but for the most part I missed out on all that casual chit-chat that goes on between very important work tasks. I found myself lingering at the biscuit tin or the microwave, hoping to catch someone on a snack run for a quick hit of social interaction. I'd hear giggling from the open plan parts of the office just outside my room, and feel desperately left out. There were times I'd heckle people as they passed by because I wanted in on whatever joke they were sharing. I started to feel like Ricky Gervais or Steve Carell in *The Office*; some sort of creep lurking around her colleagues in the hope of feeling like maybe we were friends. And I wanted to be friends with the girls at *Cosmo* — they were smart and funny and offensively chic. So, when my editor announced that we would have to knock down the walls of my office to make room for new hires, I was thrilled. We turned my office into a little cove with four desks, four chairs, four computers. I instantly got three new work buddies and it changed everything. We called our little area 'The Quad' and we adored it (studies show that work friends often come up with nicknames for themselves that they find hilarious or clever, but everyone else regards as questionable at best). The three other women in The Quad were whip-smart, hilarious, ambitious, fierce, gentle, supportive, loving, and ferociously good at what they did. They were an inspiration every day, professionally, and just the kind of diversion I needed.

The thing about full-time work in an office is that you need something to break up the monotony. In my experience, it's very difficult, if not impossible, to be motivated, alert and productive from 9 till 5 (or, more accurately, from when you wake up and first check your emails/social media till whenever you physically stop checking them at night). Procrastination, for me, is an entirely mandatory part of the process of working. So I truly can't see the harm in pressing pause on trying to collate 3,852 sex tips because your boss wants the most sex tips ever collated in one article by Wednesday for a little banter about the ridiculous time Harriet auditioned to be one of the girls on *The Bachelor* and answered the question, 'If you were a drink, what would you be?' with the most endearingly hopeless answer possible: 'Tap water'. Frankly, as long as you're meeting your deadlines, I don't see why you can't stop transcribing your interview with Khloe Kardashian momentarily so you can discuss the fact that Sean from Accounting is definitely shamelessly pursuing Harriet one very enthusiastic desk visit at a time. We have evolved to use gossip as a mechanism for intimacy, and you cannot tell me that whispering about who just asked for time off to get their breasts evened out doesn't make you feel closer to your work mates. As long as you're not being malicious or hurting anyone, a bit of banter in the office is entirely necessary for reasons of sanity and camaraderie. Work is work; your passion for it can turn up some days and abandon you on others. But good friendship is always there, if you look after it right. Good friends at work can be the difference between sinking and swimming. They can get you through mistakes, fights, deadlines, meetings, redundancies, rumours and awkward interactions at Christmas parties. They can give you professional advice over coffee, break-up solace during lunch and Tinder encouragement at Friday night drinks. They can, if you're lucky, walk an entirely delightful line between your professional and private lives, skipping between the two when you require it.

And what a beautiful moment it is, when you first realise that someone from work wants to be a part of your crew. When you start a job somewhere, befriending people can be a little bit like asking them out on a date: you can't be entirely sure they feel the same way about you, so gingerly extending an invitation to lunch or drinks after work can be awkward and nerve-racking. I spoke to Gyan, who got her start in magazines in Australia, about the exact moment she realised her mate Julia wanted to be more than just work colleagues. They'd known each other a while — Julia had come in for work experience and then, tenacious girl that she was, returned for an internship at the magazine where Gyan worked. Gyan knew she wanted to be mates with Julia, but she didn't know quite how to seal the deal. Until, that is, they were walking from the office to the train station and Julia, impromptu, started telling Gyan a story about a boy. It was the first time they'd really deviated from work-based chat, and Gyan jumped at the chance to lift the friendship out of its work-only context. She listened and then told her own story about a boy, just as they arrived at the station and had to catch different trains. Since that moment, Gyan and Julia have been really close friends; they travel to music festivals together, go out and have had so many sleepovers they've lost count. But Gyan can trace it all back to that one conversation, when she knew their friendship had crossed over from professional territory to personal. Frankly, I can't imagine having a job (or staying in a job) without having someone make that transition in your life. How do you get by without an ally in the office? Who do you painstakingly debrief with, and who else in your life cares about the minutiae of office politics and interactions?

For Agnes, that moment of friendship revelation in the office was a little more complicated. When she first met her eventual work wife, she didn't actually like her. They were both smokers so they'd see each other on smoke breaks and gently avoid one another. This woman committed some of the deadliest office sins known to man and woman: she brought in smelly lunches and she talked loudly on the phone. She gave every impression of being obnoxious, self-involved, even garish. Meanwhile, Agnes read the Communist Manifesto alone in the office cafeteria, which, she admits now, probably made her seem equally unapproachable. They went about their jobs with a faint but consistent dislike for one another, and no intention whatsoever to strike up a friendship. Then, one day, they were literally the only two people in the smoking area and social convention forced them to attempt small talk with one another. They stayed in that smoking area an unnatural length of time, chatting and discovering that the other person was not, as previously suspected, terribly disagreeable. From then on, they were inseparable and dependent upon each other for much of their job's enjoyment. They were working in IT at the time, on a product they neither believed in nor felt particularly passionate about, so their friendship became a strong reason to actually come into the office each day. Agnes's friend continued to bring in smelly lunches and eat popcorn noisily, but she forgave her because by then she knew it had no particular bearing on her personality. Eventually, they both moved on from those jobs, but they continued a morning ritual of meeting for coffee at Starbucks near Baker Street tube stop in London — the perfect way to start the work day, with a little caffeine and gossip. Agnes lives in London and her friend moved to Austria, so now they only see each other twice a year. But they do it properly: her friend's husband takes the kids away for three days so she and Agnes get a chance to have an immersive, intensive friendship love-in. The moral of Agnes's story, to me, is that everyone should conceivably be able to find a friend at work.

Befriending the noisy eater in her office turned into a lifelong friendship, and provided Agnes with sorely needed solace in an inspirationally barren workplace. It changed her entire approach to work. Sure, she had less spare time to bone up on socialist literature over lunch, but she had the true pleasure of office companionship and I would wish that upon everyone.

And yet an alarmingly small number of us actually have these important work friendships. The company Total Jobs spoke to 4,000 employees and 100 employers for their research into the 'work spouse' phenomenon and they discovered just 17 per cent of those people claimed to have a work spouse, AKA a close friend at work. This is despite the fact that 70 per cent of employers say they think friendship is good for morale, company culture and the health of the people they employ. It's despite the fact that every statistic and survey suggests friendship makes people happier, healthier, more creative and more productive. Those who do have at least one close friend at work are overwhelmingly better off: they report feeling stronger and more valued as a member of staff, more excited to come into work and more productive. In fact, in spite of all the gossiping and banter that goes on, just four per cent of those surveyed said they felt less productive because of a friendship at work. Twenty-three per cent would consider leaving their job if their 'work spouse' did and seven per cent would describe the news that their friend was leaving as bereavement.

I spoke to so many people — friends of my own, generous strangers from the Internet — who live out the statistics about friendship in the workplace. Hayley and Lauren work at a charity organisation together and they're so besotted with one another as work mates, they're known as the 'Bert and Ernie' of their office (though they of course prefer to think of themselves as the Tina Fey and Amy Poehler of the not-for-profit sector). Hayley says they're like the old guys in *The Muppets* during meetings, sitting up the back and whisper-heckling. They have come to mean so much to each other, because they are literally one another's best job perks. Amy and Frances, who work in entertainment journalism, ended up getting matching tattoos because they were so devoted to one another as work friends and then later, as life friends. Amy says the 'lols and bants' they had at work got her through severe anxiety and enabled her to keep doing her job. These sets of work buddies are demonstrably happier in their jobs and their lives in general because they have good, reliable companionship at work. A Relationships at Work study by LinkedIn found that 46 per cent of professionals worldwide believe work friends are important to their overall happiness. A study by London events company Wildgoose found that 61 per cent of people value their happiness at work — of which friendship is a major component — over financial reward. Eighty-one per cent of women and 45 per cent of men said they would take happiness at work before a salary increase. Fifty-seven per cent of people in the 120 businesses Wildgoose surveyed say friendship makes work more enjoyable — and you can only assume the remaining 43 per cent are yet to discover how completely lovely it can be.

So, then, we have to ask: with such resounding evidence in favour of workplace friendship, why is it still rare? I have a few theories. For a start, we've still got this residual feeling that offices are strictly professional places. They're not, not any more. They used to be perhaps, back when people had clear delineations between their personal and their professional lives. Back when people could arrive at work, put in their hours and return home, not to be contacted by their boss, their client or their colleagues. Back when they had a semblance of privacy, a private life they could call their own, an existence they could tap into only from the confines of their home. All of that is virtually unheard of now that we have blurred the lines between our professional and private selves so rigorously. In most industries today — certainly in your standard corporate office set-up — we bring to work a hybrid of those selves. We have to. It's become necessary to do so, because work has seeped outside of the standard 35 hours in an office and started to define who we are, not just what we do. Work is an intrinsic part of our identities now, as well as a stubborn and consuming part of our schedules. Millennials, whom I shall defend forever and a day, have had to adapt to fast-increasing demands on their time and identities. It's well documented and recognised in corporate circles that young people are more cavalier about disclosing personal information in the workplace, more likely to befriend one another and more brazen with their contacting of people from the office outside of hours. They add/follow/ like their colleagues on social media now, too, because to them, even the performativity of the personal is professional. According to a LinkedIn study, 67 per cent of millennials are likely to share personal details at work including their salary, their relationships and family issues, compared to just one-third of baby boomers. As far as casual communication outside of work goes, 28 per cent of millennials have texted their manager after hours about a non-work issue, compared to just 10 per cent of baby boomers. When you look at generational attitudes to work culture, there is a very real shift happening in how personal we are willing to get at work. If we remain professional at work at all times, without allowing our senses of humour, our humanity and our compassion to pop up at the office, then we will go utterly mad. Some people, I have to say, already have. Stress, anxiety, panic and serious existential anguish are alarmingly common side-effects of a working life now — and something must be done. In the absence of a solution that involves dialling back the presence of technology in our lives and reclaiming personal time for ourselves, the best possible thing we can do is develop positive relationships at work so we can perform the ultimate multi-task: work and friendship. All of that begins with a willingness to be our private selves in the office. It begins with a deliberate, strategic injection of kindness and candour.

How exactly, after all, do you cultivate intimacy? The fastest and most reliable way of making a friend is to share personal information with someone. Friendship is an exchange of vulnerabilities; a deal done in personal exposure. Of course it's going to be difficult for some people, especially those who began their careers in a stiff corporate environment, to feel comfortable sharing personal details with their work mates. But — and this gives me hope for the work friendships of the future — that seems to be changing. Young people, bless their catchphrase T-shirts and trendy office sneakers, are leading the charge when it comes to healthy vulnerability at work. They are finding room in their corporate lives to attend to their mental health, maintain their sanity and meet their emotional needs — and they're doing it by making buddies, I swear to Beyoncé. As we eat into our personal time with work commitments (we don't even take lunch breaks any more), it has become necessary to satisfy our emotional needs at work, too. With skyrocketing levels of stress, fatigue and burnout literally threatening and shortening people's lives, the very least we can do for ourselves is find solace and support. That is to say, we need work wives and work husbands and work BFFs more than ever because without them, all we have is the impending doom of an existence entirely defined by how well we perform at work. I don't know about you, but I'm simply not ready and not willing to surrender to that kind of apocalypse right now.

Speaking of unruly hell, things can get worse than just not having a work spouse to call your own. Being a loner at work is sad, but salvageable. What's not acceptable is workplace bullying and possibly even worse, workplace cruelty under the guise of friendship. I've known offensively disingenuous and outright cruel people in work environments, and I've watched how they can destroy a person's self-esteem, confidence and ability to function. I've known people to leave jobs with their identities in tatters because one asshole or another decides to make their life at work a living hell. And it can be so much more dangerous to encounter one of these toxic people at work because there are so many layers of secrecy and professionalism. Not to mention, of course, that you are stuck with that person by circumstance. At least if you become entangled in a toxic friendship in your own time, you can wriggle out of it with some clarity and support from a really decent therapist/friend/ally. But when you come up against an abominable person at work — either someone who shamelessly belittles you or goes about their cruelty in a sneakier fashion — it can be so much harder to find your way out.

Claudia met her toxic work friend when she started a new job in a new city. Let's call this person Pauline. Pauline was slightly senior to Claudia, say, one job title up in the office hierarchy. So, right from the beginning, there was a discrepancy in power that made their friendship complicated, even precarious. But they were both in their early-to-mid twenties, both into theatre, both particularly invested in the stories of a famous boy wizard by the name of Harry Potter. So they struck up a friendship outside of work: they'd go to Friday night drinks and Pauline would crash at Claudia's place when she got drunk because it was closer to the centre of London. As Claudia tells it, they had that enchanting sense of being kindred spirits you get when you realise you're into the same things, but even at the very beginning of their friendship, there were warning signs about Pauline. Pauline didn't get on with a lot of other people in the office; she was the sort of person who collected disagreements and sometimes, even she and Claudia would spar. But, as you do when you have that fresh, naive faith in a new friend, Claudia didn't worry too much. It was about 18 months into the friendship that cracks really began to show, and Claudia realised that perhaps Pauline had never been a friend at all; not really. Claudia started to notice, with that nauseating sort of hindsight, that Pauline had been quite cruel and controlling, and perhaps not very nice at all. She had enjoyed her seniority to Claudia a little too much, indulged in her sense of importance a little too enthusiastically, tested the limits of the friendship a little too gleefully. It was a classic toxic friendship in the sense that Claudia never knew quite where she stood, or worse, suspected she knew exactly where she stood in Pauline's estimation of things. Pauline toyed with Claudia's confidence, both professionally and personally, sometimes in a clandestine way, other times in a very open, almost outlandish way, in front of other people. She was cruel to Claudia, but Claudia didn't have many friends outside of work, so she persisted with the friendship, taking hit after hit to her self-esteem.

Then Pauline left the company to do her dream job. As it happened, Claudia could see her dream job right alongside her at this new gig. And so, disillusioned with the friendship but hardened enough by it to still see value in the connection, Claudia asked for Pauline's help getting a job in Pauline's new company. It was entirely plausible; Claudia was very good at her job and uniquely employable, given her specific set of expertise. So it wasn't an outlandish or awkward thing to ask Pauline to suss out the possibilities. Pauline, who clearly still enjoyed being of value to Claudia, promised to fight in her corner and bring her over to this new company. But it didn't exactly work out that way. Pauline's promises were empty and she let months pass without doing anything to help Claudia. It was beyond unhelpful — by this stage, things had transpired at her old job and Claudia now needed this new job to stay in the country. But Pauline kept Claudia in this cycle of promise and disappointment, which was ultimately tantamount to career sabotage, and the role never eventuated. What friendship they had left dropped off almost entirely and it became a purely transactional relationship: formal, distant, perfunctory. Looking back on the friendship, Claudia is just not convinced she ever meant anything real to Pauline; that she ever really qualified as a friend. And certainly, she wasn't treated like a friend, not really, not when she's being honest with herself about it. Claudia ended up leaving her job and searching for a new one, with the serious risk of having to leave the country looming over her, dejected and ravaged by this friendship which had always had undercurrents of emotional abuse. Claudia suspects this is just how Pauline conducts relationships in her life: with tenderness when she feels like it and it suits her, but ultimately with a strange callousness bordering on narcissism. Months later, she is still shaken by the experience of having Pauline in her life, under the guise of friendship. It seriously eroded her confidence and it will take a while to get that back.

This sort of toxic friendship in the workplace is inevitable because terrible people have day jobs, too. We cannot hope to always meet glorious, uplifting people in the context of work and we cannot always be guaranteed the Bert to our Ernie or the Tina to our Amy. Work friendship is very often to do with luck, perhaps more so than in the outside world. It's a little bit like school in the sense that you find yourself in this finite group of human beings for a period in your life, for many hours a day, five days a week, and you have to find the best companionship possible or go it alone. It can be a savage environment for so many reasons, not least the fact that bullies need to make a living, too, and they don't especially care who they destroy in order to do so. Workplace bullying is, in my opinion, one of the great scourges of corporate culture and something we are woefully mishandling as a general rule. It's very difficult to define, identify and report bullying because it's insidious and manipulative by its very nature, and besides, the victim doesn't want to make it worse or risk losing their job by getting HR involved. It's virtually impossible to report 'a growing, ominous sense that I've been emotionally abused by someone I thought was my friend' too, because it's delicate and so often happens without the full cognisance of the person embroiled in it. And so we are left with this rather stark set of options at work: find the real mates if you're lucky, detect the fake ones if you're sharp, avoid the truly abominable ones by virtue of extreme wit and, if all that fails, quit. I can't help thinking we could be doing more to eradicate bullying and set our KPIs of kindness significantly higher. I know there are so many factors at play when you're trying to find and keep a job — financial security, creative satisfaction, ambition fulfilment, career advancement strategy, all that potentially great stuff. But I have to say, my personal policy on the professional is to prioritise happiness, and therefore friendship, even at work. It's a difficult thing to do, I get it; success can be a clinical thing and we've certainly seen unkind people reach great levels of it. Friendship isn't compulsory for success, and perhaps that's why so many people forego it. We're in an era where even the contestants on reality TV shows frequently proclaim, 'I'm not here to make friends.' I just think that above pretty much all else, we bloody should be. That's all. Do me a favour, though, if you can. Just try upping your loveliness output at work and see if you can nab yourself an office spouse. Trial it for a while. Find me personally to let me know if all the stats lie and friends don't make you happier, more productive and better at your job.

CHAPTER SEVEN

Friend requests and liking people online

IF THE INTERNET was a person, she'd be Lindsay Lohan: started out as a star, lost her way, stumbled into some dark places but ultimately remains far better than her reputation would suggest. The invention of the World Wide Web in 1990 was a miraculous thing. It expanded and shrank the world at once, much like the telephone or the telegram, only more drastic. There really has been no invention quite like it. The Web elicited the kind of nerdy excitement we don't really get now except perhaps for the announcement of seven new planets in our solar system. It started out as a niche innovation for people working in technology, but in the years since its invention, it's become ubiquitous in a way we could scarcely have predicted. The growth of the Internet has been epic — not that I remember the early stages of it personally, being, as I was at the time, a toddler. While I was watching *Care Bears*, computers were changing the way we communicate, the way we think, and the way we interact forever. Not to be dramatic about it, or anything.

Now, though, the World Wide Web has a publicity problem. It's frequently blamed for our social isolation, our loneliness and our depravities. For our perversions, crimes, sickness, distraction, misery and rancid integrity as a species. The Internet is depicted, often by frightened parents, as an exclusively vicious place where teenagers have their innocence ravaged, women have their lives threatened and people log on to deceive and extort one another. It's the home of catfishing, blackmail, child pornography, revenge pornography, cyberbullying, exploitation, rape threats, misogyny, privacy invasion and the loss of innocence. You can learn how to build a bomb, elope with a terrorist, buy a weapon, score drugs, groom children and expose yourself on the Internet. And it *is* all of those things — absolutely, guilty as charged. The Internet can be a place of unspeakable horror, where people live-stream their suicides, commit hate crimes, stalk one another and destroy reputations, careers and lives. It can be a filthy, dangerous, terrifying place and it enables some of the worst human behaviour imaginable.

But — and I think you saw this coming — it's also bloody brilliant. The Internet is a magnificent beast of a thing and it's become an important part of human existence. Some days I'd like to track down the inventor of the Internet and kiss them right on the face for the astounding ways in which it makes my life liveable, possible and great. For a start, my job as a journalist would be impossible without the ability to tweet, email pitches to editors, follow news in real time, research and network. Yes, obviously journalism pre-dated the Internet and correspondents used to file their stories by phone or on typewriters. They might even consider that type of work the original, purest version of the vocation. But without the Internet, my very particular form of journalism — online social conscience and opinion pieces — would not exist. The Internet has created and now enables my livelihood and for that I am frequently grateful. Twitter has led to so many job opportunities for me, sometimes I think co-founder and CEO Jack Dorsey should get an executive producer credit for my career. As a journalist / young person, my life on the Internet is largely indistinguishable from my life as a real, in-person person. Ever since my parents put a mobile phone in my hand for safety reasons, I've had my thumbs practically fused to a tiny keyboard. From the moment the Internet started appearing in homes, my heart pumped to the sweet rhythm of a modem finding its connection. Now? I may as well be intravenously connected to Wi-Fi. The Internet is my office, a laptop is my commute to work and a mobile phone is just a way to keep the world in my pocket. Communicating online is a professional requirement for me, but it's also very much linked to my identity and sense of self: I tweet therefore I am.

And that's just my professional life online. The Internet is also extremely important to me personally — and that's where we get to relevant territory for this book. The Internet allows us to make and sustain friendships in a majestic way, and I don't think we necessarily celebrate that enough. We hear all the time that social media makes us selfish or lazy or inattentive with our friendships and that we are collectively losing the art of true connection as a species because of it. There seems to be an age divide when it comes to this issue: most 'digital natives' (people who grew up with the Internet) love the Internet. Many 'digital immigrants' (older people who have had to adapt to technological advances well after they were set in their ways) are more likely to criticise, fear or despise the Internet. That has exacerbated the usual inter-generational spat between young people coming into adulthood and the people who've been doing adulthood for a while. It's started a lot of dinner table fights between parents and kids who are on their phones all the time, too. I can empathise with the kids — a lot of essential gossip happens on those little devices and it can be devastating to fall behind on it — and with the parents, who just want old-fashioned bonding time over a shared meal because it's the only damn time the family is together. It's truly one of the great modern squabbles and frankly, I'm not sure how it'll be resolved. I do think we could ease up on the rhetoric that young people are committing some sort of godawful sin every time they pick up their phones to chat to their friends, though.

If you're a little bit in love with what your phone can do, chances are you've been teased by your family about it and treated as though eye contact is basically God's little trick for genuine emotional connection. In my experience, if you get someone over 50 in a bad mood started on the matter, they'll speak as though texting is the devil's work and young people's souls are being sucked through the screens of their iPhones. The moral panic around technology is real. Fail to answer a baby boomer's question immediately because you got distracted by the 'beep' of a message on your phone one time and you'll never hear the end of the argument that we're all going to hell in a hand basket for Internet addiction. The presumption that online friendship is somehow inferior, superficial, trivial or dangerous is widespread and well documented. That's why, for the sake of novelty and honesty, this chapter may at times read like a love letter to the Internet. I believe in its capacity to create, revive and maintain friendships in a way we've historically struggled to do. And where social media has paradoxically created a disconnect between human beings, I believe it is also the solution to that disconnect.

Some psychologists believe social media could be making us lonelier or more socially isolated. One study, done at the University of Pittsburgh School of Medicine in the US and published in the *American Journal of Preventive Medicine*, suggests that the more time young adults spend on social media, the more socially isolated they tend to feel. In 2014, lead scientist Professor Brian Primack and his team questioned 1,787 adults aged between 19 and 32 about their use of the 11 most popular social media platforms at that time (Facebook, Twitter, YouTube, Instagram, Google Plus, Snapchat, Reddit, Tumblr, Pinterest, LinkedIn and Vine). Each person was asked to detail how frequently they visited each site and how long they spent on it, then evaluate their own levels of social isolation. The results came in and it does look like more time spent on more social media makes people feel as though they are more socially isolated, even when their interaction online is ostensibly a social one. Co-author on the study, Professor Elizabeth Miller, who works in paediatrics at the university, admitted something important: they do not know which came first, the loneliness or the social media. It is possible lonely people seek out social media to feel connected, rather than the social media actually causing the loneliness. It's hard to go up against psychological research, but that seems to be what I'm doing. Despite what this study seems to indicate, I would still argue it's entirely possible to connect authentically online. I'd even say it's possible to reduce feelings of loneliness and social isolation online — not least because I have felt that exact effect.

Professors Primack and Miller both speculate that spending time scrolling through other people's social media feeds and profiles may cause feelings of exclusion and envy. Looking at photographs of an event you weren't invited to, for example, is bound to make you feel lousy. Watching Boomerang clips of someone's perfect day out in a tropical location surrounded by friends might make your life seem boring or miserable in comparison. Spying on someone's terrific day, lovely relationship, wonderful adventure or delightful party might make you feel loneliness more acutely. As an inspirational Instagram meme once said, you shouldn't compare your 'behind the scenes' to someone else's 'highlights reel'. If you're sitting at home in your pyjamas, half-watching Netflix, half-scrolling through filtered photographs of somebody else's awesome life, of course you're going to feel a little bit inferior. That, I would argue, has more to do with our inability to commit to one activity or value our alone time than it does to the actual social media. Social media is a platform for our human impulses. It's not at fault here; we are.

To me, these 'social media is making us lonely' studies only prove one thing: that we are lonely. I agree wholeheartedly with that — the human race has been struck with a loneliness epidemic and we're not sure quite how to get out of it. We are lonely, and yet we do not know how to be alone. Laying all the blame for that trend at Mark Zuckerberg's doorstep because he invented Facebook in 2004 is reductive and unhelpful; I believe our loneliness is deeper than social media and caused by myriad factors. Our loneliness has to do with the way we structure our cities and conduct our urban lives, the long hours we work, the stress our hearts take, the sacrifices we make to family and sanity, the way we squander opportunities to be part of a community. Social media may exacerbate our already existing loneliness, but if we learnt to use it responsibly and to its greatest potential, it may very well also be our saviour. The very thing that allegedly makes us lonelier has an extremely hopeful capacity to bring us back together. We could start that process by acknowledging that online communication can be as valid as in-person connection — and that we will all be better off if we can navigate both deftly and with compassion. If we continue to cast social media as the enemy, we lose an opportunity to get to know each other better.

My dearest, closest friends in the world live in different cities a minimum of 5,567 kilometres away from my current home in London, and the only way we can maintain our friendship is with loyalty and daily WhatsApp contact. I live 13,500 kilometres away from my Sydney home, so the only contact with my family is largely via Skype, text or email. Where geography prevents me from physically sharing wine, coffee or cuddles with someone, we communicate online and that makes my heart happy. I strongly object to any suggestion that digital communication like this can only be fake or hollow or damaging. I get that posting flawless photographs on Instagram all the time without making room for life's messiness can be insincere, and that chat forums, as a general rule, are creepy AF, but I don't buy the logic that all forms of online chat are evil. I don't see how we can find letters between lovers and friends so romantic, and WhatsApp banter so trivial. It's a strange modern way of shooting the messenger. Did we ever get mad at the humble postman for delivering a letter into our mailbox? No? Then why is there so much disdain for the Internet? It's a perfectly respectable medium for making acquaintances and lifelong friends.

Speaking of which, I'd like to introduce Millie. I've known and liked Millie on Twitter for a while, but we only recently met in person for the first time. We got on immediately, as I suspected we would. I already knew from her Twitter presence that she was funny, smart and sweet. I liked her writing and without much of a logical stretch, assumed I would like her. That's the lovely pragmatism of the Twitter connection: you can get to know someone surreptitiously before you commit to an actual conversation. It's an introvert's dream. As it happened, when Millie and I met, I had just walked into a party on my own and realised the room was teeming with friendships made on Twitter. Everywhere I looked, I recognised profile photographs come to life; it was a very modern affair. Later Millie would tell me this is not unusual for her — she actually met most of her best friends online. Other than two former high-school friends she holds onto mostly out of obligation, Millie's friends largely arrived in her life via the Internet. She had three bridesmaids at her wedding — Annie, Lucy and Hannah — and she met all three of them on Twitter.

Speaking to Millie one Saturday morning over coffee and baked goods, it's virtually impossible to hold onto the antiquated idea that friendships made online are in any way inferior. They operate precisely as mine and Millie's did, originating online and, where possible, crossing over into face-to-face interaction with snacks. Millie is an accomplished, kind woman whose entire social life originated on the Internet, and she conducts those friendships with every bit as much sincerity, warmth and loyalty as any you could imagine happening in more conventional ways. In fact, the Internet facilitates those lovely qualities by allowing you to quietly squirrel away observations about a person before you let them into your life. It gives you a rather delightful level of control over who qualifies for close friendship. When you meet someone online, you get the chance to preview the person they are, one tweet, picture or status update at a time. You get this strangely revealing amalgamation of who they are through what they share that you obviously don't get when you meet someone at a party, a bar, school or university. It's a screening process that allows you to build up a certain level of intimacy before you've even exchanged handshakes or kisses on the cheek. Again, I'll say, it's an introvert's dream.

Look, here's a truth: social interaction is hard. It's daunting to introduce yourself to someone, difficult to start a conversation out of nowhere and mildly terrifying to suggest a follow-up after the initial meeting. There are lucky extroverts to whom this does not apply, but generally speaking, anyone prone to vulnerability gets nervous putting themselves at risk of social rejection. It is no surprise to me that people like Millie prefer to meet people online and then shimmy towards an in-person meeting afterwards. Millie says the Internet makes it easier to be brave and that it's helped her be more herself in 'real life', so by the time she meets an online friend offline, she's actually more likely to be outgoing and comfortable. Much like a rotund polar bear, Twitter breaks the ice. It can be the start of something that morphs into an offline friendship, too. Circa 2010, Millie's friend Annie started a group called the Awesome Women of Twitter (AWoT) because she realised how many delightful souls lurked online without actually partaking in sacred friendship activities like the consumption of wine together in the same physical space. Remarkably, about 60 women — presumably all awesome — turned up to AWoT's first in-person event and many of them stayed close or organised other get-togethers. That's where Millie first met Annie and Lucy, and they decided to nuzzle further into one another's lives. They 'love each other to the bones' and spend as much time as possible together in the same room, but they also WhatsApp all the time and still go back and forth with witticisms on Twitter. And that's just the shape of a modern friendship: something that exists online and offline, much like we do.

Now, the most interesting thing Millie told me while I licked blueberry icing off my pistachio-scattered bun was that she feels like the 'real' her is the online version of herself. She is her most honest self when she's online, because that's when she feels most confident. This directly contradicts what we usually assume to be true: that our online persona is a fabrication fuelled by pride/vanity/the Amaro Instagram filter and that our real self exists exclusively in person. We even refer to this binary of identity when we use the acronym IRL: In Real Life. To meet someone In Real Life is to actually see and talk to them face to face in what we would also call 'the real world'. These little turns of phrase imply that the Internet and anything that happens there is inherently false; that it is an illusion or a construct. Along with the idea that our real selves exist offline, this relegates our online friendships to a place of alleged fantasy. But what exactly makes a conversation in person any more real than a conversation via email, WhatsApp or Facebook Messenger? Is it the eye contact? The pheromones we can smell on the other person? The possibility of physical contact? The sound of an actual voice reaching eardrums? All of those things are glorious and I would never advocate replacing them with an exclusive online existence. Sometimes what you need more than anything is to physically be in the same place as a friend, to breathe the same air. But that's not always possible, given how we set up our modern lives. I think it's time we start talking about ourselves as though we exist concurrently online and offline. It's far less menacing than this idea that we have split personalities — one in person and one on our devices.

Sociologist and Snapchat researcher Nathan Jurgenson has coined a term for this thing we do, when we separate our online and offline personalities. He calls it 'digital dualism' and he says it's a fallacy. It's absurd to pretend we have two separate realities going on: the one we exist in every day physically and the one that appears on our screens. It's time, he says, to acknowledge that we have one reality and it's made up of different sources of information: some of it is Wi-Fi-enabled and some of it is organic, or what we might have traditionally called real life. He points out, too, that technology has made friendship easier for all types of people for whom human interaction is difficult. People who have Alzheimer's, or hearing difficulties, or learning difficulties, or speech impediments, or Autism can use technology to communicate more freely than they might otherwise, and to suggest that their form of contact is any less real than our own is to create a false hierarchy of communication that belittles the way some people talk best. It is time to reject this habit of digital dualism and recognise that the real world exists online just as much as it does in person.

One of the beautiful things about the Internet is that it brings people together who may not otherwise find one another. I spoke to a lot of people who've made important friendships online, often with people from completely different walks of life, people they'd never encounter by chance or through mutual friends. What I saw becoming more and more common is the deliberate curation of friendships that meet certain needs. Looking for a particular type of friend? Great, roll on up, find one on the Internet, there's probably a forum or an app for it. There are mothers who met on Twitter and coached each other through getting tattoos when nobody else in their respective lives would indulge that particular streak of rebellion with them. There are teenagers in different corners of the world, going through the same horrors of adolescence via Facebook Messenger. There are women who've moved cities and countries so many times, they leave a scattering of friends everywhere they go and feel like they can only really start again every time by reaching out to locals online. There are all sorts of people who seek out friends by hobby, interest, location, vocation or personality type — and that's an entirely new phenomenon. Before now, friendship was about chance connection. Now, we can literally seek out the friends we crave and the people we need in our lives. Perhaps the most moving example of online friendship that came my way is the one that blossomed between two young women called Eliza and Jenna. Eliza lost her beloved husband to cancer in 2015, just three years after she herself was diagnosed with the disease. Jenna lost her husband in a car crash the same year. They met on an online bereavement forum for widows and widowers and realised they'd lost the loves of their lives at around the same time. The forum ultimately became too much for both of them; the collective grief there was overwhelming. So they added each other on Facebook, started emailing and now they call one another about once a week for a long talk. They speak on difficult days like birthdays or anniversaries and they speak when someone has said something triggering to either of them. They pick up the phone when the missing gets excruciating and the only comfort is to speak to someone else who gets it. It's a friendship based almost entirely on shared pain, and it's been essential to both Eliza's and Jenna's healing processes. Their other friends and family members are loving and they try to support them, but ultimately their kind of loss needs to be echoed in someone else's experience to make it feel real. Eliza lives in London and Jenna lives on the Isle of Wight, so they haven't met up in person, but the friendship they've built on heartbreak is priceless to both of them — and without it, perhaps the loneliness would sting even more. There are some things that are easier to say over email or on the phone, with the distance between you operating like a security blanket. There are some conversations — perhaps the achingly sad ones between Eliza and Jenna — that benefit enormously from not being in person. There's a strange but powerful intimacy in the written or spoken word, when it's done from the comfort of home, away from the pressures of physical social interaction and having to face the public world. There is immense privacy in online communication, and that can be a godsend for people like Eliza and Jenna. Theirs is just one instance of people finding the exact friendship they needed in their lives — and what a treasure it is to be able to do that. That is the future of online friendship, right there, that capacity to build your own team of comrades based on your emotional needs, rather than arbitrarily bringing friends into your life by chance and never properly asking if they deserve to stay there. Technology, when used shrewdly, is a bespoke friendship-making service and I am here for that.

Of course, it would be dangerous to replace physical social interaction completely with online communication. That, I can agree, would be isolating. I may be singing the praises of the

Internet revolution when it comes to human connection, but I wouldn't advocate a digital hermit's existence, where someone plays out their entire social life online (although I would still argue that it's better than no social interaction at all). A healthy, vibrant combination of online and offline friendship is where it's at. We know that overusing social media or relying on it as an exclusive source of human interaction will leave you lonely. Using it as a means to compare your life unfavourably to other people's will make you lonely. Scrolling through flattering Facebook photos of a life you don't have will make you lonely. Tweeting into the void and having nobody reply to you will make you lonely, as will trolls who attack your character. We do not get our requisite warmth from favourites or likes and we do not fulfil our physical touch quota via Facebook pokes. Technology, and the way we consume and deploy it in our lives, is problematic. But, again, this idea pops up: what if the very same technology that's capable of isolating us is also capable of bringing us together?

There's an exciting new burst of apps on the market that exist specifically to facilitate people meeting in person. They're a conduit between our online and offline selves and I genuinely think we might solve the problems technology presents ... with more technology. You've no doubt heard of Tinder, the dating app that allows you to swipe left to reject prospective dates, swipe right to approve them. The whole point of Tinder is to broaden your social network using technology, then shrink it again by matchmaking you with one (or, depending on your style, many) date/s. Tinder and other apps like it are designed specifically to get people together in real life. There are of course plenty of people you match with on Tinder who you have no intention of seeing in person, ever; they're there as a self-esteem boost or someone with whom to exchange flirty messages. And that's cool. But the overall purpose of the app is to introduce people online so they can follow up with actual face time. It's technology that forces you to get off your phone and actually talk to a fellow human being. And so, Tinder presents both the potential problem — a user endlessly scrolling through possible dates alone in their pyjamas at night as they contemplate the possibility that nobody will ever love them — and the solution — a smorgasbord of potential dates who are only ever a couple of logistical messages away from keeping you company within extremely close proximity.

If we are curating our romantic connections with apps, it makes sense we would start to run our friendship circles that way, too. Bumble — a dating app where the women send the first message to the men — has even branched out into 'Bumble BFF' mode, which exists to match women with other women for friendship, rather than romance. There have been websites like this before — Girl Crew, Social Jane, Girlfriend Circles, Girlfriend Social — but the advent of an app means it's really hitting the mainstream. Bumble BFF allows women to make friends in a way that is arguably easier than befriending a stranger in person. Purely by downloading the app, each woman has entered into an agreement that they are available and willing to take on new friendships, which is more than you can assume of a person you meet at a bar or a party or an evening Salsa class. The very act of being on the app implies to anyone who might want to befriend you that you are happy to acquire new buddies. And it's exactly this implicit declaration of availability that makes apps like these successful: they're actively decreasing your chances of social rejection. And what preserves loneliness better than the fear of social rejection? Or, put more hopefully, what eradicates loneliness faster than the reduced likelihood of social rejection? What we're looking at here is a proactive attempt to solve the tide of loneliness caused by the overuse, or misuse, of social media. It's fascinating to observe and now that we've watched all the seasons of *Black Mirror*, perhaps we can avoid making future interpersonal technology creepy and dystopian.

Michelle Kennedy knows the potential of apps to connect us better than just about anyone. She worked at dating apps Badoo and Bumble, where she facilitated precisely the phenomenon I'm talking about here. She worked on ways to get people dates and she was all excited about the infinite possibilities of technology to connect people ... And then she became a mother. When Michelle brought her little boy Finn into the world, she was struck by a loneliness she simply didn't predict or expect. She's quite a young mum, and the first in her group of girlfriends to procreate. Her husband is a bit older than her, so she had an impetus to reproduce, even though her closest buddies are still getting their adult lives together. As she is apt to do, Michelle instinctively looked for a way to use technology to connect with other mamas, but there was nothing. Maybe a naff chatroom or a couple of Facebook groups about breastfeeding, but nothing innovative that could actually help diminish the feeling of being the only mother on the planet. She couldn't find an app that hooked her up with other mothers, so she made one. It's called Peanut and it's basically Bumble for mums. I love the sound of it so much, it genuinely makes me feel better about the prospect of becoming a mother.

Chatting to Michelle, I can hear a certain brittleness in her voice when she talks about the early days of her son's life. She just felt all of a sudden utterly alone in the experience of being a mother, and that was only exacerbated by the requirements of having a child, like waking up in the emptiness of the night to feed, staying at home to nurse and hanging out with just your baby. That's a dramatic change when you've come from a busy career with plenty of people around you all the time. There are few things lonelier, as I understand it, than having a brand new child in your care and having nobody there to share that experience with. Michelle had her husband and family, of course, but no mum friends with whom to get coffee. She was a mama without peers, without allies. Luckily for other mamas in the same position, Michelle also had the technical skills to solve the problem.

It's not like she didn't try making friends the conventional way. Before she invented Peanut, Michelle had an excruciating experience of social awkwardness that really shook her confidence. It was very early on in Finn's life — he was maybe six weeks old, as she remembers it — and they were in Starbucks. Michelle was breastfeeding and she got chatting to another mum. They were both with their kids and as they waited for their coffee, they started chatting about breastfeeding. This other mum was giving Michelle a few tips about how to alternate breasts when you feed and they seemed to really get on. Spurred on by the apparent warmth and commonality between them, Michelle said, 'You know what? It'd be great to get coffee sometime and talk. We should swap numbers.' There was a pause, and the woman said, 'Actually, I'm really busy, and I've already got a lot of friends.' Michelle retreated to her husband, who had just seen the whole thing go down. 'Ooph,' he said, 'You crashed and burned there.' Michelle laughed it off in the moment, but secretly she was crushed. This was the first time she'd really reached out like that and she was desperate for someone to have coffee with — more than that, she was desperate for the company of another mother. Friendship so often relies on common experience, and she dearly wanted someone who was also going through the joys and agonies of raising a child, or children. Meanwhile, her own social media was only making her feel more alone, because she'd be feeding her son at 3 a.m. on a Sunday morning, scrolling through pictures of her girlfriends out at clubs or parties. Her life had become startlingly different since Finn came into it and while she loved him with all of her heart, she craved adult company and someone to talk to about motherhood.

After the Starbucks incident, Michelle really withdrew. She wouldn't dream of trying again to initiate a friendship with a stranger, so for some time, she stayed lonely. Ultimately, her mother and her husband stepped in and started setting her up on friendship dates. Her rather outspoken Irish mother approached someone in a Zara Home store, said she had seen her go to the same play group as Michelle and Finn, and said, 'Listen, my daughter really needs a friend.' They met, got along and still see each other. Michelle's husband forced an introduction to a woman Michelle was staring at in a café. He reached over and said, 'Hi, this is my wife, she's looking at you because your son is about the same age as ours.' She's a good friend of Michelle's now too. It's still possible to make friends in real actual life — a lot of people join mothers' groups for instance, though they can be intimidating, too. Michelle felt mothers deserved a new, better way to start the friendships they needed.

As Michelle started to talk more openly about her loneliness as a mother, she started to hear other new mothers echo back exactly how she was feeling. Someone she knows — a mother — told her that every single day, she wheels her pram past a little café and sees the same group of mothers and their children, chatting and having coffee. 'Tomorrow, I'll go in and say hi,' she tells herself every time, but of course tomorrow never comes because that sort of social bravery is incredibly hard to come by, especially if you're feeling vulnerable, out with your baby. Getting rejected by yourself is one thing, says Michelle; getting rejected while you've got your child with you is almost too much to handle. Think how many times little incidences of loneliness are occurring for mothers all over the world. We don't all live near our extended families, siblings or parents any more, so this idea that it 'takes a village' to raise a child is outdated now. Mothers are isolated by the very way we run our modern lives, by the layout of our cities, by the travel we do for work and adventure, by the distance we put between ourselves and our families, by the structure of our nuclear family units.

Thinking all this through, Michelle decided to try and solve the problem of motherly loneliness. It shouldn't be this hard, she thought, or this painful to make friends. She knew the technology to do something great was out there — things like intelligent algorithms, machine learning and clever user experience design. She knew how to build the app she had in mind — in fact, it was almost such an obvious step for her professionally, it seemed bizarre to her that it had taken her so long to make it happen. And, to be frank, it's such a good idea I'm surprised nobody beat her to it. That's how Peanut came to be: Michelle was simply trying to solve her own most urgent problem. She created it for herself, and for any other woman out there who has a child and suddenly feels very alone. She created it for nervous pregnant women, frightened new mums, young mums whose girlfriends haven't had babies yet, older mums whose friends have already raised children, working mums, stay-at-home mums, mums who just moved to new cities and mums who travel. She created it for anyone who needs company while mothering, but isn't brave enough to risk an incident like Michelle's at Starbucks. All this talk of motherly solidarity makes me so warm in the heart I almost downloaded the damn app before I remembered I haven't made any tiny humans yet.

When Michelle and I speak, Peanut has been available to download for about six weeks, and it's going really well. Michelle has made several acquaintances on her own app —

the kind of friends she'd happily go for coffee with on Saturday mornings when her son is at rugby. She's also made closer friends than that, one in particular whom she adores and speaks to most days. She's had all sorts of encouraging feedback from mothers and mothers-to-be who've discovered the app and connected to other women in need of friendship. She spoke to one mum who said she scrolls through Peanut during her 3 a.m. feeds — which is quite a funny image, really: a woman sitting in the dark with a suckling baby crooked in one arm, swiping through prospective friends with her free thumb. A very modern image of motherhood. It sounds as though the app has done exactly what Michelle wanted it to do. It has diminished her own loneliness and given her real friends. It's also plugged a hole in the market for a simple, innovative, usable app for mothers.

Peanut is helping lonely mamas make friends. That, to me, is the perfect example of technology being used to eradicate loneliness. The app is designed to make in-person interaction easier. First, it connects women who want to make new friends, so it takes out that painful possibility of rejection. It's also just convenient — keeping a child alive is a full-time job and many mothers have an actual paid full-time job as well, so precisely when, where and with what energy they are supposed to meet new people is frankly beyond me. Using the app should diminish the social anxiety you feel when you want to approach someone new for friendship and effectively coordinate your in-person meeting for you. It's so pleasantly efficient, it almost makes me feel like I'm ready to be a mother.

Michelle is not the only person trying to solve loneliness using technology. It's a very pleasing new trend in the apps market. One typically grey London morning, I met three men for tea in a hotel lobby to talk about their loneliness-annihilation project. British schoolmates Craig Walsh and James Murdoch were on a road trip one day in the pouring rain when the idea came up: Wouldn't it be great if you could use an app to find friends for, as they put it, 'non-sexual experiences'? They had no expertise in tech or app development, they just decided to get together outside of their day jobs to work on this app based purely on their belief in the quality and urgency of the idea. It's one of those great start-up stories where the novelty of the idea overwhelms the lack of experience of the founders. They eventually got investors on board, including St. John Hughes, who saw huge potential in the concept of a friendship-making app. All three of them recognise that we are an increasingly disconnected society, where it's becoming seriously difficult to make and keep friends, what with family, work, travel, and the general structure of modern life. When we speak, they've just launched the app and it's called HeyGreenGo (Hey for greeting a stranger, Green to indicate that another person has given you the green light to communicate, Go for the action of getting together in person). Basically, the app connects you with geographically appropriate people who are interested in the same things as you. Where Peanut matches women on the basis of their children's ages and how into dance they are, HeyGreenGo matches people based on self-selected hobbies like badminton, tennis, film or board games. So the idea is, if you wanted to make buddies, you could set up a local badminton game with some strangers and bond over an activity. It's a very male, very practical approach to friendship and these guys believe it's an antidote to our growing social isolation as a species. Their priority is creating a safe app that only allows real people (not bots, not trolls) to log on, which they've done by linking the app to Facebook and creating a ranking system of emojis that people can use after they've met someone to indicate that they're a legit human being.

If this particular app takes off and becomes a friend-making sensation, that's great. It's an easy way to use our phones to set up activities that get us to abandon our phones for a few hours of actual in-person interaction. It's using technology to decrease our dependence on technology, and that's where I'm convinced the future is when it comes to friendship. There are others like it in development at the moment. I've heard of one that allows you to sync calendars with your friends so you can easily make dates to go out, and one that sets you up with a little button to press if you need someone's support urgently. And the best part is, if you don't see the app you want, just make it. That's where we're at now with technology; whatever you want that doesn't exist yet just became your next DIY project or creative side-hustle. So, okay, maybe people do use social media to glimpse other people's perfectly curated lives and that makes them feel lonely. Maybe we live in a socially isolated, individualistic culture where it's getting harder to connect with people in person. Maybe technology enables all sorts of bad human behaviour. But we are smack-bang, right here, right now in the era of being able to fix that. We're already in the process of solving our own loneliness and there's work to be done — let's stop scrolling aimlessly through a Kardashian's Instagram feed and get to it.

CHAPTER EIGHT

Friendship break-ups

BREAK-UPS OF ANY KIND hurt. Think of the last time you broke up with a romantic partner. Break-ups ache all over: your mind, your limbs, your ego. And I swear, if you concentrate on it at the right moment, you can actually feel as though your heart is breaking. The beats seem off-kilter, like the organ has all of a sudden forgotten how to thump-thump against your chest. You feel pain, actual physical pain. You feel anguish, very real anguish. You feel as though you may never recover from it — how could you possibly resume your normal life, what are you going to do, walk around with your chest gaping open? How can you mend a broken heart? Al Green and The Bee Gees didn't seem to know. But at least when you break off a romantic relationship, there's a language for it. There's an agreed upon treatment plan and a mourning period and a set of rituals we all follow, as prescribed by our mates and pop culture. There are songs to cry to alone in a darkened room, there are movies to sob along to as you gorge on your junk food of choice, there are grace periods that allow you to wallow in your misery without the usual obligations to socialise or function. We know how to do romantic break-ups, we know what they look like and feel like and smell like. We've memorised the routine: listen to gut-wrenching ballads, watch something miserable on Netflix, binge on Ben & Jerry's cookie dough ice cream. Tubs of it. Calories don't count when you're heartbroken; neither does bad body odour or sudden-onset hermitage. Break-ups are one of the few occasions we give our friends, our acquaintances, our idols and ourselves permission to feel an emotion fully until it releases its grip. It's one of the few times we get socially sanctioned time to heal.

When I broke up with a boyfriend of seven years in my twenties, I moved back in with my dad and stepmom for a bit, played 'Magic' by Coldplay on repeat, ate only from the food group 'cookie', napped away the pain, sent woeful messages to my friends, watched endless re-runs of *Friends* on telly, and had long, animated conversations with my patient, elderly rescue dog, Lady Fluffington. These were my coping mechanisms, and I did them automatically because I knew the social protocol for break-ups. We tend to very quickly empathise with someone who's going through a break-up; it's that universal a malady. We all have hearts, they get broken, it's a bitter fact of life. But there is comfort in the banality of the pain even at the time (though it also helps to imagine that there has never been so tragic a break-up and there never will be a more tragic break-up, not now, not ever, pass the cookies). Romantic love and its demise are things we have utterly digested as a species; we live them in reality and obsessively recreate them in fiction. In fact, really, we love nothing more than the tragic ending of a romantic relationship. It is, perhaps, our most cherished form of *schadenfreude*. Just think — every time a couple get together on a TV show, the writers are obliged to throw a complication in to break them up because we simply cannot stand to watch romantic happiness or stability for more than an episode or three. We prefer the angst of wondering if they'll get together more than the satisfaction of watching it work out; such is our fascination with the end of things. We don't watch rom-coms about people in harmonious, healthy relationships who glide through their lives together uninterrupted. Oh no, we want infidelities and overseas job postings, impossible decisions and terminal illnesses, cooling affections and sexual dysfunctions, emotional cheating and intervening circumstances. When we say we like love songs, really we mean we like the sound of a famous person's heart breaking, accompanied by a catchy beat. Love songs are the poems of the broken hearted and we're sick for them because we have a cultural preoccupation with the failure of love.

And yet! And yet. We know so little and speak so little of the friendship break-up. It is a very rare thing indeed to find a candid or insightful depiction of a friendship breaking up. Because they do break up — oh yes, they break up. And it's painful. People who've experienced a true, proper savaging of a friendship say it's possibly even more painful than the end of a romantic relationship. Several people have told me it's more similar to a death than a break-up, because when you lose someone from your life that completely, it's as though they cease to exist. The grief we feel in these situations is exacerbated by the fact that we have no script for this type of break-up and no clearly marked route to recovery.

Elly and Bridie met when they were 10 years old. They were virtually inseparable, in and out of school hours. There were glimmers of disquiet even in the beginning, though: Bridie had a problem with lying. When you're a kid that doesn't really matter; if anything, it's just a sign of creativity. Elly and her other friends let Bridie get away with lies that were audacious only in the ease with which they could have been disproven. As the girls grew up and started high school, Bridie's lies grew. She started telling tales about boys kissed and virginity lost, things Elly knew weren't true largely because they spent so much of their lives together, Bridie would simply not have had time for all these alleged dalliances. But again, what real harm are those kinds of lies? So Bridie wanted to beckon the feeling of adulthood a little closer by pretending to make out with some boys, who is that really hurting? Next Bridie started inventing new friends. A whole group of them, all people she apparently had time to see outside of the tight-knit little group of friends in which she and Elly had grown up.

When Elly went to boarding school, her friendship with Bridie shrank into a series of phone calls. On these calls — those great, long chats you used to have on landlines — Bridie would tell Elly all about her new friends. At this stage, Elly thought that perhaps these friends were false, but she let Bridie have her fantasy — someone who is making up a whole group of friends is clearly clinging to the illusion of popularity because they need it. Then Facebook was invented and things got more elaborate for Bridie. She was a Catfish ahead of her time; someone who had invented people long before she even had the anonymity of the Internet to facilitate it. Facebook was a fantastic tool of deception for her. She was able, suddenly, to give her group of buddies real-looking identities online. Elly was still generous with her gullibility at this stage, perhaps believing Bridie out of a residual childhood kindness. That, and there were Facebook profiles for more than 20 of Bridie's friends, all of whom interacted with Bridie and each other. Really, it seemed too elaborate to be a lie; who has the time to invent and maintain more than 20 Facebook profiles? For whatever reason, loyalty perhaps, Elly didn't question her. So Elly and Bridie lived on as friends — for a decade.

Elly went to university, Bridie moved interstate, and then they both went through significant break-ups and decided to move in together. About a month later, Elly became very unwell. Her mental health had taken a battering after the break-up, she had serious PTSD and depression, and she ended up in a psychiatric ward. Her best friends flocked to her side in the emergency department. Bridie was there, but something was up. She kept making deep sighing noises, as though the attention Elly was receiving caused her physical discomfort. At one stage she 'fainted' or, perhaps more accurately, sat down dramatically in a nearby chair. She was paid minimal attention, mainly because Elly's friends were preoccupied caring about Elly. Bridie pulled one of them aside later and confessed that she was pregnant. The details were sketchy: she'd been whisked off by a nurse after she fainted and had a blood test and found out immediately that she was pregnant. 'Don't tell Elly,' she begged the friend, 'this is her night.' *Her night*, like being in hospital for a mental health breakdown was a wedding or a birthday party. Elly would be there for a month, and Bridie would come to visit. On one of her very first visits, Bridie told Elly about the pregnancy. Elly was alarmed, asking Bridie what she was going to do and gently broaching the subject of an abortion. Bridie was defensive, brushing off the kinds of practical suggestions that would have been helpful to a genuinely pregnant woman.

By the time Elly left hospital, Bridie would technically have been about 14 weeks' pregnant. As Bridie reached 18 and 19 weeks, Elly became really troubled because the time during which Bridie could safely terminate the pregnancy was passing. When Elly pressed Bridie on it, she got jumpy and aloofly said, 'Oh, I miscarried the other day.' What should have been devastating news was delivered with a cool kind of nonchalance, almost like she had lost interest in the lie now that Elly was better and there wasn't so much attention to be reclaimed. In a last ditch attempt to honour her friend's story, Elly insisted she go and see a doctor. When Bridie refused, Elly realised with absolute certainty that the pregnancy had been a lie. A lie designed specifically to divert sympathy from Elly to Bridie during a really traumatic time for her. It hurt, and it disturbed Elly. This was her oldest, dearest friend and she had been lied to many times before, but this time it really mattered. Bridie was one of the only people who had consistently been in Elly's life since she was little. Still, she didn't confront her.

Elly didn't mention the pregnancy, or for that matter any of the other lies from over the years, but she carried them with her. They were there between Elly and Bridie, these unspoken blotches on their friendship, nasty little silences and untruths that undermined everything they had together. In the end, it was something entirely trivial that finally broke Elly's trust in Bridie. They had a stupid, loud disagreement about a TV show one night at a birthday sleepover. Elly yelled at Bridie about her opinions on the television show, but it wasn't really about that. She was reacting to years of lies, big and little, and mainly, she was letting go of the hurt Bridie had caused when she fabricated a pregnancy to detract from Elly's mental health problems. She was also speaking out of fear and distress. Elly cared about Bridie and she was worried, even disturbed, by her behaviour.

After that night, they never saw each other again.

It was grim for Elly, this friendship break-up, because it disintegrated one of the only things she thought worth keeping from her childhood. It was devastating to find out that she never really knew Bridie. She didn't really know how to process it, except as another example of someone she loved letting her down. It took a lot to extinguish that friendship, but ultimately Elly knew she really needed to. Sixteen years of lies accumulate, until the feeling of not knowing the person behind them is just too much to bear. So Elly had to walk away from that friendship and find a way to mourn what they once had together.

Strip away the fabricated Facebook friends, the fake pregnancy, the TV-themed meltdown and the myriad other lies over the years, and this is the story of friendship broken.

It happens all the time, everywhere, to all different kinds of people. And it is my great belief that, like Elly, we haven't yet quite worked out how to deal with losing friendships.

When it comes to friendship breakdowns, we are essentially making it up as we go along. Name me a popular song about a friendship break-up. Or a sensitive scene on a prime-time sitcom about the fragility of friendship. An entire movie-length dissection of what it means to be someone's friend and then decide to cut them from your life. You're drawing a blank there because we simply do not dwell on platonic break-ups in the same way as romantic ones. We do not devote countless melodies or lyrics or storylines to them because we have ritually prioritised romantic relationships over friendships. We have been so utterly captivated by the breakdown of romantic love that we've practically forgotten to investigate how the heart aches when a friendship is, for whatever reason, over.

This does not please me. We have shorthand for the pain of a relationship break-up; simply say 'I'm going through a break-up' or 'Steve and I just broke up' and it triggers your friend or your boss or your barista to reminisce about the last time or the worst time their heart was broken. There's an ease with which we identify heartbreak, and we allow that person the space to recuperate. Try saying, 'My best friend from high school and I used to be so close, but we've sort of drifted lately and the other day we avoided eye contact on the street.' Or, 'My mate Sarah and I had an epic fight about who owed who a fiver and now I think maybe the friendship is over forever,' and you get no such emotional leniency. I hate the idea that people are aching over something that we as a society have not deemed worthy of our cultural interest. This could be changing; there do seem to be more glossy magazine articles and Buzzfeed essays about friendship break-ups. There is some momentum in the conversation there, but it's fledgling. We are still figuring out how to talk about, and validate, our friendships. It feels like a mildly revolutionary idea that a friendship could be as important to someone emotionally as a romantic relationship and that, consequentially, its ending will be just as painful.

And it is very real pain. When Elly finally fell out with Bridie, she lost years of shared memories and confidences. When a friend of mine from college drifted away, both geographically and sentimentally, we lost all the love and secrets we'd accumulated together. She had become a part of me, and all of that was wrenched away when we stopped being friends. Even though I knew it was the right thing, even though I knew we didn't make each other's lives better, it still hurts to watch someone vanish from your life. Lost friendships, whether they fall apart over a single, trivial argument or a more protracted process of drifting apart, really hurt. It's a breaking of trust and a dissolution of intimacy unlike any other, really. All the time, secrets, love and personal jokes you invest in a relationship just fade into memory, until that's all you have left of someone who once truly meant something to you. Getting over that kind of loss requires grieving — but we haven't got an instruction manual for this kind of grief yet. It's still in the works.

Because we do not have the tools to properly deal with the friendship break-up, we fumble along on our own. We haven't agreed upon a tactful or proper way to do it, so everybody's just bloody going for it in whatever way they can. That has resulted, if you ask me, in an epidemic of poorly executed friendship break-ups. People are getting away with all sorts of behaviour that we've already vetoed in a romantic break-up scenario, things we've already given trendy names to like 'ghosting' or 'breadcrumbing'. They're no longer acceptable practice in the romantic arena — in fact, if you are the victim of any such behaviour, you're entitled to at least an extra fortnight of break-up misery indulgence. Not to mention the bonus ire you're allowed to have towards the entire sex of the person who has wronged you.

For the uninitiated, by the way, ghosting is when you've been on a few dates and then your possible lover simply stops communicating with you. It's like leaving a party without saying goodbye; they simply vanish from your WhatsApp thread, Tinder inbox or text feed. They do not pay you the common courtesy of explaining they are not interested or it's not working out between you or they've met someone else, they simply stop replying to your messages. It's an especially cruel trick of the heart, because then of course you're left wondering what you did wrong, or worse, what could be so fundamentally unlovable about you that a person is incapable of explaining why they don't want to be with you. I have to admit I've done it — once. It was when I first moved to London and tried out Tinder. He was a male model and he kept referring to himself as a male model. He spent an inordinate amount of time going through his exercise regime with me and I just didn't have the heart or the words to tell him I could not be any less interested if I tried. I sent him all sorts of mixed messages and ultimately stopped communicating with him because I was confused and hadn't dated in seven years. After I'd brutally ghosted this perfectly nice young man, I saw him on the tube twice, panicked, and had to camouflage myself into the crowd, which is my penance.

Breadcrumbing, if I understand it correctly, is the act of half-heartedly communicating with someone, only ever really getting in touch in little spurts when it's convenient for you, leading someone on and then losing interest again quite quickly. Like leaving a trail of breadcrumbs in message form for a hopeful romantic interest to follow, without thinking how it might affect their heart or their ego and without the intention to actually follow through on a relationship.

Now, both of these practices are frowned upon on the dating scene. When it comes to friendships, though, ghosting and breadcrumbing are still kind-of acceptable because we haven't decided on an alternative course of action. I did a social media appeal for stories about friendship break-ups and boy, oh boy, did people deliver. It almost seems as though everyone has a painful friendship break-up they're reeling from, even if it's just one of those things where close friends drift from intimate to acquaintance territory. Evidence suggests people are hurting one another all over the damn place. Both perpetrators and victims of these bad friendship break-up techniques got in touch and it seems to me that we are, collectively, at a loss as to what to do when we want a friendship to end. The other thing I noticed is how often people said to me, 'It's so nice to talk about this with someone ...' as though they hadn't found an outlet for their stories of friendship pain until they spoke to me. That makes me immeasurably sad, that we haven't found a way to comfortably talk about broken friendships yet and so there are people walking around their lives with this lingering heartache.

One woman, Lily, was the victim of an epic friend ghosting. She's an American who'd moved to a small Australian town with her husband. They were building a house and their builder, Mikey, kept telling Lily she reminded him of his American wife, Kylie. Lily was new to town so she jumped at the suggestion of becoming friends with Mikey's wife, and quickly set up a double date for the four of them. The women got close fast — they were both American, both newly married, both looking for friendship in a sunburnt corner of rural Australia. They started having dinner and catch-ups over wine several times a week, and that lasted a year. They both got pregnant around the same time — Lily told Kylie her baby news 'the minute she peed on a stick', but Kylie kept her pregnancy a secret for 13 weeks. That, to Lily, was the first sign that things were changing. They usually told each other everything, and this was a secret they could have shared. The friendship continued in fits and bursts, both women had their second children and then Kylie announced that she, Mikey and the kids were moving back to the States. It didn't make sense — Mikey would have to start his business from scratch, they'd made their lives in Australia — but you don't question a mama of two babes who wants to move home, I suppose. Next thing Lily knows, she can't find Kylie on social media. Her Instagram account has vanished, she's not on Facebook. Lily tries to get in touch, but can't. She finally finds a sneaky private account she thinks might belong to Kylie and asks to follow her, but she's denied and blocked. Through the grapevine, Lily hears that Kylie served Mikey with divorce papers and tried to keep the kids from him. Mikey returns to Australia, distraught. Lily never hears from Kylie again. Not once. There's no explanation; just the total and abrupt erasure of a very tight friendship. Lily is mystified, left trying to come up with theories for what happened. Did Kylie have postnatal depression she kept hidden? Was she struggling more than she let on? Why did she need to leave behind her entire Australian life when she decided to leave her husband? Had their friendship been so disposable? Had Lily imagined their closeness?

Another woman, Georgie, made a dear friend when she was 20 and doing an amateur production of the musical *Cats*. Most of the cast were tone-deaf and hilariously bad, and Georgie bonded with the one other person who seemed to find the whole thing funny, a woman called Esther. Esther was Georgie's 'grown-up friend' because she had all the trappings of adulthood: a husband, a house. They both liked vintage clothes, musicals and politics, and they had one of those friendships that exists on the periphery of your usual circle; it was always just the two of them when they caught up. While Georgie was roaming the continents working as a digital nomad, Esther got divorced and decided to sell her house and travel through Europe. She got lonely on her solo adventure and came to stay with Georgie in England for a bit, where they hung out. The stay came to an end and Esther presented Georgie with a big, beautiful bunch of flowers to thank her for having her to stay. She went back to Australia on what Georgie thought were perfectly good terms. Why would you give flowers to someone you secretly hated, right? Next time Georgie was in Australia, she stayed with Esther and her new boyfriend, they had chats over tea and everything seemed fine. But the time Georgie visited Australia after that, she messaged Esther to see if she wanted to meet up and got no response. Another message, no response. Georgie checked in on Esther's Facebook to see if she could work out why she hadn't heard from her, only to discover they weren't friends any more. She'd been — you guessed it — ghosted. No explanation; simply a mysterious withdrawal of friendship.

Georgie was mystified. And then she was angry. Why dissolve a perfectly lovely friendship without so much as a goodbye? I very much like what Georgie did next. She sent Esther a message, courteously asking for an explanation. I thought we were friends, she said, but I've discovered we're not and I'd like to know why. Esther wrote back. It was a detailed, heated description of how Esther thought Georgie had failed her as a friend, abandoned her during her visit in England and exacerbated her loneliness as a new divorcée. According to Georgie, each alleged infraction was a miscommunication or a misunderstanding, and Esther knew that. And yet, here she was, definitively cutting off the friendship. The thing that gets me is this: Why didn't Esther send that message in the first place? Was she too frightened, or tongue-tied, or sad to compose a simple message alerting Georgie to the end of their years-long friendship? How could she live with that wanton absence of resolution? Did she not have the courtesy or the guts to have that conversation? Could she not have even lied about the reason, but still extricated herself from the friendship with some sort of notice to the other party?

Having spoken to a bunch of people, I now suspect this is happening again and again all over the world: people breaking off a friendship without notifying the other person. It's a matter of basic manners, to start. Confrontation is hard, I get that. Emotional transparency is difficult and sometimes friendships do just fade until your mate becomes someone you used to know. But this isn't that, this is the deliberate erasure of a connection that meant something to another person and I'm inclined to argue they deserve an explanation. It's further evidence to me that we are sentimentally ill-equipped to deal with the friendship break-up scenario. We'd sooner ghost our way out of a meaningful platonic relationship than brave the awkwardness of being honest about the situation. That ends up hurting people — people who once meant something to us.

So how do we do it properly? How do we break up with a friend like a grown-up? And then, bloody hell, how do we recover from it afterwards, breaker and breakee? I spoke to psychologist Perpetua Neo (her clients call her 'Dr P') for advice on this one. She says, first things first, look back over the friendship and try to work out whether it's been a toxic one or not. A toxic friendship is one where you feel drained, it's one-sided and the focus is always magically on the other person, and there's a lot of unnecessary drama and passive-aggressiveness. And not because they're going through something awful; just because it's their personality to be that way. It's important to decide if the friendship was toxic because it'll affect how you break it off. Toxic people thrive on drama — they're sick for a fight because it gives them adrenalin and makes them feel important — so you don't want to indulge them in that. Ain't nobody got time for some soap-opera level arguments that drag on and take over your life. If you're dealing with a toxic person, you may want to try and break it off — a simple 'this isn't working for me any more' will do — but then you may need to freeze them out. It could be the only way to avoid drama. They'll try and woo you back and they could turn aggressive when it doesn't work, but you have to stay resolved and resist 'getting back together'. If the friend isn't toxic, but your lives have diverged to a point where not even nostalgia or respect can salvage it, then you've got to pluck up the courage to say, 'We've become very different people and I've decided we shouldn't continue this friendship.' Dr P says to do it with love and try to respect what you've had between you. That's why good people deserve some sort of notice that you're ending it — because of what you've been through together. That way you're in control and you've set the tone for mutual respect — hopefully they'll respond in the same way. It's a whole other story when you're the person being broken up with.

Lizzie got in touch to tell me about a friend who'd broken up with her. She met this friend, Kimmy, in their first year at university. They became entwined in that lovely way young women can: they stayed at each other's houses after nights out, travelled together, studied together, went on double dates and really grew into early adulthood side by side. It was a formative friendship for both of them because they were busily working out what it was to be an adult person in the world, with a close ally. They'd always been supportive of one another, but then suddenly they found themselves competing for things: jobs, grades, boyfriends. It blew up, in the end, over a man, but that man became symbolic of everything that didn't work between them any more. Kimmy told Lizzie she didn't want to be her friend any more. Lizzie was devastated; she says it was worse than any romantic break-up she's ever had because it felt more personal. As she says, there are any number of reasons a romantic partner might break up with you: perhaps they're allergic to commitment or scared of relationships, maybe their family doesn't like you or he's decided he loves you but not enough. There are familiar events that break up a romantic relationship: the cooling of passion, the pressures of long distance, the boredom of the heart. But with a friend? With a friend, it feels as though a person has got to know you intimately, spent all this time with you and made an analysis of who you are as a human being — and somehow you've fallen short. Most of us only have room for one romantic partner, so it makes sense that multiple people won't make the cut. We have room in our lives for plenty of friends, so when someone decides they would like you to cease and desist with your companionship, it's a huge and very hurtful move.

A friend of mine, Melanie, lost her childhood best friend to Jesus. They'd been, as she puts it, 'wild, crazy savages that always came in a two-for-one deal for all things in life'. You know those childhood friendships; you become inseparable in a very intense, almost obsessive way that defines the way you see the world and yourself. You grow up side by side, companions in everything, allies through the process of becoming teenagers and then adults. Friendships like this are so important; who could possibly know and adore your spirit more than someone who learnt to love you as a child? Imagine, then, growing up and growing apart. Imagine the pain in hearing they no longer want to be in your life — they know you so well, better than anyone, they know you to the core of your being, and they make the decision to eject you from their life. When Melanie's friend found Jesus — unexpectedly, as an adult — she changed. She morphed into someone Melanie didn't recognise, and suddenly there was this great disconnect between them. It all came undone officially when Melanie hooked up with someone at her friend's wedding, and her friend used that as an excuse to end the whole friendship — supposedly because an act of lust like that was so far removed from her new religious life, it had 'embarrassed' her on her wedding day. Melanie was dumbfounded and devastated. She felt she hadn't done anything wrong, certainly nothing worthy of a break-up. She was distraught in a way that truly has no equivalent. It felt more like a death than anything else — the friendship ceased to exist with the brutal suddenness of death — but we have no way to really mourn someone who is still alive, so she's just left with this aching feeling of inexplicable loss.

Dr Perpetua Neo has some tips on how to recover from such a thing. She says it's really important to mourn properly, and that starts with giving yourself permission to feel broken. We mourn all sorts of things in life that are not technically deaths — the parent we wish we'd had but never got, the future we thought we'd have with a partner, a missed opportunity. When a friendship breaks, we will grieve. It's normal and natural. Dr P suggests maybe trying to set a time limit for your mourning, like some cultures do with their grieving rituals. Allow yourself to cry and scream and binge on ice cream. Allow yourself to fully experience the pain of the break-up because there is no way of avoiding it, or distracting yourself away from it. You can try and postpone it, but when you try to play tricks with it, pain has a way of smacking you in the face when you least expect. It's important to know this sort of pain is natural and universal, so normalise it and get on with it. Don't judge yourself or blame yourself, it's a waste of time and energy. Then, says Dr P, do a friendship post-mortem. Try to work out what went wrong and draw it all into a narrative so you can understand it and package it away. Our minds love closure. Talk to the good friends you have in your life to remind you how fabulous friendship can be and make a note not to settle for anything less than what they give you.

Now, as I said, there are friendships that naturally come to an end — and then there are toxic friendships. Not all broken friendships were toxic friendships, but in my opinion, all toxic friendships should end up broken. We are coming to terms with the idea that domestic abuse is not always physical, and that sometimes emotional abuse can be just as excruciating. We are getting more comfortable talking about that concept in the context of a marriage or romantic relationship, but we don't often expect or even realise when it's happening between friends. It is entirely possible for someone to emotionally abuse, belittle and demean their platonic friend — it happens all the damn time and it's dangerous. It's insidious and sinister, the way some people coerce and control their friends, some of whom may not even be aware of just what's happening. When I put out a call, people came forward on Twitter, Facebook and email who had been in toxic friendships for some time before they understood something was very wrong. People who've had to take out court orders against former friends, move states or countries to escape them, and alter their lives dramatically to move on. People who've had their lives utterly torn apart by other human beings they once called friends. More often than not, it's a gradual process — an erosion of the soul, one nasty gesture or remark at a time. But sometimes it's just all-out harassment.

A woman called Alice had a friend once, a guy we'll call Ben. She and Ben struck up a friendship over work and started writing comedy together. They'd write for hours a day, for a period of about six months, before things started falling apart. Ben spiralled into a depressive episode right at the time Alice's mother was dying. At first, Ben depended on Alice for support, depended on her to do things like hold him at 3 a.m. and stop him from killing himself. It was too much for one person to bear, let alone someone who was having to care for her ailing mother, who had begun to lose herself in psychosis. Alice felt like she was desperately holding up two people who were sinking and she didn't have the buoyancy for both, so she tactfully told Ben she simply couldn't be there for him, not as his primary carer and not in the way he needed. She suggested he move home to get support, but he never forgave Alice for prioritising her mother over him. It was an act of desperate necessity for Alice; one person cannot tend to two people in such severe states without crumbling herself. But to Ben, she had abandoned him when he needed her most.

Ben's way of dealing with this alleged betrayal was to attack Alice with as much vitriol as he could muster. He began sending long, abusive emails, accusing her of all sorts of things that never happened, things like physical violence against him. Alice took Ben out for a cuppa a few times to try and work things out, and he'd always claim not to have meant any of it. But then he'd do it again, berating Alice and inventing crimes she'd committed against him. After four or five rounds of this sort of abuse, Alice felt she had no choice but to cut him out of her life. She blocked his email, his Facebook and his phone number. He started texting her from payphones so he could get through to her phone, alternating between declarations of love, threats of suicide and accusations. He started showing up at her house. He sent emails using Alice's website contact form. He found whatever way he could to stalk and harass a woman who was being unambiguous about her desire not to be friends. He started spreading rumours about Alice — serious things, things about sex and violence. Alice began to wonder how much of this Ben was making up to damage her reputation, and how much he truly believed had happened. An opportunity to move interstate came up and Alice gratefully took it, relieved finally to escape the threatening presence of a man she once called a friend.

There are so many incarnations of danger in friendships. Lara, who got in touch via Twitter, made a close friend when she was about 16 years old. She has asked to call this friend 'A', and given it's an allusion to the villain in the TV show *Pretty Little Liars*, I am more than happy to oblige. That show is a master class in toxic friendship — four high-school girls are threatened and blackmailed by a mysterious person who signs their dangerous text messages with a single 'A' and over seven glorious seasons, they steal, lie and kill in the name of friendship — so it seems especially relevant. Anyway, Lara and A picked up a new friend about a year into their friendship — let's call her Belinda. A started fairly quickly to play Lara and Belinda off one another, testing their loyalties and pitting them against one another in a complex web of lies. She'd tell Lara awful things about Belinda, and Belinda awful things about Lara. She led them to believe that the other was a terrible friend, which only secured her position as the alpha friend in the group. Lara lent A a substantial amount of money, an insultingly small percentage of which was ever paid back. Basically, under the guise of friendship, A terrorised Lara and Belinda from point-blank range, keeping them in a constant state of confusion, hurt and worry. Ultimately, Lara and Belinda had enough of A's surreptitious bullying, worked out they'd been lied to and forged a friendship of their own, without A. They never hear from or speak to A now, and deliberately surround themselves with genuine friends. It's an example of two people cleanly, strategically removing a toxic friend from their lives.

Aristotle believed friendship wasn't for everyone. He said it was a fine skill, to be mastered over a lifetime of devotion, generosity, and attention. For him, it should be time-consuming and challenging, requiring a person to draw on their greatest stores of humanity. The implicit idea, really, is that some people don't deserve friendship; that some people are simply not cut out for the task; that some people cannot muster the requisite humility and care to be a proper, true friend. Look, I'd like to believe everyone deserves friendship; truly, I'd like to be so generous. But the more stories I hear of betrayal, deception, theft, racism, bigotry, cruelty, coercion and abuse, the more I find myself agreeing with old mate Aristotle. In some circumstances, perhaps friendship could be healing or even redemptive for someone who is deviant and unkind. If a person has the superhuman patience to care for someone cruel without being damaged themselves, fantastic. There but for the grace of Beyoncé go I. But if I'm being ruthlessly truthful, I think perhaps there are people who are simply incapable of genuine friendship. People who do nasty, calculated things. People who siphon kindness from others, steal their confidence and mangle their self-esteem. People who wilfully endanger, threaten, harass or frighten others. People who are so self-centred and self-absorbed they cannot perform the act of genuinely caring for another human being.

Stories about people like this came pouring in on Twitter: Peter had to cut his good mate Stuart from his life when he got married because Stuart didn't 'approve' of Peter's wife's ethnicity. Leanne had to distance herself from Kaley when Kaley got physically violent with Leanne's child. Nicola had to move on from Fran when she refused to get help for her excessive drinking and started seriously verbally abusing Nicola every time she got drunk. There were tales of a more insidious sort of toxicity too, the sort of thing that develops over time rather than being defined by a single act of awfulness. Those friendships are the real fuckers — the ones that carry on for years, slowly destroying one person's sense of self until they feel drained of identity. Like any kind of abuse, the toxic friendship experience can be extremely difficult to identify when you're going through it. Some people, thankfully, recognise what's going on and can extricate themselves effectively. Other people get trapped in these friendships for a lifetime, unable or unsure how to get out, perhaps even unaware they need to.

London psychotherapist Samantha De Bono sees a lot of clients trapped in toxic friendships, some of whom don't even realise until they come in to talk it through. Just like domestic abuse, toxicity in a friendship can be difficult to detect, mostly because we deflect, make excuses for the perpetrator and blame ourselves. Just like the victims of an abusive relationship, people who find themselves enmeshed in an abusive friendship are very quick to think 'it must just be me' or 'it's not that bad, remember that time she made me breakfast?' Dr De Bono says the first thing you should do is trust your gut: if something doesn't feel right in a friendship, it probably isn't. She says toxic friendships are almost identical to an abusive relationship, primarily in that they feature manipulation and emotional control. If a friend is doing things entirely on their terms, isolating you from your other friends and loved ones, turning you against other people in your life, stealing your friends or demeaning you, then that's abuse. We're just hesitant to call it abuse in a friendship situation because it's embarrassing, because we don't take friendships as seriously as romantic relationships and because we haven't got a properly developed understanding of it. There are so many incarnations of toxicity, and it ranges from mild to extreme: being negative all the time, body shaming you, insulting you under the guise of a joke and criticising your life choices all the way up to openly disparaging you, spreading rumours about you, ignoring your requests for space, controlling who you can and can't see, and making your life a living hell. If all bad behaviour is on a spectrum, it's about working out where your deal-breaker line sits. How many surreptitious, nasty comments can you take before you need that person out of your life? How many times does your sister, father, boyfriend or mate have to tell you that someone is bad news before you believe them? How many insults, taunts, or let-downs does it take to break a friendship? All of that is completely subjective. You've got to decide for yourself what you're willing to tolerate and when it's healthier to get someone out of your life for good.

Dr De Bono had a toxic friend of her own. She essentially forced herself into Dr De Bono's life, befriending her other friends and inviting herself to things she hadn't been invited to until she infiltrated her social circle. As Dr De Bono says, narcissists move very quickly, and this one weaseled her way into her life at breakneck pace, with emphatic declarations of friend-love and expensive gestures very early on. She'd organise things for the two of them to do and then get very angry when Dr De Bono couldn't make a particular date or activity. She'd demean and insult Dr De Bono, taking a place in her life as an emotional sort of parasite. They'd been friends a while and the doctor is a fallible human like the rest of us, so she kept thinking it was her problem and it became very difficult to cleanly end the friendship — especially because every time she tried, this person would turn up at her house with flowers or wait outside her office. This toxic friendship had the markings of an obsessive relationship: the attempts to bully, belittle and control, the sending of flowers to try and woo Dr De Bono back, the turning up without an invitation. Finally, Dr De Bono broached the subject and told this person her behaviour really bothered her. 'I'm going to be the way I am and you'll have to deal with it,' the friend said, in a text. That gave Dr De Bono her way out because, actually, no she didn't. She composed a very calm message that simply said, 'You are wrong, and this is where our friendship ends.'

Getting out of a toxic friendship can be very difficult, especially if you're dealing with a narcissist, whose whole modus operandi is to coerce and charm you in turns. The truth is that you have to be very clear about your boundaries (but first you have to know what they are, which can require some serious self-awareness — might I recommend a therapist?). If someone contravenes what you think is right or decent or good, then you must calmly escape the friendship. To get to a place where you're able to do that, you have to start by setting yourself free a little. For example, it ain't your responsibility to care for this person during the fallout of your friendship. In fact, you've probably been taking responsibility for the friendship too long and it's time they were accountable for their own behaviour. Give yourself permission to say no: no to invitations, no to apologies, no to the whole friendship if that's what you want. Dr De Bono's advice is not to lie, but to very simply and unambiguously declare that the friendship is over. Yep, it'll probably wound the other person, but ultimately that's not your responsibility. Oh and — praise be! — Dr De Bono also says you can totally break up with a toxic friend over text. It doesn't have to be a big, dramatic sit-down affair (the sort of person who abuses a friend might quite like the drama of that scenario). It just has to be a clean, assertive notification: 'I don't think we should hang out any more', 'This friendship is over', 'You make me feel small and sad, please don't contact me again'.

And then ... Duck down the road to the shops, pick up a tub of Ben & Jerry's, get in your pyjamas, whack on the telly and mourn that friendship like you would a romantic relationship. You deserve it.

CHAPTER NINE

The loneliness epidemic

LONELINESS IS A SINISTER, capricious sneak. It wraps itself around the hearts of all sorts of people, from every demographic, from every walk of life. In fact its very mundanity is its best disguise; it gets away with taunting people for ages before it's properly detected. That, and there's the shame that cleaves to loneliness like a pilot fish. What has struck me most, after talking to so many generous people about their loneliness, is just how tenacious it can be. And how common. We often think of loneliness as an affliction of old age; something the elderly must confront the closer they get to death. It is, of course, a very real and disturbing problem for old people, particularly as their mobility, mental alertness, confidence and actual number of living friends diminish. But actually, we are vulnerable to loneliness at any age. The tenderness of youth seems to be a particular trigger for loneliness, as kids, teenagers and young adults struggle to establish who they are in the world and end up doing so on their own. We're susceptible in middle-age too. Well after we've gone through the initial rounds of identity building we are so often struck with some kind of existential crisis: have we ever truly known who we are? Truth be told, we can get hit by loneliness at any stage from birth until death. Frankly, it seems loneliness can get to anyone, regardless of how buoyed by Facebook friendships they are, regardless of how outwardly confident they may seem, regardless of how often they venture outside the house. Loneliness does not discriminate.

'Hello, I'd like to speak to people about loneliness. If you've ever been lonely, please get in touch. #journorequest,' I write in a tweet. The 140-character limit isn't quite enough room to make the appeal properly though, so I do another couple: 'I promise to be gentle about it and we can talk on whatever platform suits you. #thefriendshipcure.' And then, finally: 'Lonely, unable to make friends, isolated, feeling alone. I know it's a tricky, vulnerable one but I'd like to chat to you.' What happens next is both heartening and devastating. I get an influx of tweets from brave lonely people who want to talk about their experiences. It is exactly what I need and just what I asked for, obviously, but I am instantly saddened by the sheer volume of people ready to speak. Not just ready, some of them, but needing to speak. The candour and generosity with which some of my interviewees talk makes me think this might be the first time they've opened up about their loneliness. That's not surprising, really, because we certainly do not make it easy to talk with any degree of honesty about feeling lonely. We are, generally speaking, made to feel like social pariahs if we utter the words 'I am lonely' in any company except the most empathetic. So I am extremely grateful to the people who come forward, volunteering to speak to me about one of the most intimate emotional experiences you can have. I'm impressed, too, because it takes a level of courage to talk to a stranger about it. During the week after my initial tweets, I speak to people on the phone, by email and in person, and as I listen to their stories of loneliness I am truly taken aback by how common the experience is, how varied and how persistent. I am also deeply moved by the tenderness and insight with which they tell me their stories.

Amy says loneliness hit her hardest just after the birth of her second son, Joe. He's six and a half months old when we speak, and probably extremely sweet, as children of that age tend to be. But the sweetness of a baby is not enough to quell loneliness; in fact, their silent presence seems to be, by so many accounts, a lonely sort of company to be in. Around the time Amy fell pregnant with Joe, she and her partner Tim had just moved from Melbourne to the Surf Coast of Victoria in Australia, to a little beach house by the ocean. They moved away from their parents, who had helped so much with the first baby, and all their friends. It was beautiful, but isolating. When Joe arrived, Amy started feeling anxious and sad in a way she just hadn't the first time around, when she had her son, Alfie. She felt so distraught, so little like herself, that she thought perhaps she had postnatal depression. In a teary conversation with her partner, Tim, one day, Amy was really trying to get to the bottom of why she was feeling so utterly awful. She'd had a difficult pregnancy — the kind where you alternate between vomiting enthusiastically and feeling violently nauseated for the majority of nine months. She was away from her people, her tribe, her family. 'I'm just really, really lonely,' she told Tim, through sobs. It was a light-bulb moment for them both, to give her anguish a label. Amy was, and still is, quite isolated. She hadn't been doing the school pick-ups or drop-offs for Alfie because she'd been too ill with the pregnancy, so she didn't even have those 8 a.m. and 3 p.m. interactions at the school gate. Tim did; he started accumulating some friendships from school. Whenever Amy joined in or spent time with some of the kinder mums, she ended up feeling even lonelier, in that peculiar way the wrong company can actually make you feel even more alone. She'd come home from a night out with the local mums, burst into tears and tell Tim, 'They're not my people!' Amy's people were in Melbourne. She had a few close friends back there, but as a general rule, she'd always struggled to make decent female friendships. She used to have a lot of best friends, but they were more like whirlwind romances that burnt themselves out than real, lasting, friendships. She has a friend called Mim, whom she adores. She and Mim lift each other up, support each other and make each other better. Amy's other people are sort of drifting away from her, distracted by their own lives. One of her closest friends has been trying to have a baby, with no success, so she's particularly sensitive about spending time with families. Another has started having an affair, which has really put a strain on the friendship, as poor romantic decisions and infidelity can.

When I ask Amy to describe loneliness to me as though I'm someone who has never experienced it myself, she asks if I've ever been to a silent disco. Yes, I have, I say. Hundreds of people turn up at a big venue and dance, only they're all wearing headphones and dancing to the music that blares through them. So you can have this eerie experience where you slip your headphones down around your neck, away from your ears, and watch people dancing in the silence. Amy says she saw one once, at a festival, and it made her feel brittle and sick because it reminded her so strongly of how she feels in all social situations. Loneliness, to Amy, is like going to a silent disco, but she's the only one without any music playing in her headphones. It's alienating, it's isolating, it makes her the only person unable to sway or swing or boogie to the same beat as everyone else. I love this description of loneliness; it's so perfectly bleak. Imagine the sort of panic you'd feel if you were the only one in a room of hundreds unable to hear what everyone else is hearing.

Amy isn't the only mum stuck in a silent disco sort of purgatory. Ella came to me with a similar distress. She has a five-year-old son and she left her husband when the little one was just four months old. Ella's loneliness is compounded by the looming guilt that being a mother isn't enough. She loves her son, but she's lonely with him and lonely without him. When he goes to stay with his dad some weekends, Ella sits at home with this yawning stretch of time to fill, and she only ever really sees her mother. 'I often think I might as well be dead,' she says to me. 'Every day is the same, I'm just marking time until I die.' What exacerbates the whole thing is how alone Ella is in her own loneliness; she can't really talk to anyone about it. She tried, once, but it didn't exactly work out. She mentioned how she was feeling to her brother, but he just said, 'You have a lovely son and a great job, you should be thankful.' She never brought it up again. Now, just like when her son was a baby, the highlight of Ella's week is her trip to the supermarket. For some people it's a chore, but for her, it's the only time she really has a chance to interact with other people.

Dave can actually pinpoint a moment of extreme loneliness in his life: it was 23 April 2009. He was at a hostel in Portugal and someone had just teased him about reading David Beckham's book. He remembers lying back on his little bunk bed and feeling utterly alone and 'like an imposter'. I jump on that phrase when he says it because that's an important part of the loneliness experience, feeling like you don't belong, like you're an imposter in your own life. The way Dave explains it, loneliness is a void, an emptiness, a hollowness. It's that sense of languishing in the space between the versions of ourselves we save for other people. Dave actually feels pangs of loneliness most days. Usually when he's sitting on the train on the way home from work, in between being 'work Dave' and 'home Dave'. I love that he makes that distinction between Daves because it makes loneliness out to be this strange space we occupy when we're not performing our public and private selves. It's what happens when we press pause on our identities and we don't know, for a moment, who we are. 'I feel like everyone's watching but no one is paying attention,' Dave says, rather aptly describing the feelings of paranoia and negligence that so often accompany loneliness. It's the silent disco scenario all over again.

The people who talked to me kept echoing the same sentiments: loneliness is emptiness, loneliness is rejection, loneliness happens just as often in the presence of other people as it does when you're alone. Lauren is particularly lonely at the moment because she just lost her beloved gran, her flatmate has started dating someone she had feelings for and sometimes she doesn't leave the house because she hates the way she looks. She says loneliness hits her most when she's actually with other people, like their company only isolates her more. When her gran was still alive, she'd come home after a night out and complain to her that she'd had an awful time. 'Why do you go out with them, then?' her gran would ask. All Lauren could say was, 'I'd rather go out with them than be alone.' And therein lies the great conundrum of loneliness: how can you keep yourself motivated to seek out social interaction when it only makes you prefer to curl up inside your loneliness? What sort of incentive do we have to spend time with friends, if they only make us feel lonelier? And what the very hell is loneliness, if we still feel it in the presence of other people?

There's a difference between social isolation and loneliness. A difference between not being able to make real friends and losing the ability to connect with the ones you have. Steph told me about the time she moved from London to Exeter to write her PhD. She was 22 years old and let's just say Exeter is not exactly an early-twenties paradise. She was friendly with some of the other students, but she just didn't feel like she was with her people. Her people were back in London. She made an effort to socialise, but every time she did she just felt the distance from home all the more keenly. She shared an office with people she refers to as profoundly lovely, but hanging out with them was confronting: it just made her ache for the friends she'd left behind and the person she could be with them. Loneliness made her angry and she started to doubt her own academic abilities. She ended up spending most of her scholarship money on trains back to London to see her real mates and when it all became too much, she decided to move back after six months. Being reunited with her tribe calmed the loneliness but didn't dissipate it altogether. Even back in her city with her people, something like a strange man shouting at her on the street can make Steph feel alone in her own existence. She suspects most people get little pangs of loneliness like that and I'm inclined to agree.

Becky told me a similar story of circumstantial loneliness. She left school and got a job in her home town straightaway, so she skipped university, where so many of her friends made new friends. She has a few close friends, maybe three or four, but beyond that she just feels like there's a gaping chasm between her life and the life promised to her by the sitcom *Friends*. She has no omnipresent gang of buddies to get giant cups of coffee with every day and debrief about life, and I think she feels betrayed by that somehow, like popular culture promised her a form of friendship that just doesn't exist in real life. The friends she does have are disparate by circumstance: one is planning a wedding, one has just bought a house with her long-term boyfriend, one is a shift worker and one lives in Australia. They talk on WhatsApp, but that doesn't mean that when Becky buys tickets to see the band Paramore, she'll actually have someone to go with. She technically has friends, but she doesn't feel like she actually gets to see them often enough and that distance hurts. And so Becky does things on her own: dances at Paramore with thousands of strangers, goes to the movies, eats dinner in restaurants, goes on organised group trips to America with other people who like to travel solo. She's learnt to enjoy her own company by necessity, and I think that's a really great thing. It doesn't abate the loneliness, but it gives her something to do with her time.

And that's where I have to emphasise a really important point: I think it's vital that we know how to exist on our own. I think so many of us have lost the ability to be on our own healthily, or perhaps never had it at all. Being in our own company comfortably is crucial if we're going to survive the disparate nature of modern existence. You can actually be on your own without being lonely, and that's one of the most important skills you can have as a grown-up human being. Loneliness can still infiltrate our alone time, but it's not necessarily caused by it. It's a complex social emotion, loneliness, brought on by a culture of individualism we don't know how to actually inhabit. We don't truly know how to be on our own or with people, and we get stuck somewhere awkwardly between the two, unsure how to proceed with our own lives. We are both frightened of the possibility of loneliness and already very much in its clutches. The people I've spoken to about loneliness have simply confirmed something I've always suspected: that loneliness is one of the most frightening certainties of the human experience. Very few people are immune, and those who claim never to have experienced it are most likely unwilling or unsure how to identify it. Let me be honest with you: I've always been scared of loneliness, my whole life.

When I was little, my sweet, fabulous first grade teacher got us to cut paper into little shapes and write the personality trait we most valued on it, over and over. She got us to store those little cut-outs in a box of our choice, kept somewhere special so that when we needed our chosen quality, we could take out the box and sprinkle the pieces of paper over our heads and bodies, like magic confetti. I cut my paper into stars and scribbled the word 'courage' on them, and I kept them in a little box, inside a slightly larger box, in the bottom drawer of my bedside table. In fact, I suspect they're still there. They survived several rounds of clearing out childhood belongings, because who can bring themselves to throw out homemade courage? Everyone needs it, at some time or another. As I grew up and started keeping diaries, a single fear started to emerge, the one thing that most frightened me about becoming an adult, the one thing that may require me to inoculate myself with my secret stash of cut-out courage. 'Please let me never be lonely,' I'd write in my early teenage diaries. I'd wish the same for my parents, my grandparents, my sister, my friends. It became like a persistent little atheist prayer, to nobody in particular: please let me never be lonely. Several times, I used my confetti of courage to try and protect myself from the impending feeling of loneliness. I sat on the edge of my bed or stood alone in my bedroom, reverent, and emptied those little scraps of paper over my head, my eyes closed with the significance of it. It felt necessary, even important, and I was still enough a child to have the placebo of sheer imagination. I needed it then: we are, of course, strangely alone when we make our way into adolescence. I felt the sting of loneliness first then and it only exacerbated my fear of feeling it for the rest of my life. It occurred to me then that adults are in no way immune to loneliness; in fact, the more I saw of adult life, the more I suspected everyone was moving about their lives, secretly paralysed by loneliness, or the fear of its arrival. I thought a lot about loneliness and what it was to be alone, so much so that a psychiatrist chided me for worrying too much when I was 12 and forbade me from watching the news. She suspected my tender almost-teenage soul couldn't take the constant coverage of atrocities across the world, but she wasn't quite right. The thing that frightened me most was more private and less obvious than bad news on the telly. It was loneliness. I started seeing it everywhere: in my parents, in my schoolteachers, in my classmates at school.

When my beloved Papa died and left my grandma on her own in their home with only the dog for company, I started seeing it in her. I started smelling it, this entirely tangible feeling of being alone in the world, but for an American cocker spaniel with ears long enough to fall into his food. Perhaps that's when I truly fell in love with dogs; that stout, blond creature seemed to be the one thing between my grandma and an all-consuming loneliness, the encroachment of which even we, her family who adored her more than we could ever say, could not stop. It is not always within our power to eradicate loneliness for other people, not always. Grief steals something from a person, something that cannot truly be replaced. Becoming a widow is an experience of acute, excruciating loneliness. The person you chose to accompany you through life is gone, and no matter who else is still around, there's a conspicuous emptiness you can't shift, a deep sense of emotional isolation that sets in and never gives up on you. Loneliness, strangely, becomes your greatest companion.

But loneliness is not just a companion to grief. Loneliness can slip into our lives, undetected for some time, for all sorts of reasons. It could slither in alongside tragedy or trauma. Profound distress has a way of making you feel like you could be the only person who has ever been through such pain, and it can leave you alone just when you need people the most. Loneliness can strike when you literally remove yourself from the people you know and adore: when you move to a new city, go to a new school, start at university or get a new job. There's something particularly vulnerable about young adulthood, just when you're trying to work out who you are. Loneliness can accompany chronic illness, mental illness and disability. It can hit you when you're down and out, when you've lost your job, when you've broken up with someone, when you're addicted. It might be chronic; a feeling of being alone in the world that's been there as long as you can remember. It could be fleeting; an ephemeral sense of existential dread. It might arrive as you age and your friends start to die. It might hit you young or middle-aged. Whenever it comes and whatever it looks like, it hurts. It hurts in that numb, melancholy, empty sort of way that makes you believe in having a soul just so you can explain where the pain is.

The scariest thing about loneliness is that it can exist in the presence of love. Loneliness isn't frightened of company; it doesn't scamper at the sound of another human's voice or disappear in the company of others. Loneliness is perfectly happy to come to a party with you, pleased as punch to accompany you on outings with people you know and perhaps even adore. Loneliness is audacious like that: it doesn't care who you're with and it doesn't care what you're doing. It will tag along on any outing, then stay, nuzzled into your psyche, when you're physically alone at night. And that's the most important thing there is to understand about loneliness: loneliness doesn't always mean you're alone. Solitude is a deeply necessary part of being human; there are things you simply cannot know about yourself without the space to see it on your own. No, loneliness doesn't always accompany solitude. It's a lot sneakier than that.

Loneliness exists in the gap between company and companionship. It lurks in between the quantity and quality of our relationships. It comes for us when we leave enough emotional space unoccupied in our lives. It feeds on our insecurities and it echoes our greatest fears back to us in the quiet. It is cruel and unforgiving, opportunistic and greedy. On its kinder days, loneliness will whisper to you all the reasons you might be alone forever. On its crueller days, it will take you by the hand and lead you to the precipice of life. We have long suspected that loneliness shortens our days on Earth; that heartbreak and grief and unwanted solitude could bring us ever closer to death. We have played with this idea a long time, the idea that emotional distress can inflict physical pain. Poems and ballads have toyed with the notion of psychosomatic pain for as long as we've analysed the human condition in prose. We've sensed, without proof, that something like loneliness could harm us irreparably, perhaps more seriously than any purely physical ailment. And now we have the evidence to back it up. The science is here to validate those suspicions and to prove how deadly loneliness can be.

Researchers at Brigham Young University in Utah, USA, looked back over the scientific literature on loneliness from the years 1980 to 2014. The studies they reviewed covered 3.4 million people all up, which of course is a stunning sample size. Pulling all this research together, they concluded loneliness can increase the risk of death by at least 30 per cent — although some estimates are as high as 60 per cent. This hastened mortality rate applies to people experiencing both actual and perceived social isolation. It is a complex thing, to break down the lethality of loneliness. For a start, there are practicalities. Lonely people are less likely to seek help if they need it, for either mental or physical problems. They're less accountable to others for their behaviour and so more likely to hold onto bad habits. And then there's the rather bleak scenario that something happens to them, and there's literally nobody there to call emergency services. It's what Bridget Jones famously worried about: being found alone, partly devoured by Alsatians. But loneliness is much more insidious than that, too. Scientists are just beginning to understand that loneliness has a direct physiological effect on the body. It's not merely the circumstances of loneliness that cause us bodily harm; it's loneliness itself.

Loneliness is more dangerous than smoking 15 cigarettes a day and deadlier than obesity. It might be the most significant threat to our health since the discovery that cigarettes blacken our lungs and line our insides with tar; it is the new smoking. Loneliness can increase our chances of developing clinical dementia by 64 per cent. It can tighten our arteries, raise our blood pressure, increase our rates of infection, diminish our heart health, and lead to higher rates of cancer. Lonely people develop tumours faster, have weaker immune systems and lower thresholds for pain. Loneliness raises the level of the stress hormone cortisol in our blood, which puts us at a higher risk of heart attack and stroke. When we're lonely, we wake up every day with higher levels of morning cortisol because we are bracing for yet another stressful day of feeling alone. Loneliness disrupts our sleep and makes us prone to depression. Lonely people over the age of 55 die at twice the rate of people who have regular contact with friends and family. Loneliness is associated with accelerated cognitive decline in older adults. It is, unequivocally, a very real danger to us all.

Loneliness is the next great public health epidemic, unfurling faster than we can keep up with and getting stronger the longer we let it fester. Loneliness is killing people the world over and we have barely stopped to work out how to halt it, how to cure it, how to prevent it. Psychologists and biologists are starting to argue that we should treat loneliness like any chronic illness. John Cacioppo — Professor of Psychology, Psychiatry and Behavioural Neuroscience at the University of Chicago — says the effects of loneliness, social isolation and rejection are 'as real as thirst, hunger or pain'. Professor Cacioppo has been studying loneliness since the early '90s and is now an authoritative voice in the fight to have it taken seriously as a major health risk. He is convinced it is the *feeling* of loneliness that does such damage to the body. Some scientists do not agree an emotion could be so potent, but I think you only have to look at the ways in which heartbreak, grief and depression ravage our bodies to know that Professor Cacioppo is absolutely, chillingly correct.

Back in the early '90s, Professor Cacioppo did a loneliness study on his undergraduate students. He started by asking how lonely they felt and splitting them into three categories: the lonely, the sometimes sort-of lonely and the not lonely. He strapped blood pressure cuffs, biosensors and beepers to all of them. Nine times a day for seven days, the students were contacted on those beepers and prompted to fill out a questionnaire about how they felt. They stayed overnight in a hospital so Professor Cacioppo could monitor their sleep patterns. He took regular saliva samples to measure the students' levels of cortisol, the infamous stress hormone. As it turned out, the students who slept poorly and had higher levels of cortisol were also the ones who said they were unhappy because they hadn't made close friends. They also had higher than normal vascular resistance, which is when the arteries narrow because tissue is inflamed. All of this led Professor Cacioppo to the conclusion that the lonely kids were in survival mode.

Loneliness raises our levels of cortisol because the perception that we are unworthy of social contact is deeply distressing. And that's what loneliness is, amongst other things: the persistent belief that we either have been or will be rejected. That's why the feeling comes laced with such shame; we associate the state of loneliness with inferiority, undesirability and worthlessness. That's why it's a silent killer; people are too ashamed to talk about it, to even consider it could be loneliness they're experiencing. We are hardwired as a species to seek out social contact — we are social animals and we have always had our greatest chances of survival in a group. Human beings have evolved to need social interaction to survive. So if we are isolating ourselves or feeling profoundly dissatisfied with our connections to other people, then we are naturally put on high alert. We know instinctively that it is dangerous to be alone, so feelings of loneliness can make us hyperaware of our own mortality. This is a state psychologists call hypervigilance, and in the case of loneliness, people become hypervigilant to signs of rejection.

A study conducted at the Centre for Cognitive and Social Neuroscience at the University of Chicago and published in the journal *Cortex* tested this idea. Dr Stephanie Cacioppo (John's wife, as it happens) enlisted a group of healthy young volunteers and asked them to complete a loneliness questionnaire. Thirty-two of the group were classified as socially well integrated and 38 as lonely. All participants were hooked up to sensors that register electrical activity in the brain and sat in front of computer screens. They watched as words in various colours flashed onto those screens: 'misery', 'pleasure', 'unwanted', 'accepted'. The experiment was designed to test the students' reactions to words that were associated with social acceptance or rejection. When the lonely participants saw words relating to social exclusion — things like 'detached', 'unwanted' or 'excluded' — the area in their brains related to attention lit up faster than those students who did not identify as lonely. The lonely students' brains were less affected by happy words like 'accepted'. This showed, say both Cacioppos, that lonely people are preoccupied with the idea of social rejection. The ever-present fear of being rejected tends to make lonely people behave in a more hostile manner, which starts off a vicious cycle of loneliness, whereby the lonely get lonelier because they rebuff social interaction and make it difficult for people to get close. Lonely people are more likely to interpret the actions of others as being hostile or unkind, because they are in a state of constant suspicion and fear. Loneliness is cruel that way: it taints the actions of the very people who could infiltrate the solitude. It puts us in a state of short-term self-preservation, and that can include keeping people at a distance for fear of their rejecting us.

Most people are, to some extent, concerned about social rejection. Every interaction with another human being is darkened, initially, by the possibility they could reject us. Even worse, that someone could move from being a stranger to being a friend, and still find reason to reject us. We are powerfully hardwired to avoid social rejection, which means protecting ourselves from situations in which it may be likely. If you started looking at the world like it's an obstacle course of possible social rejection, you'd never leave the house — and indeed, some people do not, for this very reason. Loneliness breeds a fear of social rejection, which in some cases can cause agoraphobia or coax people into staying inside their loneliness. Some people feel lonely for long enough and find social interaction difficult enough, that they come to prefer their own loneliness to the possibility of company. It is easier, for some, to nestle further into their loneliness than it is to venture out of it, to make friends, to see people. And if you find yourself feeling alone even in the company of other people, then where exactly is the imperative to change? If contact with other human beings makes you feel even more alone, why not simply settle into the loneliness you know so well? I believe that is happening in households and hearts the world over and, to be frank with you, I'm not entirely sure how we tackle the problem. The only thing we can conceivably do is launch such an aggressive campaign of kindness that it overwhelms the fear of social rejection long enough to allow people to make real connections again. But more on the treatment for loneliness later; for now, a little more about the pain of social rejection.

You see, as it turns out, social rejection can cause us physical pain. If you've ever felt the sting of being excluded from a group of people you like, admire or respect, then perhaps you know precisely how visceral it can be. Let me tell you about a now-famous experiment by Professor Naomi Eisenberger at the University of California, Los Angeles. To test how social rejection affects us, Eisenberger hooked people up to sensors and had them play a game called Cyberball. Participants in the study would start playing the game, where they threw a virtual ball between themselves and two other virtual people. As the game progressed, the virtual people started leaving out the participant, instead just throwing the ball between themselves. This feeling of being excluded lit up the dorsal anterior cingulate cortex in the brains of the participants — the very same area of the brain that registers physical pain. Physical pain lights up other parts of the brain too; this area is specifically to do with the emotional fact that pain is distressing. Social exclusion alerted that part of the brain because the feeling of being unwanted or ignored is like physical pain; it's that powerful. It's no wonder we avoid it at any cost.

Social rejection feels deeply shameful, too. Loneliness has this veneer of shame because we tend to think it's caused by our being unlovable in some way. We very much frame loneliness as a personal failing, rather than the result of a cultural malaise or a side-effect of modernity. Richard S. Schwartz — Associate Professor of Psychiatry at Harvard Medical School, senior consultant at McLean Hospital and author of *The Lonely American: Drifting Apart in the 21st Century* — has been preoccupied with the social problem of loneliness for many years. Long ago, as he tells me, he and his wife, Dr Jacqueline Olds, began to notice that patients who came to see them were struggling with social isolation and loneliness. Curiously, people were more inclined to say they were depressed than lonely. As Schwartz and Olds got to know their patients better, they started to see signs of profound loneliness, rather than depression. But of course, as we've discussed, loneliness often comes with great shame and secrecy. Schwartz says he thinks his patients believed loneliness made them a 'loser', rather than, say, someone who is simply experiencing a volatile, common part of human existence. That really got Schwartz and Olds thinking about loneliness and how important it is to bring it out into the open. Since then, they've researched and written a lot on the topic of social isolation and they truly believe it is a major global problem.

'Why are people so lonely?' I ask Professor Schwartz, with more than a trace of desperation in my voice because I'd just spent the past six hours pulling up stats about how lonely we all are. He sighs — a sweet sigh, the sigh of someone who has spent many years trying to answer precisely this question with some semblance of hope and certainty. In short, he thinks we are doing it to ourselves. We have become obsessed with work and productivity, and come to define ourselves by those things, so much so that at the end of a long work day, we tend to step back voluntarily from other people. We retreat into our home lives, whatever they may be. And that becomes a trap: we start out isolating ourselves but then we notice socialising going on without us and we begin to feel left out. But so often our reaction to feelings of exclusion is to isolate ourselves further, to retreat further from the possibility of outright rejection. We get demoralised, Professor Schwartz says, and pull back further into ourselves. He thinks we are meeting less and less face to face, and that it's that much easier to disappear when you've only got social media to keep you accountable for interacting with someone. We have lost the quality of our connections to other people and we are not quite sure how to get that back.

'What do you tell your patients?' I ask. 'What do you tell them to do about their loneliness?' The answer sounds relatively simple, but is no doubt more difficult than it appears: first, Professor Schwartz tells his patients to recognise what is going on. He says to pay attention to the loneliness, to acknowledge it is there. Then he urges people to redefine their experiences of it. It is not, as we first suspect, a personal failure to be lonely. It is a complex state with many factors, but a significant one is actually the current state of our society as a whole, and there's very little point internalising guilt over that. So he says to look at the changes you can make in your life to reconnect with other human beings and allay those fears of social rejection. Look at how you might meet new people or revive friendships you once had and abandoned. That could simply be reaching out to someone you know for a phone conversation that leads to a coffee that leads to a more regular sort of contact that might constitute friendship. It could be joining a chess club or a netball team or a local choir; something that literally gets you out of the house and into physical proximity with other people. But I think what's so interesting about Professor Schwartz's take on this whole thing is that before we can sign up to any kind of organised fun, we have to get past this deep-set idea that loneliness is somehow shameful. We have to wriggle out of any feelings of guilt, shame and discomfort with ourselves if we are going to have any hope of addressing loneliness in any real way. Nothing, Schwartz says, is a complete solution. You could start going to Salsa-dancing lessons every Tuesday and still come home with a gnawing sense of being alone in the world; you could strike up a sweet conversation with someone at Spanish class and still feel that hollowness in your heart. The point is, these are little steps you can take towards regaining a sense of genuine social connectedness. The real danger is in the self-perpetuating nature of loneliness, its tendency to cycle back on itself and get more ferocious the longer you leave it unattended. The most chronically lonely among us have reached a stage where they are actively resisting company and connection with other people, so surely the simplest and most powerful first step anyone can take is to literally place themselves in the presence of other human beings. It's not a perfect balm for loneliness, but it's a step in the right direction.

So, I hear you ask, what the bloody hell do we do? How do we solve the global epidemic of loneliness? Whose responsibility is it to act? There are organisations, clubs, groups, charities, business and initiatives popping up all over the place, happily. Progress is being made in the United Kingdom, where several key organisations have made research and awareness a priority. Jo Cox, the genuinely inspiring British Labour minister who was murdered in 2016, started The Jo Cox Commission on Loneliness just months before she died. She was devoted to helping the lonely, and that's just one of the things that made her extraordinary. The continuation of the Commission, which is chaired by both a Labour and a Conservative minister, is just part of Jo's remarkable legacy. Apparently, she first became invested in the plight of lonely people when she was little and she'd do the mail rounds with her grandfather, who was a postman. She realised some people actually went days without seeing anyone and their only interaction was with their postman. This idea distressed Jo so much that, as an adult, she did what she always did: she took real action to make people's lives better. She would no doubt have been thrilled that in January 2018 the UK got its very own minister for loneliness. And so, 13 charities across the UK came together to form her Commission on Loneliness, and their mission is first to break down the stigma of loneliness. The Commission tries to shine a light on different groups of lonely people each month: the elderly, men, people living with disabilities, carers, refugees, parents and children. They recognise better than anyone that loneliness is becoming alarmingly prevalent. A study by Co-op and the Red Cross revealed that nine million people in the UK are always or often lonely. According to Action for Children, 43 per cent of 17- to 25-year-olds experience loneliness and less than half of them feel loved. Twenty-four per cent of parents always or often feel lonely. The charity Sense claims 50 per cent of disabled people feel lonely on any given day and The Forum says 58 per cent of migrants and refugees do. Carers UK says that eight out of 10 carers feel lonely while looking after a loved one and Age UK says 3.6 million people over the age of 65 identify television as their main form of company. In an Australian study by Lifeline, 60 per cent of more than 3,000 people said they 'often felt lonely' and 82.5 per cent said that loneliness was increasing in society.

The Commission on Loneliness is working within the community and with government bodies to address loneliness on an individual and a state level. The Commission has seen some endearing success handing out badges that say 'Happy to chat' and they've spoken to health services about helping the chronically lonely re-enter community life. Jo's legacy is bigger than that, though. She wanted to ask the big, awkward questions about loneliness: Should the government be measuring our levels of happiness, as well as the gross domestic product? Should GPs be prescribing social interaction for people who need it? Has modernity caused loneliness? The Commission is hard at work trying to answer these questions and we may not see results for years to come. But at least we know the work has been started. Hopefully other countries will follow suit.

There are other people who recognise that loneliness is an urgent social issue, to be ignored at our own peril. In the UK, Executive Director of The Campaign to End Loneliness, Laura Alcock-Ferguson, has been doggedly working on it for about seven years. When we speak, her determination practically reverberates down the phone line and I become fond of her very quickly. She, like Jo Cox, is an ambassador for the lonely among us and I cannot help but feel a little better that people like her are on the case. Laura's mission is to make people understand that loneliness is a major public health issue, one that needs to be addressed urgently. She has issued a critical call to action to business, statutory bodies and members of the public because she believes solving loneliness is everybody's business. She wants to launch a campaign of kindness, pleading with people to perform even small acts of kindness towards their fellow human beings. While she is busy putting out the message that we need an assault on loneliness and a surge in kindness, she is also targeting community and national leaders to take action on behalf of the lonely among us. And this is where we get closer to talking about some practical action: first, there's this idea that we need micro actions of kindness from every single person in society. Then, there's the action we need from small businesses and corporations, who have a responsibility to make their interactions with customers and employees more inclusive and socially fulfilling. Laura wants to make it a corporate responsibility to create spaces of social inclusion and friendship.

There are, you'll be pleased to know, already places that take this responsibility seriously. There's a café in Cardiff in the UK that offers free tea and coffee every Tuesday to people who might like to make friends with strangers on their premises. There's a retirement village and elderly services community across England that run activities like 'craft and chatter' and 'knit and natter' for old people to make friends. There's an organisation that started in Australia and now operates across England, Scotland and Ireland called Men's Sheds that sets up workshops for men to hang out in and make mates. There's a supermarket in the UK that does 'slow shopping Sundays', where they switch off the automated machines and allow shoppers to actually interact with each other and the checkout staff. There are groups that organise choir practice, sport, chess, afternoon tea, supper or breakfast clubs, lunches, language classes, sewing classes and book clubs all over the place to encourage new and strengthening friendship. Laura Alcock-Ferguson is heartened by all of this, as am I. But it's not enough; Laura's not satisfied and neither am I. Getting down to your local netball club requires a certain level of motivation, one that many severely lonely people simply do not have. And who is to say you won't feel that gnawing sense of aloneness exactly at the moment you swivel and throw the ball? Social clubs and befriending services are lovely and charming and helpful, but they're not reaching the people who are so tightly encased in their own loneliness, they don't even know how to leave the house, let alone play sport or knit in the presence of strangers. Groups can solve social isolation, perhaps, but not necessarily loneliness.

To solve loneliness, I think we need a major overhaul of how we interact as a species. We need a global uptake in kindness so dramatic, it alters our capacity to fully experience each other's company. We need to value and invest in the friendships we already have, as well as making new ones when the opportunity arises. We need to teach ourselves and each other how to be resilient in our own company. We need to revive our attention to our emotional needs and decide to actively define ourselves by our character, not just by what we do for a living or how hard we can work or how much success we can accrue in a lifetime. We need to prioritise compassion over fame, empathy over ambition and kindness over wealth. That's a series of decisions we can each make on our own time and with our own consciences. Until we work out how to make human connection a priority again, both in our personal and public lives, we will continue to be plagued by loneliness. Go to any party or concert or club meeting of your choice to remind yourself what it is to be with other human beings. Do whatever you can and whatever you like to ease the feelings of loneliness.

But please, take the time to acknowledge what loneliness is and how your actions affect other people. Increase your quota of kindness and deliberately implement a policy of empathy in your life. Be the friend you wish you had in this world, and maybe we will start to chip away at this epidemic of loneliness.

That, and please consider adopting a dog. They are the single greatest companions you could want. Or a cat, I suppose, if you're into that kind of thing.

CHAPTER TEN

Misery needs company

I'M IN BED, lying dead still, staring at the ceiling. A particularly nasty depression has got me by the heart and I can't function. I've just inhaled a family-size packet of home brand chocolate chip cookies, the only thing I've eaten in days. At once panicked and numb, I reach for my phone, open WhatsApp and text one of my best friends. She tries to FaceTime me but I watch her name flash on my screen until it disappears, unanswered. An exchange of vocal communication is too much for me right now. It's okay, Sammie knows to text me at times like these, and she does. I briefly describe my state — immobile, sardonic, lost, tired, unsleeping, desperate. Sammie gives me flawless, tailored advice. 'Have you seen the movie *Twister*?' she says. 'Helen Hunt survives because she finds a single piece of leather, wraps it around a strong pole and holds on until the tornado passes. That's what you've got to do: find your piece of leather, hold it tight, and wait for this to pass.' Luckily, I'm a whimsical depressive with a particular nostalgia for '90s films; this analogy speaks to me and I find one thing worth living for and hold onto it with my mind until the chemicals in my brain find balance again. That one thing, on this occasion, is my friends. I hold onto a single happy moment — the last time I was with my best friends, who are now all scattered across the globe in various locations — like I'm about to conjure a Patronus. I survive this day, Helen Hunt style.

Another time, I'm in Edinburgh for the Fringe Festival, a frivolous, fabulous event where you pay professionally funny people to make you laugh. It's a painful sort of irony, to be depressed at a comedy festival, but there I was. I was climbing to Arthur's Seat when my limbs started to get so heavy I could barely move. It was sunny, it was sort of warm in that autumnal Scottish way, it was beautiful. But none of the loveliness could reach me, not through the sudden, awkward armour of depression that encased me. We didn't make it to the top of Arthur's Seat, we had to turn around and go back down to the little Airbnb flat we were staying in. I was physically surrounded by friends this time, even my sister was there, but it didn't help. I felt strangely, utterly alone, even in company, estranged from the loveliness around me and profoundly low. My darling friend Elise, who was pregnant at the time and wonderful all the time, tucked me into bed, drew the curtains, pulled a blanket over me and gently closed the door. She went out to get a bucket-size punnet of fresh Scottish strawberries and a family-size block of chocolate — objectively two of the greatest comfort foods available. She came back in, sat softly on the edge of the bed, hand-fed me berries and chocolate, and started to sing me One Direction songs, a capella. She has the voice of an angel, so her cover of 'Live While We're Young' is truly worth hearing. And then she left me to nap heavily, which I do when I need an escape from existing. She checked back in on me throughout the day, and listened when I needed to whisper about how I was feeling. She was also perfectly happy to sit in silence, a warm, welcome presence on the edge of the bed as I waited, again, for the storm to pass.

I've been living with depression most of my life. I was seeing a psychiatrist for excessive melancholy by the time I was 11, on anti-depressant medication by the time I was 12, in a treatment clinic for anorexia by the time I was 15 and diagnosed with bipolar disorder by the time I was 17. I have known long, hollow stretches of depression and brief, frenetic bursts of mania. There are few things more emotionally isolating than the experience of chemical instability; it's sort of like heartbreak in that way it makes you feel as though maybe, just maybe, you are the only person to have ever felt this way, maybe the only person who ever will. There's something utterly, pervasively, exhaustingly lonely about living with a mental illness. Even when you're with friends and family and people who adore you — in fact, cruelly, sometimes more so when you are.

I've been obscenely lucky, really, throughout the whole thing. My parents and family have been and continue to be beautifully supportive (my mum and dad call me every day when I'm unwell and I know they have little tele-conferences afterwards about how my voice sounded on every call) and some of the teachers at school were actively wonderful ('I can't imagine you would need it, but if it was ever helpful to have the perspective of someone who has been through depression, I am here,' said one rather fabulous teacher). My friends at school knew to keep inviting me out to things on weekends, even though I barely ever turned up. They, for the most part, held me up in whatever way they could, given that their own adolescent angst was taking up most of their energies. My friends at college used to gingerly make fun of me for the long daily naps I'd take when I was on medication that knocked me out for the majority of the day, but they were still gentle and sweet to me. My teenage boyfriend was doggedly supportive, in the sort of way that would make him the perfect teen heartthrob if they ever made a movie about a guy who visited his depressed, anorexic girlfriend in hospital all the time. I found my soul buddies, my greatest friends, the ones who tell me *Twister* analogies and sing One Direction a capella by my bedside, at university. I have collected various other delightful friends through my early adulthood, when I moved from Sydney to London, through work, on Twitter and just serendipitously. Intensely pleasantly, I have fallen in love with a man who seems to naturally know how to be there for me and is therefore worth his weight in gold. I have actively recruited a group of people in London, Sydney and flung around the world, who know how to be kind to someone who is struggling. Since reaching adulthood proper, I've only really kept friends in my life who know how to be there for me when I'm low or down or desperate. If I don't feel comfortable even disclosing that I have bipolar, then the friendship is over before it began. My mental illness is like a litmus test for compassion, and frankly I have culled anyone from my life who doesn't pass it.

It has to be like that, really. Curating the friendships in my life on a secret criterion of kindness and mental health wokeness is a necessity for me. Frankly, everyone should do it. I've watched people keep toxic, good-for-nothing friends in their life and suffer excruciatingly for it. I don't do that, I can't do that. I already fill my quota of anxiety without that. A man once told me he could never love or trust someone with a mental illness; I drunkenly informed him that an attitude like that was a deal-breaker and promptly removed him from my life. A girlfriend once told me she didn't believe I was depressed; I called an end to the friendship immediately. In my life, there is simply no room for meanness or weakness of character. I deliberately surround myself with good, kind, patient people because it is delightful but also because it is part of my mental healthcare plan. Keeping strong, smart friends is strategic for me because they know how to keep me alive when I need them to. They are wonderful enough to act as an incentive to survive. Along with anti-depressants, therapy, eating well and exercising, friendship is a crucial part of my version of what we now call 'self-care'. Depression can leave you languishing in bed on your own for days, even weeks at a time, unable to participate in your own life or venture outside into society. Even when I'm languid with depression like that, I still try and book in safe little social interactions with friends — a WhatsApp chat, a Skype call, a coffee, a dinner, an afternoon screening of my main man Harry Styles in his first big movie, *Dunkirk* — to top up my feeling of existing. It's difficult, I'm not going to lie; socialising can be exhausting and you can still feel empty in the soul even when you're sitting in a sweet little café across from someone perfectly lovely, eating a cinnamon scroll.

Friendship doesn't cure mental illness, nor does love (no, Jennifer Lawrence's character did not quirkily cure Bradley Cooper's character of bipolar in that movie, *Silver Linings Playbook*). It's really important to make that point, on behalf of people who live with mental illness and addressed to the people who care about them: love is not medicine. Sadly, you cannot be adored out of depression, in much the same way you cannot simply 'snap out of it' or 'get it together'. It's a pernicious, stubborn illness that claws at you until you believe you may be alone in this world. But with all that self-doubt and self-harm and self-loathing going on, love and friendship can be exquisitely helpful. It can make the difference, sometimes between life and death. I do believe love can reach you, somehow, even when you're at your most vulnerable or destitute or angry. It is crucially important to love someone through their depression, to love someone in spite of their depression and sometimes, although it might sound odd, to love someone because of their depression. And when I say depression, substitute your own ailment, of course, may it be bipolar or schizophrenia or borderline personality disorder or anorexia or bulimia or anxiety or PTSD. The people who live with these things are brave human beings — believe me, it takes extraordinary courage just to survive when your brain is not producing or absorbing the right chemicals. They deserve love and friendship as much, if not more, than any other human.

Tragically, I just don't think that's happening. Not enough, not as a general rule. People are failing each other left, right and centre; they are abandoning, neglecting, abusing or wilfully forgetting their former or alleged friends for the precise reason they need them the most: their mental illness. People are frightened or confused or confronted by the presence of illness and choose to run away, rather than bunker down and be there. If you've ever lost someone you love, you'll notice a similar pattern in the way people deal with grief. They will offer their condolences all at once, in a rush, and send flowers, those delicate symbols of sympathy that die, too, just days after someone's brush with mortality. They go to the funeral, if they feel like it's necessary, and maybe they send a text or a card or a casserole afterwards to reiterate that they care. And then, generally, just when they should be stepping closer to the grief, they step away from it. Just when the ceremony of death is over and the real grief sets in, people tend to scatter. It's too confronting for them, or too difficult to know what to do, so they do nothing. It is a particular form of cowardice that people excuse as politeness or respect, and frankly I think it's not good enough. It's not difficult, actually, to do the right thing by someone who is in mourning. It's very simple: you keep being in that person's life, perhaps even more conspicuously than usual. You keep checking in on that person, keep making sure they've eaten, keep making yourself available to chat and even more importantly, to listen. You acknowledge how awful death is, you allow the person to talk about the void that's been left in their life and you gently but persistently make sure this person is not falling apart. It's a very similar protocol for people with mental illness: distance may be more comfortable for you and I'm sure you can convince yourself that it's polite or respectful, but it's not. Smothering someone isn't advisable either; I'm not advocating 24–7 surveillance of your depressed friend and I'm certainly not suggesting you cross any boundaries that person has put up in defence. What I am saying is that abandoning someone with a mental illness because it is too confronting or too weird or too hard is inexcusable.

Harriet first went to the GP, at the behest of her mother, at about 14 years old. Harriet had been hurting herself, she was depressed and she was being bullied at school. She would start taking anti-depressants two years later, at 16, attempt suicide at 18, and be admitted to an outpatient program for anorexia, bulimia and depression at 19. By the age of 21, she would have a new diagnosis: borderline personality disorder. She was put on more medication, this time anti-depressants and anti-psychotics. Throughout school, she felt like she had to hide her illness — kids can be cruel, and they were to Harriet. When she got to university, she was undone by a new sort of life, partying, drinking, taking drugs, starving and purging herself. She shrank to an extremely unhealthy weight, her hair started falling out, her nails turned blue and her brain started to fail her. She'd spend nights howling, she'd get into abusive relationships with older men, she'd become someone else, someone who was probably difficult to be around. Surely her friends started out being supportive, urging her to eat something, making sure she was okay. She can't remember exactly, because starvation can steal your memories like that. She does remember the friends she was living with at the time starting to ignore her, starting to leave her out of social events, starting to taunt her. She remembers how they'd stop talking whenever she walked into the kitchen and she definitely remembers the girl who used to stand outside her door and sing, maliciously, 'We're going out and you're not invited.' She remembers when they informed her they would no longer be living with her the next year and she remembers when they vanished from her life.

Harriet lost a lot of friends in those fledgling adult years, mostly because they thought she had become 'too much trouble'. A close friend told her she was pathetic and he wanted to shake her out of it; others called her a drama queen and an attention seeker. To these alleged friends, Harriet was an inconvenience and an embarrassment, right at a time in their lives when all they wanted to do was study hard enough to get their degrees and go out a whole bunch to find out who they were. They didn't have time, or make time, to look out for someone they used to care about, to make sure she was okay. They didn't make her feel comfortable enough or perhaps even give her the chance to explain that any abnormal behaviour on her part was due to the borderline personality disorder and the anorexia and the depression. That happens in young adulthood the world over; people not working out how to be there for someone who is going through an internal hell. They could have rallied around her for support, they could have shown her kindness, they could have made their shared home a safe space in which she could exist and confide in them. They didn't. Harriet has forgiven them, but frankly, on her behalf, I have not.

Luckily for Harriet, she has since found people who belong in her life, people who know how to look after her when she needs it. Her fiancé Matt has been an enormous support and so has her best friend, Ebony. At times, Matt and Ebony have colluded to make sure Harriet is alive and well, which is just the sort of teamwork required sometimes. Two years ago, they jumped in a car and drove all around Manchester, where Harriet lives, searching for her because she had gone AWOL. She had decided she was too much of a burden on the people in her life, so she had taken herself on a mission to disappear. Finally, in a stroke of genius that did not even occur to the police, Ebony decided to use 'Find my iPhone' software to locate Harriet. They brought her back to safety. At other times, during other episodes, Harriet has had friends come around to her place, clean her up and just sit with her. Sometimes this is all you need: a companion in the silence of pain.

I ask Harriet what she recommends people do, to actually be a good friend to someone with a mental illness like her. Research their condition, she says first. If you really care about them, open Google and start learning. It's not difficult; the public conversation about mental health is getting louder by the day and the Internet is swarming with great resources (Mind, Young Minds, the Mental Health Foundation and the NHS website in the UK; Beyond Blue, The Black Dog, Mind and the Australian government site in Australia; Mental Health America and the National Alliance on Mental Health in

America and a quick Google anywhere else). Harriet lost friends partly because they didn't understand what was going on with her, especially when she started to behave differently. If they'd educated themselves, perhaps things would have been different (I'm still mad at Harriet's former friends). Understanding what someone is going through — the effects of starvation on your brain, the way depression manifests as exhaustion, the physical effects of a panic attack — makes it easier to be there for them. Knowledge is extremely powerful for anyone living with a mental illness — to know what is happening to you and why you feel a certain way is to reclaim some of its power over you — and the same applies to the friends of those affected. Mental illness is still, despite how astonishingly common it is, shrouded in this shameful sort of mystery. As a friend, demystify and destigmatise it with knowledge. It is a great kindness, to try and understand what someone is going through.

The other things Harriet recommends are listening without judgment, offering advice if your friend is open to it, physically going around to hang out if they've had a bad day and understanding if they have to cancel plans because they're not well. She says it's really helpful for friends to encourage people to get professional help — and that is such an important one. I think perhaps some people assume that if they offer their services as a friend to someone with mental illness, they will end up shouldering all the responsibility for their survival. That's simply not the case and it shouldn't be. A friend can only function as a friend, not as a doctor or a therapist or a psychiatrist. Medical treatment, talk therapy and the prescription of medication are vital parts of a mental healthcare plan; the best gesture a friend can give is to point their beleaguered friend in the right direction of the appropriate services. Even better, if they can, accompany them to the doctor or pick them up from therapy for a cheer-up cupcake and a debrief. Friends should not be expected to take on the full brunt of mental healthcare; that's not the responsibility or the requirement here. They should, however, learn how to be there for someone in their capacity as a buddy.

To get some wisdom on this complicated matter, I rang Dr Andrew Solomon, psychiatrist and author of *The Noonday Demon: An Atlas of Depression*, as well as a number of other popular books on everything from politics to identity and child-rearing. He is also, if I may be bold enough to venture it, a sort of friend of mine. We once ate cheese toasties and cinnamon cake out of baskets in a Notting Hill café and spoke about the seasons of depression, love, hope and recovery. He is the single sagest voice on the topic of depression in the world right now, in my opinion. His TED Talk, 'Depression: The Secret We Share', is the greatest 29 minutes and 21 seconds you can possibly spend on your personal mission to understand depression. I have forwarded that video to my parents, my friends, my lovers and my bosses because it is the most elegant, cogent description of mental illness I could find. One of the things Andrew has said over and over is that depression is a disease of loneliness. When we talk — he in New York, me in London, a slight crackle on the line but otherwise all clarity — he is quick to point out that friendship is profoundly difficult when you're depressed.

Depression can sap the vitality that friendship usually requires, making it difficult if not sometimes impossible for the person to engage in normal social interaction. Love on its own is not, as I have said, a cure. People with plenty of friends still choose to end their lives; friendship does not guarantee survival and indeed depression coaxes you to hide all sorts of brutal realities from the people who care about you most. It is a cruel illness that can render you incapable of exactly the sort of human connection you need, and that is why friends of the depressed need to stick around, even through this ineptitude. That, to me, is the greatest mark of a true friendship: the tenacity to stay in someone's life, even though you may not necessarily feel welcome.

Now, I happen to know that Andrew has great love in his life and that it has truly helped him survive. His resilience through a lifetime of depression has been partly biological, partly the presence of other people — his husband, his friends, his children. Love, in the form of both romance and friendship, has been evidence for him that life is worth living, if only he can get well. It is an incentive to keep going; it is, if you'll excuse the cliché, the light at the end of a very dark tunnel. Friends give a person with mental illness the ability to see through their own despair, to glimpse a lighter, brighter reality in which they can actually enjoy company again — in which they might feel as though their life is their own. They are a reminder of a former lightness, too, an emblem of the life that came before the depression or anxiety or trauma. Good, stubbornly present friends are mascots of joy, ambassadors for normalcy and symbols of a life more fully lived. Perhaps we forget how transformative friendship can be for people with mental health problems because a doctor cannot prescribe it and a pharmaceutical company cannot monetise it or print its brand name on a pen or a mug. But we should reacquaint ourselves with its power, because friendship can be a lifeline.

Ever since Andrew has had a contact form on his website, he has received hundreds of emails from depressed people, many of whom are utterly isolated from the world. They get up every day, chemically depleted and alone, they go to a job where their only interaction is with a computer, they come home, make dinner, eat with the television for company, tuck themselves into bed alone and do it all over again the next day. For these people in severe social isolation, getting back into the throes of humanity might seem impossible. Even for people who are more socially integrated than that, it might seem that way. But depression lies to you like that. It is entirely possible to enter back into society. It takes courage and resilience and what might feel like a superhuman effort, but it's doable. You could start out getting a pet or, as Andrew suggests, even a potted fern might do. Just a living thing that depends on you for its survival, a living thing to demonstrate the basic process of staying alive. Harriet, who we met earlier, was once given a rose plant and she's kept it alive a full year. That's a genuine achievement, a helpful little reminder that something outside of her relies on her for sustenance. Watering that plant could be the only thing Harriet does on a bad day, but it's a gesture of survival and an act of hope. This is why I insist on getting a dog as soon as my living arrangements allow it; the very act of nurturing a little creature can give your days a purpose. Their little waggle tails and munchkin faces can give your heart a lightness you might have forgotten how to feel, too. Having a plant-based, canine or even, if you insist on it, feline, friend can be enormously helpful, but I would also recommend getting some human ones, when and if you can.

Doing that could be as simple as getting in touch with an old friend or gingerly setting up time to spend with a new one. It could be a to-and-fro of texts from the safety of your home that leads to some companionship when you're up to it. Or, if you're feeling brave enough, it could be an actual outing with a person you like. During a recent depressive episode, I made a concerted effort to see one friend per week for a coffee/wine/apricot danish. Actually speaking to another human being, even if it didn't fill me with joy because that emotion was unavailable to me at the time, was a matter of pride for me. It made me feel as though I was acting out the life I wanted to get back, the life I wanted to own again. And I was even able to chuckle a little, buoyed by the presence of someone who cared about me. It was tricky and possibly the last thing I felt like doing, but I treated it like a compulsory part of my mental healthcare regime, just like going to the gym, taking my meds and putting food in my mouth. It helped because it reminded me of the person I want to be.

Friendship is a human instinct, says Andrew, but it is also a skill — one that can be learnt and one that can be taught. As a parent, he believes one of his great responsibilities is to teach his children to understand how friendship works. We can do this, he says, by observing how kids behave and talking about the dynamics of social interactions. It's a process of praise and correction, as so much of parenting seems to be. He tells me about a sweet moment with his god-daughter, India, who was learning how to be a friend when he visited her recently. They were sitting on a sofa — Andrew, India and India's mum — and Andrew had been asking India a bunch of questions about her life. As you do, when you're interacting with a child. 'Now, remember one of the things we've been working on,' said India's mum. 'People like to be asked questions, too.' And so India thought for a moment and turned to Andrew. 'What things do you like most about your life?' she asked. A big question, to be sure, but a rather lovely example of a child being coached in the art of friendship. I particularly love this little anecdote because it reminds me of my childhood. You know how parents tend to dispense their favourite bits of advice so often as you grow up that you start remembering them like their own personal catchphrases? My dad used to tell my sister and me, again and again, to ask people questions. When in doubt, ask a question, he'd say; people love to be asked questions. When we were meeting a new person or catching up with a friend, he'd tell us to ask them questions. Obviously I listened to him; I essentially ask people questions for a living. That fatherly advice has been helpful to me literally on a daily basis; asking questions is how you put someone at ease, how you get to know someone, how to put listening ahead of talking. It is a basic gesture of interest in someone else's life and it is a seriously useful tool of friendship.

If you were looking for a way to be a good friend to a depressed person, you could do a lot worse than listen to India's mum and my dad. Gently asking how someone is and genuinely showing interest in their wellbeing is a very strong start to making them feel valued. From there, as Andrew reiterates, it's all about dogged persistence and conspicuous presence. A depressed person may well push you away. They might try and wriggle out of your friendship because they do not think they are worthy or capable of maintaining it. They might not be up to performing the rituals of friendship: coffee dates, phone calls, long chats over rosé. But just because they cannot or do not engage in the friendship in the way you're used to, doesn't mean they don't need it in their lives. In fact, that's when they need it the most.

A man came to Andrew and said, 'My daughter is depressed and she won't talk to me. I call her and she won't take my calls, what do I do?' Just as I would have, Andrew told the man to keep calling, every day. If the daughter doesn't answer the phone, leave a voicemail. If she doesn't return your call, pick up the phone the very next day and call again. Do not interpret her lack of contact as an excuse to give up. Do not take her inability to communicate as a sign that she needs to be left alone. Those voicemails, or even the notification on her phone that she has them, are little reminders that someone else wants her to continue existing. They are urgent little interruptions to a monotony of despair and they could just bring that man's daughter back from the brink. You must do the same with a friend; be in regular, kind, persistent contact regardless of whether it is reciprocated. Don't be brash about it and turn up at their door unannounced — that could be terrifying for someone feeling vulnerable. Contact your friend in a consistent but reasonable manner. I recommend WhatsApp, text, Facebook Messenger or even email because it's less invasive than a phone call or a visit. Just something that will infiltrate the loneliness of existing while depressed or anxious or whatever it may be.

The other thing Andrew and I would both recommend is to acknowledge the awfulness of the situation. So many people get it wrong with depression, just like they do with grief — they mean well, but they parrot these deeply unhelpful phrases like 'You'll be right as rain any day now' or 'Try not to worry so much.' Imposing cheer or nonchalance on a person who is chemically incapable of feeling it will only make them feel more bleak. Trivialising or ignoring the sadness they feel can just make them feel more alone. Try, instead, to directly acknowledge what they're going through. Say, 'I can only imagine how awful this must be for you' or 'This really sucks.' It can be incredibly validating to hear from another person that what you're going through is terrible. Offer your help, with the disclaimer that you know it may never be enough. Say, 'You know what, whatever I can do is insufficient, I get that, but I am here for you.' Being human and honest and realistic is much better than trying to erase the pain, when you both know that is not within your power. And then of course there is the practical help you could provide. Depressed or traumatised people can forget to eat, or exist on cookies, so bringing or preparing them fresh food is helpful. Checking whether they've eaten is helpful. Offering to drop around a batch of chicken soup without necessarily staying for chats is helpful. Caring for a friend with a mental illness is actually quite straightforward and quite similar to nursing someone with any illness; it's all about gestures of kindness. The main thing is not to be frightened or judgmental if your friend is, for instance, unable to get out of her pyjamas for days at a time.

And so, to the person in pyjamas. The person who lives with a mental illness. The person who may or may not be able to leave the house every day. There are a lot of us. If we all turned up in one place we'd make one great, almighty, seething army of human beings. Mental illness is a startlingly common affliction: it affects one in five Australians (though 45 per cent of Australians will experience a mental health issue over the course of their lifetimes), one in five Americans (that's 42.5 million people), and one in four British adults (disturbingly, 19 per cent of British adults thought 'one of the main causes of mental illness is a lack of self-discipline and willpower'). This is one of the great modern medical emergencies, with an alarming chunk of these sufferers either not seeking or not receiving appropriate professional care. Millions and millions of people exist in a chemically bereft state every day. Many of them probably feel alone in their experience of depression, anxiety or trauma; that feeling of utter isolation is just part of the deal. And because there is still prejudice, judgment and mystery shrouding the experience of mental health, many of these people probably feel ashamed of their condition. That shame only exacerbates the loneliness, and makes it more difficult to open up to the people around them.

Before we even get to the gestures of kindness we've spoken about that a person with a mental illness should expect and perhaps even chase, there's the matter of disclosure. A lot of people feel too embarrassed or uncomfortable to even tell their friends about what they're going through. Moments where they could have said, 'Mate, I've got to tell you something, I've got depression' or 'You know what? I've been feeling really fragile recently, maybe I should see someone' come and go unspoken in lives around the world. It's really difficult to be honest about emotional despair and there's still such a stigma around mental illness, it actually prevents people from telling each other what they're going through. According to a study done by the Mental Health Foundation in the UK, four out of 10 people were worried about telling their friends they live with a mental illness. One in three felt their friendships had become strained or had lost them altogether. These attitudes lead to a prominent silence between peers: One in four people only discovered their friend was having problems when they ended up in hospital and one in 20 only when they attempted suicide. Thirty-four per cent of the 543 people in this study said that they felt like they could tell none or very few of their friends about their mental distress. In fact, only 28 per cent said they could tell most of their friends.

This is all, if you ask me, down to the fear of vulnerability and the fear of judgment. According to the Stigma Shout Survey by the UK organisation, Time to Change, 87 per cent of people living with a mental illness reported the negative impact of stigma and discrimination because of their condition. That's a great walloping lot of people still being treated unfairly purely because their brains are broken. It is profoundly unfair and distressing, and only compounds the suffering of people living with a mental illness. It is also an alarming disincentive for them to talk to people, be they buddies or doctors. It makes it more difficult to function, to go to work, to fall in love and to engage in social interaction with the completely legitimate expectation of fair and just treatment. I believe this stigma is also the reason mental healthcare is so woefully underfunded by government bodies the world over, and so systematically deprioritised. A callous absence of compassion informs policy decisions just as powerfully as it motivates ordinary people to abandon their ailing friends.

And this brings me to an important point: mental healthcare is both a deeply private experience and a public health issue. It is absolutely crucial that we relearn to be kind to one another and educate ourselves on how to be there for someone with mental health issues. We have a profound personal responsibility to care for and contribute to the lives of the people around us, particularly the ones we do and could love. But it is also on our politicians, our governments, our businesses and our leaders to make change at a structural level that allows individual people to live fully and kindly alongside one another. That reality is both hopeful and frustrating — the powers that be actually have viable solutions to this mental health crisis, but they so often wilfully ignore them. The fact that experts do actually know what needs to be done is enormously comforting to me because if you think about the loneliness of depression long enough, you begin to think it might not be solvable.

To talk me through what can be done, I call Isabella Goldie, Development Director at the Mental Health Foundation in the UK. She was lead author of their report, 'Relationships in the 21st Century', which is essentially a manifesto on the importance of personal relationships for mental health and wellbeing. She has a Master's in public mental health from the University of Glasgow (she is very, very Scottish) and is a registered mental health nurse. In other words, when it comes to these issues, she knows where it's at. I kick off our phone call by quoting back my favourite line from the Foundation's report on the importance of relationships for mental health because I fancy it as our shared mission statement: 'As a society and as individuals, we must urgently prioritise investing in, building and maintaining good relationships and tackling the barriers to forming them.' I take a breath and then I ask, 'How do we do that, Isabella?' Fifty-six minutes of detailed explanation later, I have a much clearer idea. In short, we have to do better by our children, our parents, our neighbours, our refugees, our teenagers, our young people, our adults and our elderly. We have to embark on a broad-reaching, comprehensive campaign of structural kindness and emotional intelligence that reaches every demographic in society. That includes education programs, social and financial support for families, volunteer outreach programs for the elderly, city planning that explicitly prioritises social interaction, improved neighbourliness, empowering our school teachers, protecting our children and changing the conversation around immigration. To solve the crisis of mental healthcare, we need to be providing support at every stage of life.

Let's start at the beginning. Our capacity to form and maintain good, healthy social relationships begins at birth. In fact, if we're going to get finicky about it, it really begins before then, when our mothers get pregnant. Harmony and strength is essential in our lives even at the time of our conception and throughout our development in-utero, so it's vital that we are supporting prospective parents. If it were up to Isabella, mental health support would technically begin before conception, by empowering and educating parents-to-be on the importance of bonding and love for their children. Research confirms over and over how vitally important the beginnings of our lives are for social and psychological development. Attachment to our parents sets the template for how we will conduct ourselves in every relationship we ever have. We need to make parents aware that family relationships inform a child's capacity to form healthy relationships as they grow up, and put them in a position to provide the best possible love and care. Having a stable, secure, loving family life is key to a child's mental health and social intelligence. So the societal support really needs to start there, if we're going to enable the next generation of kids to grow into mentally resilient adults.

From there, when kids start going to school, their peer relationships become extremely influential. Isabella says this is when we must call on schools to enforce anti-bullying campaigns and protect their students from social rejection. Being bullied at school is a significant predictor of mental health issues later on, so it is extremely important we make sure kids aren't victimised or left behind in classrooms and playgrounds. We can do that by making teachers custodians of mental health and classroom harmony, by teaching them skills to deal with bullying and also how to nurture children and provide a mental-health friendly environment. Children's brains are wired to absorb and pick up cues from the adults around them, so it's also really important we look after the mental wellbeing of our teachers, too, who are already under immense pressure. There's a significant opportunity for schools to make a real difference in this regard, by becoming safe, socially inclusive spaces. When schools teach students about health and sexuality, they should also be running programs on the importance of friendships and healthy family relationships. The same should really be happening in our universities.

Then, of course, when children become adults, they spend most of their time at work. Isabella believes — and I agree with her — that we critically over-focus on productivity when it comes to objectives in the workplace. Scandinavian countries have lead by example, showing that if businesses invest in the emotional wellbeing of their employees, productivity is a pleasing by-product. If workplaces invest in things like team building and relationship forming as well as mental health policies that actually work, they see positive results, not to mention the fact that people would take fewer sick days to attend to their mental health. In fact, if Isabella could narrow our focus to three types of relationships in our life, it would be these: 1) the attachment we have with our parents; 2) the teachers we have at school; 3) our line managers at work. So long as those three relationships are healthy and supportive throughout a lifetime, you can promote mental health and social interaction at all the right times. As far as line managers are concerned, it would be great if they could take on more of a custodial role, supporting their employees on a personal level as well as professionally.

Outside of home, school and work, we used to have a delightful sense of community. The way we structure our modern lives and our public spaces has meant we have lost a lot of that. Governments are actively shutting down the venues we used to have for basic social interaction between neighbours, locals and strangers. Think about the closure of libraries, community centres, parks and post offices; places where people used to physically gather. Schools are being built without playgrounds and community spaces without access to nature are popping up. We have fewer outdoor and indoor spaces to actually congregate for the sort of natural, spontaneous social interaction that used to define community spirit. Isabella tells me about a property development in Sydney, Australia, which is specifically designed to enable the kind of living behaviour that's good for your mental health. They've made sure, when they're building places for people to live in the ever-growing city, that there is access to blue and green space, room for families to sit and eat together, and enough personal space to be conducive to harmony between co-habitants. That kind of emotionally intelligent city planning is precisely the sort of action we need to support mental health and social engagement on a structural level. We need to invest in our sense of community again, and build safe spaces for us to engage with our neighbours and our friends. Having a friendly relationship with a neighbour can improve your wellbeing, so it's absolutely worth making that happen.

There are other things we need to do to prevent mental illness and promote social wellbeing. We need to allow GPs to prescribe social activities, like yoga or mindfulness classes or book clubs. We need to run volunteer befriending programs for the elderly, so they don't suffer so much from social isolation. We need to campaign for a more inclusive, compassionate approach to refugees, for whom loneliness can be a major problem, particularly if there are language barriers between them and their new community. We need to run a concerted, dedicated public health campaign on the importance of social interaction for our mental, psychological and physical health. Because this concerns all of us. Mental illness does not just affect the person stuck in their pyjamas at home, destitute because their psyche is broken. Mental illness is not just me, lying in bed at home, gorging myself on cookies and contemplating what it would be like to stop living. Mental illness is a public health crisis that deserves the urgent attention of our leaders and our friends.

CHAPTER ELEVEN

Friends with health benefits

LET'S TAKE A LITTLE TRIP to Sardinia, an island about 321 kilometres off the coast of Italy. It's got the kind of rustic, lyrical beauty you can only get in the Mediterranean, and in the summer it has its trademark heat. Specifically, let's visit Villagrande, a little Sardinian village that takes up about 211 square kilometres of Earth. It's home to a population of roughly 4,000 people, an unusual number of whom are over the age of 100. The extraordinary thing about this little Sardinian village is that it's the only place in the world where the men live as long as the women (whereas usually women live six to eight years longer than men) and there are more than six times the amount of centenarians living in Villagrande than on the Italian mainland. In fact, oddly, there are 10 times more centenarians living in Villagrande than there are in North America. It's a strange, beautiful little concentration of people living beyond their 100th birthdays. A geographical anomaly that might just hold the secret to living a long life.

For psychologist Susan Pinker, this phenomenon in Villagrande was fascinating enough to warrant a visit. She packed her bags, got a visa, convinced her daughter to join her and went on a little research trip to find out exactly why so many people in this little village, on this little island, live so long. When Pinker arrives, she has the distinct feeling of being watched through the gaps between curtains and shutters. She walks through this densely populated little place, which is crowded with buildings that sit very close to one another, and senses how cohesive and how close these villagers are. It is truly the kind of intimacy you can only find in a small rural town or a seaside village, the kind where everyone's business is public and real privacy is sacrificed for the proximity of neighbours and friends and family. Villagrande is a remarkable place, where everybody seems to know each other. And so it isn't difficult to interview many centenarians, their families and their friends, inevitably in their kitchens because they're Italian. You speak to one, you get to speak to them all, that's how these villages work.

And so, Pinker interrogated the oldest people in Villagrande, one by one, usually with their sons, daughters, aunts, nephews, great-nieces, granddaughters or cousins nearby. She thinks she found the answer to super longevity, and it's not what she expected when she set out. She started out thinking that perhaps the secret to a long life might be positivity, a cheery disposition that gets you through life's mundane stretches. Apparently not, according to the curmudgeonly 101-year-old man who was, Susan says, the grumpiest person she's ever met. We cannot possibly reach 100 by way of positive affirmation or optimism, if this man is anything to go by. Perhaps the secret is in a low-fat, low-carb, gluten-free diet, she thought. Nope, apparently not that either, she realises when she meets a nonna over the age of 100 who every Sunday makes culurgiones, the local specialty: big parcels of pasta crimped round the edges and filled with ricotta and mint, doused in tomato sauce, which she distributes to people throughout the village. No, in fact, the longevity of these Italian lives has nothing to do with diet, weight, exercise, or even whether they smoke or drink, though of course all those factors might be relevant. The reason these people are living so long, according to Pinker, is because they are so comprehensively socially integrated. Not one of the centenarians she interviewed has been left to grow old alone; they are all surrounded by friends and cared for by their families. They usually live with family members, be they children, siblings, grandchildren, nieces or nephews, and they are frequently visited by others. The physical proximity of the people they love — remember those crowded buildings — and the culture of family intimacy means these villagers are escaping loneliness. They are living proof of something we have come to realise about humanity: that our greatest chance at survival is companionship.

Relatively new research from all over the world suggests friendship has a very real and powerful effect on our physical health. Especially, in a poetic sort of way, on our heart health. It is particularly lovely, I think, that friendship has cardiovascular health benefits because we so often refer to the organ that pumps blood around our bodies as a place of love. It is fitting that we should bolster our hearts with camaraderie. As it turns out, having a stable, warm, high-quality social network can not only improve heart health, but also give you a potentially stronger defence against Alzheimer's disease, delay cognitive disrepair, make you fitter, lower your chances of obesity, change your dietary habits, lower your blood pressure and give you a higher pain threshold. Having friends is every bit as important as getting regular exercise and having a nutritionally balanced diet. It is, science tells us, imperative for our survival.

Let me hit you with a bit of research. For starters, let's look at a 2010 meta-analysis of 148 studies covering 300,000 people who were tracked for seven and a half years. Researchers at Brigham Young University in the United States, led by Dr Julianne Holt-Lunstad, looked at all that data linking socialisation to mortality factors and concluded that having social connections makes you live longer — they're not sure how much longer, but the mere fact that friends can literally extend the amount of time we exist here on Earth is impressive enough for now. Holt-Lunstad and her team took into account all sorts of lifestyle and health factors such as bad lifestyle habits, mental health and pre-existing physical conditions and then essentially waited seven and a half years to see who was left standing. In that time, they found there was a 50 per cent increased likelihood of survival for participants with stronger social relationships. This remained consistent across sex, age, initial health status and cause of death. The impact of friendship on the risk of death is comparable with well-established risk factors for mortality like alcohol consumption and smoking. The link between social interaction and mortality is stronger than other, more renowned risk factors like physical inactivity and obesity. In fact, social integration and close relationships are the two most important predictors of mortality, well above things like alcohol consumption, exercise and diet. Julianne Holt-Lunstad decided to look into this issue in the first place because she suspected much of what Susan Pinker concluded on the island of Sardinia: that our level of social integration is profoundly linked to our rates of mortality. Holt-Lunstad believes the way we live in most industrialised countries, so often far-flung from our families and therefore separated from our natural support networks, is making us increasingly socially isolated and in more and more cases, lonely. More people in industrialised countries are living alone, which obviously increases their chances of becoming isolated and lonely. She thinks that while, as a society, we recognise traditional mortality risk factors like obesity and physical inaction as real threats to our health, we are yet to publicly acknowledge the effects of loneliness. This ignorance, this blind spot in our public consciousness, is potentially very dangerous.

Having close friendship support is equivalent, in health terms, to giving up smoking. People who reported having an adequate number of good friends also had lower rates of heart disease, fewer infections and illnesses thanks to a stronger immune system, less abnormal inflammatory responses to stress and lower rates of dementia. It seems as though being social reduces the harmful effects of stress because friendship can literally guard us from that nasty little hormone called cortisol that sends our stress levels skyrocketing. Friendship can also act as a powerful pain reliever, perhaps even more effective at relieving pain than morphine. Oxford PhD student Katerina Johnson conducted a remarkable study in 2016 on the link between friendship groups and pain relief. She rounded up a group of participants and quizzed them on the size and quality of their friendship groups and interactions, asking them to identify who and how many people they could go to in a crisis, for example. After Johnson and her team had established the strength or weakness of the participants' social ties, they got them to perform a simple endurance test: stand with your back against a wall with your legs bent so the body weight is resting on the thighs. The team timed how long participants could stay in this surprisingly painful position and found the ones with stronger friendship connections were able to tolerate the physical discomfort for longer. They controlled for other factors like physical fitness and the results remained the same, leading them to conclude that strong friendship associations can increase our tolerance of pain. This could very well be something to do with the dopamine and oxytocin that contact with other human beings releases in our systems, a primal reaction to intimacy that generates feelings of trust and comfort in us. The better buoyed we are by friendship, the better prepared we are for physical pain because our bodies are in better condition to withstand it.

Friendship has surprisingly tangible effects on the physicality of being human. As we've covered so far, it can improve heart health and alleviate physical pain. It is also a strong positive influence on our behaviour patterns and our habits. We are, practically speaking, more likely to conduct ourselves in a healthy way if we have friends because there's a sweet sort of peer pressure that makes us more inclined to eat well, leave the house, exercise, take our medication, shower and generally make ourselves tolerable, vaguely presentable human beings to be around. I can personally attest to that one: the prospect of seeing friends is (sometimes, but not always) enough to raise me from a depressive and/or slothful stupor to put clothes on, physically remove myself from my flat, go out into the world, move my body, eat good things and stimulate my brain with some good old-fashioned conversation. Speaking of which, science also suggests that friendship may contribute to building up a 'cognitive reserve', which is like a cool little stash of mental energy we mightn't have otherwise. Mentally stimulating activities like feeling, thinking, sensing and talking — all of which you do in the presence and at the behest of your buddies — can build up a reserve of healthy brain cells and promote the formation of new synapses. It is all very, very good for you.

Meanwhile, in another study, 60 international students arrive in Montreal, Canada. They're there to go to university, where they'll hopefully make the sorts of friends you hold onto for life. Those sublime, important friendships you make just as you're becoming an adult, when your identity is trying to settle. These students are as alone as you can be in a new city, though; they've been specifically selected because they have no family or friends in Montreal and they're not in a romantic relationship. They are, as far as one could tell from looking at a group of strangers, as likely as possible to be lonely in their new Canadian home. When they first arrive, researchers from Concordia University give them questionnaires about their social networks — things like how many people they see and speak to each week. They also measure their heart rates and book them in for a further two appointments. Two and five months later, these ostensibly lonely students return to the researchers for further questioning and another heart-rate test. The purpose, of course, is to test how making friends is affecting their heart health. The study, published in the *Annals of Behavioural Medicine*, showed that those students who became better integrated socially had better heart health. The researchers measured something called heart rate variability, which is the time between each beat of the heart. Having low heart rate variability is not good; it can be a predictor of poor heart health. High frequency heart rate variability (HF-HRV if you fancy an acronym) is a marker of how well your parasympathetic nervous system is functioning. People with more friends at the two- and five-month marks after moving to Montreal had better heart rate variability than those who remained lonely — which is a clear and very interesting connection between cardiovascular health and friendship.

Jean-Philippe Gouin, lead researcher on this study, which was conducted between Concordia University in Montreal and Rush University Medical Centre in Chicago, couldn't help but dispense some advice to his lonely subjects after he'd listened to their hearts beating. Reach out to people, he said, especially at this stage in your life. The more quickly you manage to integrate socially (make buddies, collect pals) in your new home, the healthier you'll be. That certainly does seem to be good advice, which is given further weight the more science goes about the business of testing the importance of social connection for human beings. Gouin and his team are actually not the only ones who have sought to find a connection between heart health and companionship. A three-year Swedish study concerning 13,600 women and men found that people who reported having only a few or no close friends increased their risk of having a first-time heart attack by 50 per cent. Another two-year study of 500 women with suspected coronary artery disease reported that those women with the lowest levels of social support were twice as likely to die during the study. Women with good levels of close friendship support were not only more likely to survive the study, they also had lower rates of high blood pressure and diabetes, and were less likely to have excessive abdominal fat.

Four studies done at the University of North Carolina by an academic called Yang Claire Yang, featuring hundreds of thousands of people aged 12 to 91, found significant evidence of friendship's health benefits. Yang compared biomarkers such as blood pressure, body mass index, waist circumference and levels of the inflammation marker C-reactive protein in groups of people with and without friends, and found they were all considerably worse in people with weaker social ties. A study in the 2015 medical journal *Proceedings of the National Academy of Science* found that a lack of social connections more than doubled the risk of a person developing high blood pressure. Those social ties that keep us healthier throughout life also have the capacity to literally keep us alive longer, too. A 2012 study conducted by researchers at the Kaiser Permanente division of research in North Carolina looked at 4,530 women with breast cancer and found that women with stronger social support had significantly lower rates of mortality than those without friends. Researchers asked the participants questions about who in their lives would listen to them when they needed to talk, be there for them in times of crisis, and lend them money or give them a place to stay when they needed it. Quite simply, the ones who answered those questions positively outlived the ones who didn't. When you put all of this together, the revelation is startling and the evidence is plentiful: friendship is extremely good for your overall physical health.

Friendship is also, as it turns out, extremely good for your brain health. An academic called Ugo Lucca and his team at the Istituto di Ricerche Farmacologiche in Milan, Italy, looked into the correlation between strong social ties and dementia. Lucca's team recruited all residents over the age of 80 in the eight municipalities of the Varese province in Italy for their study. Psychologists collected data from them all, questioning subjects about the presence of friends in their life and how often they had contact with them. As is standard, they used that hefty medical bible, the DSM-IV, to diagnose dementia. Of the 958 non-demented elderly subjects, 28 per cent said they had no friends at all. Within three years, 41 per cent of subjects without friends became demented, as opposed to 28 per cent of people who had at least one friend. These results stayed significant even after factoring in age, sex and level of education as well as the presence of diabetes, hypertension, Parkinson's disease, depressive symptoms and a history of stroke. The conclusion the researchers made is this: having at least one friend is linked with a delay in the incidence of dementia in the very old.

A study of 2,249 Californian women published in the *American Journal of Public Health* in 2008 corroborates that link. Over four years of interviews, researchers found that women with good social networks reduced their risk of dementia and delayed or prevented cognitive impairment. Participants were asked things like, 'How many people can you rely on?' and 'How often do you talk to friends?' to ascertain the strength of the women's friendship networks, and then assessed for risk of dementia. Women with social networks were 26 per cent less likely to develop dementia and women in daily contact with friends cut their risk of dementia by half. Half! A 2012 study in the Netherlands followed 2,000 people over the ages of 65 over three years. None of the participants had dementia when they started the study but, by the time it ended, 13.4 per cent of those who said they were lonely developed dementia, compared to 5.7 per cent of the people who said they had friends. It's difficult to say, definitively, what exactly protects someone from dementia. The scientists involved in this study suggest friendship is powerful here because it promotes healthier behaviour. Having friends, particularly as you age, will more likely inspire you to live an active, healthy lifestyle — especially if they're looking after themselves, too. Wellbeing is contagious among friends. Exercise stimulates the formation of synapses, enhances blood flow in the brain and increases the formation of nerve cells — so getting out for a walk in the park with friends (or a walk to the pub, as the case may be) is extremely beneficial. Social interaction can help to protect the ageing brain in much the same way doing puzzles and playing word games can.

In fact, the more we look into it, the more obvious it becomes that friendship is especially important as we get older. William Chopik, Assistant Professor in Psychology at Michigan State University, conducted two studies on friendship. In the first, he got 271,000 people from more than 100 countries involved in an extensive questionnaire about friendship, their lives and their health. He asked about who people had to confide in, how happy they were, how healthy they were and whether they suffered from any chronic conditions like heart disease or stroke. Chopik found that people who valued friendship more in life functioned better as a whole, indicating to him that friendship has a very real effect on our health. In the second study, Chopik spoke to 7,481 older adults and found that friendship support predicted higher subjective wellbeing over an eight-year period. That is to say, more casually, that people with buddies were healthier overall than the lonely and the friendless. People who felt the strain of their friendships, or indeed the absence of friendship altogether, were more likely to develop chronic illness over a six-year period. Chopik tells me over the phone one Michigan morning that friends are actually more important than family as we age. Our social ties are stronger predictors of happiness than our relationships with spouses or family members, particularly as we get older.

Earlier on in life, friendship makes us a little bit happier, but as we get older and reach, say, our forties, the difference between the people with mates and the people without is extremely noticeable. He suspects this is because our friendships are selective relationships, so we are more likely to extricate ourselves from the toxic ones over time and keep the ones that are good for our health and wellbeing. We naturally shrink the size of our social networks over time, probably focusing more on the quality of those connections than the quantity. We tend to trim back our friendships at certain junctures in our life spans, like when we get married, move away from home or get a new job. Friends are either actively decommissioned or they simply fade from our everyday lives until they no longer really qualify as friends. Either way, we tend to get better at quality control as we age and keep the people in our lives who make us feel healthier and happier. Chopik thinks this is probably down to that sweet revelation that comes with age and wisdom: that life is short, too short for bad friends.

There is other evidence to support the view that, as we age, friendships are a more significant factor in our health than our connections to family members and our partners. An Australian study from 2005, for example, looked at the lives and friendship patterns of more than 1,500 women and men over the age of 70. Researchers from the University of Adelaide and Flinders University interviewed participants once a year for four years and then every three years after that, always asking about their closeness to friends, family and their spouse. The study found that more than any factor, including family and their beloved, the

THE FRIENDSHIP CURE

size and strength of the subject's circle of friends predicted their survival a decade into the study. Really, this should be a stark reminder to avoid social isolation and loneliness as we age and a prompt to perhaps visit your grandmother, but it should also form the basis of a new, urgent approach to healthcare and social policy. If friendship connections and the intimacy of lifelong friendship is this vital to our health, it should be classified as preventive medicine and inspire social policy makers to prioritise campaigns that promote connectedness, kindness and social outreach. You can barely read a newspaper, go on social media or exist in the outside world without seeing some sort of reference to diet, exercise, weight management and smoking. These are all highly publicised personal behaviours that have crossed over into the territory of public policy. We take them extremely seriously; enough to run national campaigns to get people eating their five a day, moving their bodies, staying within a healthy weight range and giving up their little tar-lined nicotine sticks. But we have no such public acknowledgment of the dangers of social isolation and consequently no proactive campaigns to get people to prioritise social interaction for the sake of their physical and mental health. That needs to change — urgently. This is one of those issues that touches both our private and public lives; loneliness is a deeply private affliction but it has far-reaching and sinister effects on public health, morale, population, productivity and the economy. It is our responsibility as individuals to practise smart, consistent social integration, now and as we age, but it is also extremely important that we have structural support from the government, our leaders and the healthcare system.

Becoming socially isolated is as dangerous as smoking 15 cigarettes a day. We have been warned that ingesting tar, smoke and nicotine is extremely damaging to our physical health. Now we need that sort of awareness for the threat of social isolation. If we are going to lead the fullest, happiest, healthiest lives we can possibly lead — if we have any hope of celebrating our 100th birthdays like our Sardinian villager friends — then we have to recognise the vital importance of friendship, companionship and social integration now, for ourselves, the people we know and love, and the strangers watching their lives dissipate into loneliness. So, make like a 102-year-old Sardinian nonna and make it past the century mark by protecting yourself with friendship, spending time with family, staying close to people you know and placing urgent value on the quality of your closest relationships.

CHAPTER TWELVE

Happily ever after

ON THE 22ND OF OCTOBER, 2015, something changed me. I had made Hyde Park my office for the day and was sitting underneath a tree, in extremely picturesque circumstances. It was a rare sunny day in London, but crisp and a little bit cool. Cyclists and picnickers, lovers and families, tourists and pensioners were scattered across the grass, all engrossed in their own lives. They weren't to know that I was about to read a horrifying article on the subject of friendship breakdown. The headline read: 'How Friendships Change in Adulthood (We *need* to catch up soon!)' and it was by Julie Beck for *The Atlantic*. It was a very good article, for the record, it just happened to alight in me a singular fear: that my current golden age of friendship might end one day and I'd be stranded in the territory of real adulthood without my soul buddies. In the article, Beck writes: 'The voluntary nature of friendship makes it subject to life's whims in a way more formal relationships aren't. In adulthood, as people grow up and go away, friendships are the relationships most likely to take a hit. You're stuck with your family, and you'll prioritise your spouse.' So basically, a marriage certificate and blood ties will keep your spouse and family in your life but there's nothing quite so legally or genetically binding to keep your friendships locked down. Your friendships will be the first things to go when shit gets real in life. With this bleak but possibly realistic argument, Julie Beck seemed to lay out my future as one without secure friendships. It felt like she was talking directly to me. When you get married and have kids, Kate Leaver, if you choose to do so, you will watch as your beloved friends fall away from your life. Your identity will shrink every time you type the words 'we really need to catch up' until it's just you, a battered maternal instinct and one other person to whom you are legally bound.

And so I sat beneath my tree, whipping through this manifesto on the disappearance of friendship as we age, dry retching and texting my close friends elaborate plans for some sort of platonic marriage-like pledge of solidarity with a clause built in to ensure a minimum number of contact hours a week until roughly 2065. I made desperate little vows to myself that I would never let this friendless future eventuate; that I would always keep the friends I've spent so long loving in my life, front and centre. Julie Beck's elegantly written horror story about ageing into friendlessness frightened me into a promise to myself and my buddies: that I would always find a way, no matter what, to keep my friends in my life. Even if it meant somehow reversing or rejecting the natural progression of life as we know it. This whole revelation was, in some part, the very reason for this book's existence.

Don't get me wrong, I get it. I can see why friendships might get bumped down the priority list when people find their beloved, settle down, throw a party where they declare eternal love to one another and then possibly make some tiny human beings in their image. We allow romantic love to supersede other types of love in many instances and maybe it's necessary, even lovely, to devote more time to your partner as you build a life together. The activities that make up romantic togetherness are time-consuming and the feelings that come with it seem bigger than others, somehow. It happens every time we get into a significant romantic relationship: on average, we lose three friends when we start seriously seeing someone new. That makes sense, if you think about the nature of love or if you've ever seen a Rachel McAdams film. The initial stages of romance and courting can be all-consuming. You suddenly find this person you like and there's all this irresistible chemistry and you just want to go on picnics and gaze at each other and flirt and hold hands all the time. And all of that is wonderful. So wonderful that dates tend to take up a special place in the social calendar, above other forms of social interaction, like seeing people you don't want to shag. It's just the way things are: our romantic lives seem to take precedence over our other social engagements when we are all floaty and happy and falling in love. I don't begrudge someone a little all-consuming romance; all I'm saying is that perhaps it makes us develop a dangerous habit of prioritising romantic love over all else, including ourselves and what we might truthfully need. I'm trying not to sound bitter or heartless or even unsentimental here — I love love, love is great. I am currently in love — it's a glorious feeling and it makes my life better every day. My beloved is a terrific human being and

I am a better person for having him around. But! I would never treat my boyfriend as though he were my everything in life, as though he could single-handedly satisfy all my emotional needs, as though he is the one person I need in my life to survive.

For some reason — rabid sentimentality and Hugh Grant's career have a lot to do with it — this idea, that one person could be your all, is supposed to be romantic. We, as a society, are utterly transfixed by it. We are so desperate to track down The One that we sacrifice other relationships and little pieces of our identity along the way. Someone told me recently that she stayed in a bad relationship because she liked the story of the way they met too much to leave him; that's how deeply rom-com morals have infiltrated our psyches (rom-coms are great — when I am old I will hit play on the film *Leap Year* starring Amy Adams and a handsome Irishman and watch it on repeat until I die — but I do think they've fed us some damaging ideals). In reality and with overwhelming likelihood, there are multiple suitable partners for each human being and it is a nonsense to abdicate the responsibility of choosing one to some sort of fate or destiny. And I do think this is happening; people genuinely leave the rather important life-partner decision partially if not completely up to the universe, as though it's sentient and might know best what they need in a companion. Intelligent, good people do this all the damn time, wildly interpreting quirks of behaviour or circumstance as 'signs' that they should be with someone, instead of scrupulously choosing who they want to be with based on a very diligently thought out criteria of things like kindness, compatibility and integrity. A friend of mine has always said she chose her husband with her head, not her heart. She deliberately, strategically turned a good friend of hers into a love interest because he had the qualities she most admired and desired in another human being. She auditioned many men by way of dating, but settled on the one who made the most sense for the future she wanted. She also made her friends an enormous part of the process, and continues to do so now that they are married. This is how we should really all be conducting ourselves when it comes to love — with a deliberate, if somewhat unsentimental, intelligence. Frankly, it's irresponsible to do otherwise.

Marriage (and when I say marriage, I also mean long-term relationships and de facto couples) has changed a lot in the past century. It used to be a more transactional affair, an exchange of property, wealth and intimacy between a man and a woman that usually resulted in children. It could be a rather formal, mercenary, even grim sort of relationship as a woman was essentially passed from her father to her husband like an accessory or a possession. Indeed, in parts of the world, this is still the case. For many of us, though, we are privileged to be able to marry/settle down for love and increasingly, I think we are doing it for friendship, too. Go to any engagement party, wedding or love celebration and you are almost guaranteed to hear about how excited the betrothed are to 'marry their best friend'. Our spouses and long-term, live-in partners are allies and confidants in a way they never necessarily used to be. That closeness is a modern phenomenon and has largely been enabled by the progression of women's rights. Women are now able to be equal participants in a marriage (though overwhelmingly the domestic chores and child-rearing duties fall to them both in greater volume and with a more persistent social pressure). This means we are able to expect and cultivate an emotional bond in marriage that hasn't necessarily always been there. And that's extremely lovely. Again and again, research tells us that marriage and co-habitation increase our happiness and wellbeing. But, the thing is, the by-product of all this loveliness is that now we expect one person to be the Swiss Army Knife of partners: best friend, lover, co-parent, confidant, therapist, problem solver, drinking buddy, travel companion, financial advisor, career cheerleader, mentor, spirit animal, one true love. We have come to expect the person we spend our lives with to satisfy all our emotional needs, which puts enormous pressure on one relationship and in my opinion (perhaps being a child of divorce with two step-parents and three step-siblings has somewhat influenced me here), sets it up to fail. We are complex social animals, humans, and we need to get our emotional, psychological, intellectual and social stimulation from multiple sources. Rather than putting all our eggs into one basket and hoping for the best, we should be distributing our love more sensibly and more widely. Put some eggs in your friends' baskets, is what I'm saying here. Treat friendship as a non-negotiable in your life because it can be an invaluable source of strength, resilience, love and wisdom.

A venture capitalist friend of mine once put it beautifully. We need to diversify our happiness portfolio, he said, rather pleased with himself, I think, at his wisdom. He was actually talking about our satisfaction with our careers at the time, but I'm going to appropriate it for my own purposes here. We need to invest our love and hope and vitality into more diverse accounts, to better our chances of return on investment. Putting all our emotional resources into a single other person is simply not a safe or smart bet, if you're looking at it with a ruthless sort of pragmatism (which we should, more often than we do). Our staggering divorce rates prove that romantic relationships fail all the time, everywhere in the world (see also: the period of global mourning that followed the demise of Anna Faris and Chris Pratt's seemingly perfect marriage for an idea of how profoundly we elevate these types of relationships and do not expect them to crumble). And then what? What happens when you've put everything you have into that one relationship and it falls apart? Then you have to pick up the pieces of your identity, take a deep breath and work out how the hell to get back the people you abandoned when you fell in love. You have to rebuild your life without that one person you'd chosen as a romantic partner, without that one person you'd made the centre of your existence — and that can be excruciatingly hard. It would be much easier — still hard, still hard, but easier — to recover from a relationship breakdown if you already have a solid support network in place. If you have several other healthy friendships going on in your life, then you have something to fall back on, rather than having to scramble some together at short notice when your major relationship breaks up. You have people to help pick up the pieces and move on. You have a more complete life. You have to plan for these sorts of things in life, because they can happen to anyone.

All of this realism has to start when you very first get together with someone — that's when you really decide how much space in your life they will take up. It certainly has to happen before your wedding day: you can't just throw a big party where you declare your love for someone in front of all the other people you adore without acknowledging that you need everyone in that room. As a small side note, a lot of married people have told me that working out the guest list for their wedding has been a task in friendship appraisal: it's one of those big lifetime milestone events and it's also bleeding expensive so you tend to only invite people you actually care about (throw in a few you are obliged to invite for reasons of awkwardness or family connection) and want to be there. Several people said they actually realised friendships were over or had run their course while they were listing the people who would get invitations to their wedding. It's an exercise in self-awareness, really, and you have to look at who is in your life and who deserves to be. The same goes for any significant party or event you throw — if you're arriving at an age with a zero at the end, for example — because they seem to have this way of coaxing us into working out who matters enough to attend. Use that! Give a party a purpose and do a little friendship audit while you're planning which sparkling rosé to get.

Not being married myself, I sought wisdom on the matter of friendship and marriage from, fittingly, my friends. A great number of kind strangers from the Internet were also willing to help me dispel my fear that you lose friends when you tie the knot. It does happen, judging by my poll of married people; friends do tend to drop off as you enter that chapter of your life. It can be a logistical thing: maybe people move away to be with their beloved, maybe they dedicate more time to relationship maintenance than friendship upkeep, maybe they're consumed by some sort of life obstacle like depression or infertility or financial difficulty and they sort of nestle, hermit-like, into their relationships. Maybe they become flippant about their friendships because they're distracted by how charming their love-friend is, maybe they stop seeing the point in friendships that were predicated on being single, maybe they change their minds about what they want from their mates. Encouragingly, a lot of people actually said it wasn't a horrible accident of circumstance, an erosion of friendship by negligence. A lot of people deliberately culled friends when they got married because something about that grown-up party made them re-evaluate who they wanted in their lives. I'm all for a strategic friendship cull when and if you have people in your life who shouldn't be there — for every piece of evidence we have that says friendship is good for us, there is an equally damning one that says bad, abusive, negative or toxic ones are doing us harm. So if getting married inspires you to do a little friendship audit of your life, that's great. It has always been and will always be about the quality of the friendships you have, not the quantity of them. It's the ones we let go out of laziness, negligence, ignorance or nonchalance that concern me. It's the ones we sacrifice at the altar of all-consuming romantic love.

My friend Amy seems to have nailed the marriage–
friendship balance particularly well. She has a healthy, loving
relationship with her husband, Garry, and a lot of delightful,
strong friendships to buoy her up. Contrary to the narrative
we are so often expected to write for ourselves, Amy actually
didn't consider her wedding a happy ending. It was not, as
she so rightly points out, an ending at all. Her marriage to
Garry (whom I desperately want to call Gazza because I'm
Australian like that) was not the glowing, fairytale ending
we're meant to have, if we are to obey the industrial marriage
complex imposed on all women from a very early age. It was
a beautiful, important day, but Amy simply never thought of
it as a culmination of anything. It wasn't a beginning, exactly,
either, because Amy and Garry already had a life together. A
life that featured everyone who attended that wedding, not just
Gaz. Amy didn't actually expect anything to change when she
got married and perhaps that's the secret: it's a continuation
of the life you've built with someone you love very much and,
as such, nothing much should really change. Including your
friendships. Amy is a writer and so I particularly love it when
she gets all lyrical with me: 'I love my husband dearly,' she says,
'but he's the person I'm building my life *with*, not the person
I'm building it *around*.' That is such an important distinction to
make, and it is music to my ears. Amy and Garry are partners
in love, but neither is relying entirely on the other to fulfil their
every emotional need. They're totally wild about each other. In
fact, when we speak, Amy is actually at the supermarket and
she tears up in one of the aisles just thinking about how much

Garry means to her. But in her heart of hearts, Amy knows that if they split up, she'd be okay because she knows she can live without him. She'd be heartbroken but she'd fix herself, with the help of her friends and family. The day we chat, she's actually meeting up with a friend — a man! — without her husband and then going to swim laps by herself. Amy and Garry often have little friendship outings on their own like this, and it's really important for their relationship. Garry is a policeman and he often works the night shift, so Amy has quite a bit of time to herself, which she often fills with friendship catch-ups. She and Garry have been together eight years, so they've found a rhythm in their relationship that works for them and they have always allowed each other time and emotional space to have separate friendships in their lives. Amy thinks it's about respect: her husband respects her enough to realise she needs friends and time to spend with them, and in turn she does the same for him. She never saw her friendships as stopgaps until she got married, she's always loved them and intends to keep them in her life forever.

Amy and Garry have made gestures towards that eternity throughout their relationship: on her wedding day, Amy danced with her girlfriends because Garry's not much of a dancer and the day after, instead of absconding together in the direction of a sunset, they had a roast lunch with their friends. They even had a little clause in their wedding vows to make sure they get to keep their friends around. It went a little something like this: 'Family who are friends and friends who are family, before you stand two people who love you very much and who I'm sure you will agree have brought as much joy to your lives, as I know you have to theirs. Will you promise to support their relationship and inspire their future? To love them not only as individuals, but as husband and wife? To be their friends and confidants today, tomorrow, and every day to follow?' The congregation of more than 100 people all answered with a chorus: 'We will.' That clause is the closest thing to a friendship contract I've seen — except for two dudes in the Netherlands who drew themselves up a literal friendship contract, signed it and had it made legally binding, but that's not as sweet a story. The very act of going to someone's wedding is an implicit gesture of support for their love, but I do like the ones that actively involve the friends and especially this one that made everyone promise to stick around forever and ever and ever.

Maintaining friendships forever and ever and ever is a challenge, though. Loneliness as we get older is a very real and devastating problem. As we age, we tend to shed friends, as we go for quality over quantity and get better at working out who is good for us and who is not. We could, all of us, find ourselves at the end of our lives alone — and so we must act now, and urgently, to stop our own possibly bleak futures from eventuating. Holding onto our good close friends (apparently it's four for middle-aged women, six for middle-aged men) requires deliberate, strategic time management. Getting married or getting into a serious, committed, long-term relationship is one way to deplete the time you spend with buddies; having kids is another altogether. Boy oh boy, oh boy, oh boy, becoming a parent is hectic. It seems to be one of the most time-consuming, all-consuming things a human being can do with their lives. If the testimonies of people I've spoken to, people I've known and the general public consensus on the matter are anything to go by, parenthood can completely change the way you see the world and therefore the people in it. It can change your priorities, big time. Suddenly you have these tiny humans you cherish and not only have you got to keep them alive, you also want to be there for every waking moment just in case they do something adorable for the first time, like walk or talk or fart. I'm an aunty to two little boys and, by the time this book is out, a little girl, and frankly it's a great vantage point for seeing how children affect a family and a relationship. It's this great, joyous event that brings so much love into the family, but it is also utterly consuming. I get to hang out with my nephews and niece, squeeze them, play with them, give them presents and treats, and then give them back to their exhausted parents. It's the perfect kind of try-before-you-buy experiment, because I get to feel the love with only little glimpses at the responsibility that comes with it. But glimpses are enough to know how difficult it is, and how dramatically it can transform your life. It's enough to make me want to do it, but not enough to stop me from being terrified. Parenting, as far as I can tell, is hella difficult. Great! So great, so great. But hard. Possibly one of the hardest things you can decide to do — and I'm trying to be realistic here, not dramatic.

You can guess where I'm going with this: when you've got to keep children alive and happy, where do you get the energy or the time to attend to your friendships? Seriously, how do you have a baby, toddler, child or teenager and still have time to shower, let alone get out of the house and interact with other human beings? It seems like an almighty juggle, and I'm sure people struggle to do it. We know they do, actually. An American parenting magazine called *Child* commissioned Fairfield Research to do a study on what changes when you have kids. They spoke to 901 people about how parenthood affected their friendships and the results were interesting. While 69 per cent of women felt satisfied with their friendships before having kids, only 54 per cent felt that way afterwards. Men went from 67 per cent satisfied to 56 per cent. And, as expected, having kids significantly diminished the number of contact hours between parents and their friends: before children, women spent 14 hours a week with their friends, and only five hours after. Before children, men spent 16 hours with their friends, and only six hours after. Just over half of parents who are unhappy with their friendships feel forced to choose between family and friends because of time constraints. This is perhaps compounded by incompatibilities like having single friends who don't necessarily fit in with the family schedule, moving away to start a family in a new place, taking on the workload of being a single parent, or simply dealing with the myriad chaotic logistics of keeping kids safe, fed, watered and rested. Marriage/commitment and parenthood are greedy for your time, that much is unequivocally true.

Having children is an extremely stressful (yep, yep, beautiful, wonderful, etc.) thing to do and it is perhaps one of those times we need our friends most, particularly with modern families often more fragmented than ever. And yet, it is just the time we tend to get rid of them, neglect them, lose them or discover some sort of practical mismatch with them. In this *Child* study, 45 per cent of women and 38 per cent of men said they had fewer friends after they had kids. Now, this could be for any number or combination of reasons. It is partly the time factor: children require an enormous time investment. But it is also possibly a shift in priorities and interests as well as the fast encroaching awareness of mortality that sort of makes you more inclined to shed the friendships you don't truly need. And perhaps what you actually look for in a relationship changes: 90 per cent of the women in this study said the main thing they depended on their friends for before having children was fun. After having kids, that number dropped to 50 per cent. Fifty-six per cent said that having friends who are good listeners was more important. Interestingly, men always rely on their friends for a sense of fun, both before and after becoming fathers. That could be a result of the sometimes crushing and disproportionate pressures of motherhood compared to fatherhood, or it could speak to the difference in how we operate our friendships.

Next, the study asked participants who they turned to in hard times. Most people rely on their spouses for support before anyone else, with just 32 per cent of women turning to a friend and only 13 per cent of men going to a mate. At first, this might seem perfectly natural and even lovely; of course people go to their significant other for emotional support in tough times — how sweet, how fitting, how normal. But think about it a little deeper and consider the burden we are putting on one other person, repeatedly, throughout our lifetimes. If we turn to our partner first or our partner only every time we go through trauma, doubt, confusion, pain or loss, we are relying on them in an extremely onerous and powerful sort of way. We are also limiting our options for perspective and advice on whatever the issue might be. We'd be better off mixing it up a little, in my opinion, and going to our friends for advice and support as well as or even, sometimes, instead of our spouse. Lifelong companionship is a lot to ask of someone and sometimes, let's face it, you need to talk about someone rather than to them. That's where friends come in: I treat mine as my brains trust in life, my emotional, intellectual and professional support team. My boyfriend is a beautiful support and gives excellent advice (he also makes a wicked roast lunch, which always helps), but I would never ask him to be my one and only source of emotional sustenance. That is too much for one person. No, no, instead, I consult my family, my friends and that dear friend of mine whom I pay to listen to me for an hour a fortnight, my very well-dressed therapist. Divvying up your life concerns and asking for back-up from multiple sources is a brilliant strategy; take it from someone who does it on the regular. If we distributed our love and our pain more evenly and more wisely than we currently do, perhaps we would have more resilience. We would certainly be better insured for the inevitable situation when one or more of the members of our support team retire.

But again, it should be said, I am not a parent. Not yet. I do not yet know the unique joys of parenthood: the sleepless nights, the little cuddles, the constant nappy changing, the weight of a newborn baby's head on my chest, the birthday cakes, the tantrums, the negotiations, the bedtime stories, the bath times, the squabbles, the playground visits, the grandparent fawning, the Christmas mornings, the childcare struggles, the school gate meetings, the crying, the games of hide-and-seek, the reruns of *Peppa the Pig*, the sibling rivalry, the giant bag of everything you need to have with you at all times, the feeling of a tiny hand holding mine, the eternal snack preparedness, the sound of a first word uttered, the thrill of a first step taken, the fear of a life so fragile, the disappearance of alone time, the teamwork, the breast leakage, the absence of personal space, the family picnics, the parenting books, the Wiggles soundtrack, the unprecedented love. And so, I asked my friends who have made small humans how they manage to stay sane and whether it's possible to sustain friendships in all that beautiful chaos.

The overwhelming reality, going by their responses, is that it becomes infinitely more difficult to prioritise and even schedule friendship once you have kids. My friend Scott (he is also, just to make the point that you can stay friends with people you once loved, my high-school ex-boyfriend) said the one thing he just never really thought about before his daughter arrived was how difficult, almost impossible, it would be to just go out to dinner. If their little girl isn't on a strict evening schedule of dinner, bath time and pyjama o'clock, she gets tired and the whole routine of child rearing is upset. Just popping down the pub for beers with the guys is a significant event now, because it takes serious scheduling prowess to even organise it. Scott and his wife are from Australia and moved to the outskirts of Sydney, so they're a little bit geographically removed from some of their friends, which raises the difficulty level of social interaction. But their friends are really important to them so even if it's not as often as they'd like, they make time for brunches and lunches and daytime activities that allow for baby nap times and meal times.

Timothy, who I met on Twitter, spoke about a similar logistical difficulty in becoming a dad. He's lucky, though, because one of his best mates actually became a dad five weeks after him, so they text about dad stuff all the time and swap notes on raising kids. And that is an important point to make, too: parenthood can actually facilitate or strengthen friendships, if you go about it right. A number of people told me they've gone through parenthood with their friends or made new friends through prenatal classes, childcare, nursery or school. So if your single mates don't want to hang out with you and the kids for a bit because they're at a different life stage, you can actually be out there trying to make new friends predicated on the very experience that lost you some other friendships. Parenting can be a powerfully bonding experience and you've got to have allies. For this book I have spoken to more lonely new mothers than I ever expected to — every time I asked for stories of friendship or loneliness, they put their hands up to speak. Becoming a mama (or a papa) can be extremely isolating, so it is more important than ever to work out how to keep friends around or make new ones with whom you can swap breastfeeding tips. It sounds to me as though friendship while parenting is logistically difficult but crucially important. And the onus is not just on the parent here; I think we need to get better at supporting our parent friends, too.

My darling friend Elise (the one who sings me One Direction songs and feeds me strawberries during depressive episodes) is mama to a 20-month-old called Felix. Felix is offensively cute, not least because he knocked out a tooth when he tried to bite a door handle and the gap is impossibly endearing. He can say his own name and a terrific number of animal names and noises, and I saw him eat his first piece of solid food (a little sliver of avocado because his mum is a millennial). Elise's husband, Phillip, is also fantastic. I am an enormous fan of their little family and, really, watching them together is my truest glimpse at what it's like to raise a child. I see Elise on her own on the days Felix is at nursery, I see Elise together with Felix and totally dote on him, and I see Elise and Phillip on nights when they get a babysitter so they can venture out and drink wine with other adults. So I see Elise in all her incarnations: as girlfriend, as mother, as wife. We have been close for more than a decade now and it's been an absolute delight to watch her find the man she loves and have a child with him. Watching your friends become mothers is a true and serious joy — and a learning experience.

Elise moved from Sydney to London to be with Phillip several years ago and is now a British citizen. So she's 12,500 kilometres away from her family, just like me, and trying to raise a bebe largely without their immediate help. There's FaceTime and Skype and holidays home and visits from family members, but mostly it's just Elise and Phillip and Felix, surrounded by their friends. Their mates have become surrogate aunties and uncles in that rather lovely way that friends can become family when you need them to. And although Elise admits she sees her friends less frequently than she used to and when she does it's a lot harder to organise and actually do, her friendships mean more to her than ever. There are some that have fallen away as she's settled down and that's okay; some friendships have finite lifespans and some friends are not meant to be in your life forever. But Elise recognises how important her close ones are for her health, happiness and sense of self. Before she left Australia, her father — not usually an emotionally open man — gave her some sage advice. He said you can lose your identity in a marriage if you're not careful, so to always look after her own. Elise's friendships have always been intrinsically linked to her identity and emotional wellbeing, so she's really made sure they are nurtured. She also never wants her participation in a marriage to limit how much she can be there for her friends to support them because she cares deeply about their happiness — and as one of those people lucky enough to be her friend, I can say that is truly appreciated and acknowledged. Elise is extremely diligent and thoughtful in her friendship; she is always, always generous with her time and her love, no matter what is going on in her life. She has learnt, or perhaps simply naturally knew, how to be a very excellent friend, and that has not stopped just because she has also taken on the roles of mother and wife. She has deliberately, fastidiously maintained her important pre-marriage, pre-Felix friendships and that is a real sign of her strength and loveliness. And friendship has been absolutely crucial to her sanity as a parent: since having Felix, she has needed to talk about the joys and challenges of motherhood with her friends over coffees and drinks, both with and without him. It's important to her that Felix has a relationship with her friends, too. She made him! A little human being! Made of her genes! Of course her friends should love him, too. For his part, he gets excited to see his surrogate aunties and uncles, mainly because he senses that they are important to his parents and because he loves having a wider audience to show off his latest skills to (standing, walking, speed-waddling, reciting colours). Elise has successfully kept her important, close friends in her life throughout the first 20 months of motherhood and, if anything, drawn the ones she loves most even closer. She could be up at 1 a.m., 4 a.m. and 7 a.m. breastfeeding and she'd still find the energy the next day to be there for me if I needed her. That's just how she operates. Just like Elise has shown me up close what it's like to be a mum at our age, she's also shown me it's possible to be a mama with friends and that's infinitely encouraging to me. She, Phillip and Felix make my future look a little happier, if only I can multi-task with even half of Elise's grace.

And so, that article, 'How Friendships Change in Adulthood (we *need* to catch up soon!)' becomes just an article; a passing collection of thoughts by one person. Not, as it first was, an ominous prediction of my adult life without friends. It is, as it turns out, entirely possible to be in a committed romantic relationship, be realistic about the power of love, bring little humans into your life and still retain some of your pre-romance, pre-baby identity. It is entirely possible to keep good, genuine friendships in your orbit, even if it means you have fewer direct contact hours. Even if it means conducting a lot of the friendship over WhatsApp or FaceTime. Even if it means grabbing whatever coffee/wine/pastry time you can get in the beautiful chaos of your life, and simply learning to cherish it even more for its rarity. Not enough people are doing it, not enough people are actively cherishing their existing friendships or cultivating new ones. We have, I believe, a sort of cultural amnesia when it comes to the peculiar importance and power of friendship. Frantic, career-focused, time-poor and riled up by modernity, we are consistently forgetting how crucial friendships are for our identity, our sanity and our physical wellbeing.

Please, let this be a little reminder: make time for the people who lift you up in life, who stick around when things get rough, who listen, who make you laugh, who care. Do it, even when you get married or find the love of your life — in fact, do it even more then. It's powerfully lovely to have big romantic love in your life and it's sublime to have family, but it's also the people we actively select to have in our lives, independent of romance or biology, that make us, and keep us, who we are. They are, so often, if you're doing it right, the ones who remind us what matters, who make life lighter, and who choose to stay in in our lives despite all the madness of human existence. If the sleep-deprived mother of a newborn baby can make time to be an actively good friend, any of us can.

If you take anything away from my ramblings here, please let it be a sweet little prompt to pick up the phone and text someone you haven't spoken to in a while. It can be a tiny, simple gesture — a dancing-girl emoji on a WhatsApp thread, a quick 'thinking of you' private message on Facebook, a stupid joke with a new friend — but tiny, simple gestures add up and all together they defend us from the encroaching loneliness that age, distance, circumstance, fear and melancholy can bring. Please, please start to think of loneliness as a very real threat: it can happen to any of us, even the ones who were popular in high school or surrounded by mates at university. Age comes for us all and we need to find ways to protect ourselves from being isolated, depressed and alone. It is just smart to gather your good friends around you and keep them there, no matter what life throws at you. It is scientifically incontestable that friendship is good for our health; it has curative, restorative, preventative qualities and we should be ingesting it liberally in our lives. If you want a chance at companionship when you become elderly, better heart health, more resilient mental health, a decreased chance of developing dementia, a better chance at survival through chronic illness and a longer life on this planet, then you know what to do. Value your friendships. Nurture and cherish the good people in your life. Get rid of the toxic, abusive, negative people. Give yourself the strongest chance at health and happiness — because to borrow a sentiment from a shampoo commercial, you are worth it. We all deserve to know and feel love, and that includes the indispensable, exquisite form of love that is friendship.

It might not be easy. Battling loneliness is hard, socialising can be awkward, making time for friendship dates is logistically difficult. We're not all naturally predisposed to be good friends, as Aristotle would argue, but I think friendship is something that can be learnt and can be taught. It should be a skill we pride ourselves on and actively develop throughout our lives. If we teach ourselves and each other to become better friends to one another, we can genuinely make the experience of humanity a bit more delightful. You know my feelings on this: we need an aggressive, worldwide campaign of greater kindness and a dramatic revamp of our values as a human race so that we prioritise things like compassion and integrity more than we currently do. We need systemic change in the way we treat vulnerable people and we need real solutions to the global epidemic of loneliness that is threatening, darkening and taking lives. We need to commit to this on a deeply private level, and campaign for it in public. We need to shift our singular dependence on one romantic partner and diversify our portfolio of emotional investment to include proper, healthy friendships, so we can become better, safer, wiser human beings. We need to encourage and lobby for structural change in public policy to support the disenfranchised, the vulnerable, the homeless, the mentally ill and the poor, so we can solve the epidemic of loneliness. Look at the signs — the scientific proof, the academic studies, the social trends — and you'll see that friendship is our future and our salvation. It is the one thing that could save us from ourselves.

Not to be dramatic about it or anything.

Acknowledgments

THE FIRST THANK YOU has to go to Robyn Drury, without whom this book would probably not exist. As my agent, she was calm, badass and integral to the development of this whole idea. She also has an admirable commitment to Italian carbs which improved the whole process. Thank you, too, to Diane Banks and Martin Redfern at Diane Banks Associates for their representation, drinks, and particularly their loyal support during a tough incident.

Thank you to my fantastic publisher, Catherine Milne at Harper Collins, whose initial response to my proposal for this book is printed on a tiny piece of paper and lodged in my wallet. Thank you to Gesche Ipsen at Duckworth for seeing the potential and to Matt Casbourne and Thogdin Ripley. Thank you also to Belinda Yuille and Jeanmarie Morosin for their hawk-like attention to detail. It takes more people than you can imagine to make a book like this and I'd like to thank everyone who has worked on it in any capacity — there are some whose names I do not even know. Writing is a lonely pursuit, so it is a strange and extreme delight to have an entire team help you execute an idea you had sitting in Hyde Park in 2015.

Thank you to every single person who spoke to me for this book, be they stranger from the Internet, academic, scientist, therapist, entrepreneur or evolutionary psychologist. Thank you, especially, to the strangers who gallantly volunteered their private stories of friendship, love and heartache. I very much hope I have done them justice and ask forgiveness for the ones that didn't make it into the final version of this book.

Thank you, of course, to my friends: to everyone who liked my Facebook updates about the book, everyone who did me the great honour of reading this book, everyone who kept me company over wine or coffee or on Twitter. Thank you to Rosie Waterland and Jamila Rizvi for being my own personal Oprahs. The most special, loving, adoring, effusive, eternal and infinite thank you to the members of the following WhatsApp groups: Greece 2017, Bridesmaids, Brotato Chips and XXX Girls Girls Girls XXX. This book is for you.

Thank you to my beautiful family for their relentless enthusiasm, love, support, loyalty and cuteness. Thank you especially to my mum and my dad, who have been such patient, wonderful cheerleaders for this book and for my mad decision to make a living out of writing words. Thank you to my grandma and my papa, who are no longer here but taught me to love the English language.

And finally, thank you to my darling Jono. Our life together is a dream.